THE SPIRIT AND CULTURE OF YOUTH MINISTRY

THE SPIRIT AND CULTURE OF YOUTH MINISTRY

LEADING CONGREGATIONS TOWARD EXEMPLARY YOUTH MINISTRY

Roland Martinson • Wes Black • John Roberto

EYM Publishing
St. Paul, MN

THE SPIRIT AND CULTURE OF YOUTH MINISTRY
Leading Congregations Toward Exemplary Youth Ministry

Funded through a generous grant by the Lilly Endowment.

Cover image © istockphoto. Male hand model courtesy of Claudio Calcagni.

Researchers: Dr. Thomas Berkas, Mark Brekke, Dr. Merton Strommen, and Rev. Hal C. Weldin
Publishing consultant: Huff Publishing Associates, LLC
Cover and book design: Hillspring Books, Inc.

ISBN 978-0-9823031-2-2

Library of Congress Cataloging-in-Publication Data is available

EYM Publishing
2481 W. Como Ave.
St. Paul, MN 55108

www.exemplarym.com

Manufactured in the U.S.A.

CONTENTS

CASE STUDIES, TABLES, AND APPLICATION TOOLS

The following denominations were involved in the study: Assemblies of God, Evangelical Covenant, Evangelical Lutheran Church of America (ELCA), Presbyterian Church (USA), Roman Catholic, Southern Baptist, and United Methodist Church.

CASE STUDIES

TABLES

APPLICATION TOOLS

this changes everything

E very now and then, one comes across an idea or a piece of work that reorients one's way of thinking. For us, the material you hold in your hand has done just that. The work of the Exemplary Youth Ministry (EYM) study is a brilliant gift to the church. It's a gift in that the study is ecumenical and national. It's a gift that offers statistics and stories. And it's a gift because of its focus on the faith maturity of young people. Simply stated, no one has ever done a study like this before. No one has ever identified what works in youth ministry based on *that* goal, with this depth, and with these conversation partners. Wow!

Sometimes ideas that reorient are hard to get one's head around. For many, that's been the case with this work. The findings of this study are not a map or set of programs, rather they are more of an "inside the closet" examination of youth ministry in congregations. We know that youth ministry literature often offers the former. Yet many of you also know that such approaches, at best, offer short-term solutions to deeper realities. Consequently many of you have been searching for an "inside the closet" perspective. Well, here it is.

If you are someone searching for a deeper analysis of youth ministry, open the pages of this book and look inside congregations that are seeking to and having some success at helping young people mature in their Christian faith. But be warned, looking inside has the risk of changing everything.

It has changed everything for us. For the past seven years, we, the Children, Youth, and Family Ministry leadership and teaching team at Luther Seminary, have sought to allow the Exemplary Youth Ministry study findings to both permeate and shape how we teach and equip leaders in the church. In so doing, we have developed a very different kind of degree program because of what we now understand about the practice of youth ministry, and we now are asking different questions of congregations and church leaders. Let us explain.

I (Nancy) had the privilege of going behind the Exemplary Youth Ministry research for my PhD research, doing in-depth interviewing of young people from some of these congregations. My goal was to listen to and describe the specific theological foci of committed adolescent faith. The youth minister in me loved the amazing students I was able to meet. I could see the rich results of focused attention to maturing Christian faith by their congregations and their families. I was able to hear the nuances of the EYM forty-four Faith Assets in action. I could recognize the difference that maturing faith makes in what they had to say and how they *had* to live. I was also convinced that their conversations about faith need to shape not only the practice of youth ministry but the very essence of our beliefs about adolescent development.

I (Terri) had the opportunity to coach congregational youth ministry teams based on the EYM study results. My main question whether congregations can be coached to create a new culture and spirit around ministry with young people. After five years, my answer is *yes*. But it's not for everyone. It takes time, a committed and diverse leadership team, and a shift in thinking.

Some of the primary findings of this study center on the life and spirit of the congregation as a whole, as well as its leadership, namely the senior pastor. No longer can ministry with and for young people be handed off to a sole youth worker, paid or volunteer, and take place in the "youth room." That reality not only changes the congregation's posture toward youth ministry but also changes the expectations and ideas of what constitutes vibrant youth ministry. This makes youth ministry more complex, but it also makes it more central to congregational ministry.

These discoveries not only changed *what* we are teaching in the classroom but also call forth *new conversations*. My PhD work with missional congregations ties directly into these findings. Looking behind the curtain of youth ministry calls into question a congregation's view of church. In other words, what are God's people called to be and do? This means we are not only calling the purpose of youth ministry into question but also asking congregations to revisit their understanding of the mission of the church. This has changed our focus from teaching youth ministry practices to shaping leaders who can ask particular questions and guide congregations to discern God's movement within their midst.

At the same time the two of us were working directly with the EYM findings, our colleague Andrew Root was offering a corrective on youth ministry's understanding of relational ministry. The EYM findings highlight, as one might expect, that relationships matter. Yet over the years relational ministry has been based on certain assumptions and been bound by programmatic initiatives. The EYM findings call out some of these assumptions and offer the opportunity for reconstructing relational ministry. Andrew's brilliant theological framing of incarnational ministry offers a way forward and names "placesharing" as our calling as God's people. The churches in this study embody this idea.

EYM has changed everything about our work at Luther Seminary and reframed our goals for youth ministry and the church. It has allowed us not just to proclaim but claim:

> Like newborn infants, long for the pure spiritual milk, that by it you may
> grow up into salvation— if indeed you have tasted that the Lord is good.
> As you come to him, a living stone rejected by men but in the sight of God
> chosen and precious, you yourselves like living stones are being built up as
> a spiritual house, to be a holy priesthood, to offer spiritual sacrifices acceptable to God through Jesus Christ. But you are a chosen race, a royal priesthood, a holy nation, a people for his own possession, that you may proclaim
> the excellencies of him who called you out of darkness into his marvelous
> light. Once you were not a people, but now you are God's people; once you
> had not received mercy, but now you have received mercy. 1 Peter 2: 2-4, 9-10

As you work through this book, its data, its findings and its tools, we'd like to encourage you. We know there is a lot here. We know it will take a while to digest what it says and what it means for ministry within your context. But don't give up. Keep at it. Sit with it. Let it stir within you. And be open to letting it ignite a new way of seeing ministry with young people. We believe congregational ministry with young people is vital if young people are going to have a vibrant and mature Christian faith. The price for not wrestling with these ideas is high. So join the adventure. But be warned, it changes everything.

Dr. Terri Martinson Elton
Dr. Nancy S. Going
Children, Youth, and Family Ministry
Luther Seminary, Saint Paul, Minnesota

PREFACE

O ur goal in *The Spirit and Culture of Youth Ministry* is to present the findings from the Study of Exemplary Congregations in Youth Ministry and to provide you and your congregation with research-based practices and approaches for developing and enhancing ministry with young people today. As a preview we suggest that you keep in mind several important findings from the study as you read the book.

Congregations Consistently Develop Vibrant, Committed Youth

We all have read research studies and reports about the lack of committed faith in teenagers today, but that is not the whole picture. While the young people in the study are typical teens in so many ways, in matters of faith, they possess a desire to know and follow God that defines them, shapes their character, and guides their lives. It is clear from the study's findings that congregations *can* and *do* nurture youth of vibrant Christian faith. The study found congregations with high percentages of committed Christian youth with committed Christian parents who possess a vibrant faith that can be described in these seven ways:

1. *Seeking Spiritual Growth*—pursue spiritual growth through conversation, study, reading the Bible, prayer, small groups, retreats.
2. *Possessing a Vital Faith*—are keenly aware of God present and active in their own life, the lives of others, and the life of the world.
3. *Practicing Faith in Community*—actively practice their faith in Jesus Christ, privately and publicly, through participation in the congregation's worship, ministries, and leadership.
4. *Making the Christian Faith a Way of Life*—recognize God's call and integrate their beliefs into the conversation, decisions, and actions of daily life.
5. *Living a Life of Service*—are involved in activities caring for others, reaching out to others in need, and addressing injustice.
6. *Exercising Moral Responsibility*—live with integrity utilizing their Christian faith in making moral decisions.
7. *Possessing a Positive Spirit*—reflect loving and hopeful attitudes toward others and life.

As you will soon discover, the purpose of youth ministry in the congregations we studied can be summarized in a single goal: making disciples of Jesus Christ. These congregations focus their youth ministries on Jesus Christ and engage young people in discipleship, witness, and service that transforms their lives. Effective youth ministries make a significant impact on the personal of faith of young people by deepening their relationship with Jesus, helping them understand the Christian faith better, applying their faith to daily life and serious life choices, and sharing their faith with others.

The Faith of the Whole Congregation

The Study of Exemplary Congregations in Youth Ministry discovered that it is the culture of the whole church that is most influential in nurturing youth of vital Christian faith. The research points to the value of a congregation's culture endowed with a palpable sense of the living, active presence of God at work among the people of the whole congregation, its ministries with youth, its parents, the ministries of the congregation, and its congregational leaders (pastor, youth minister, youth and adult leaders) as providing the most powerful, pervasive influence these congregations have on young people long-term. It is the communal awareness of participation in God's presence and action that permeates the values, relationships, and activities of these congregations, giving rise to an atmosphere, a culture of the Spirit focused on mission and the transformation of life that seems to make them so influential in the lives and faith of young people. The congregations in the study present a portrait of the strong impact faith communities can have on the faith and lives of young people when churches set their minds to fully enfranchise young people in their life and ministry. When pastors, congregational leaders, parents and adult youth leaders work together to promote real commitment to young people as full members of the body of Christ and carry that commitment across the life and mission of the entire congregation, teenagers mature in faith and grow to respect and love their church. The study demonstrates how age-level youth ministry and ministries with family are dependent upon and greatly enhanced by congregations setting young people and youth ministry as one of its essential priorities. If a congregation is not willing to make this commitment, youth and youth ministry will always be tangential and second rate. Congregational commitment to young people is at the heart of effective ministry with youth.

A Holistic and Comprehensive Approach to Youth Ministry

The Study of Exemplary Congregations in Youth Ministry identified forty-four Faith Assets that contribute to developing a vibrant, committed Christian faith in young people. The forty-four Faith Assets present a holistic, comprehensive, and research-based framework that congregations can use in developing and enhancing their ministries with young people and their families.

CHART 1

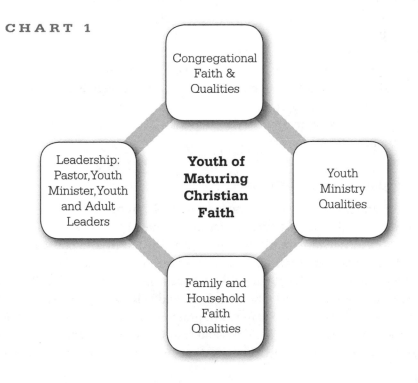

Congregational Faith and Qualities

The congregational Faith Assets describe the values and dynamics of the intergenerational life and ministry of the whole congregation. The congregational Faith Assets reflect attributes the congregation as a whole brings to its relationships with youth. They describe aspects of the congregation's theological orientation, faith maturity, values, attitudes, and practices that bear directly on its capacity to engage and influence the faith of young people. Each faith asset identifies an element of the congregation's overall functioning that contributes to effective ministries with youth. Most importantly, the research shows that the theological commitments of the congregation as a whole become the theological commitments of the congregation's youth ministry: because of the centrality of the gospel and discipleship in congregational life, knowing Jesus Christ and following him in discipleship are at the core of these congregations' youth ministries. We believe this faithfulness to the Christian tradition to be one of the factors in the depth and breadth of a congregation's effectiveness.

Youth Ministry Qualities

The Youth Ministry Faith Assets describe the quality of the congregation's age-level ministries with youth. They indicate the attitudes, expectations and practices of the congregation's age-level ministries with youth within the larger intergenerational culture of quality ministry with young people. The study identified nine youth ministry practices that were incorporated in each congregation's youth ministry: (1) peer ministry and youth leadership, (2) retreats, (3) service and mission trips, (4) Bible study and religious education, (5) prayer and spiritual formation, (6) spiritual support groups, (7) youth-oriented worship, (8) special events, and (9) family and intergenerational activities. Congregations take these common practices and approaches of youth ministry and develop custom-designed, innovative ways to address the particular needs of youth, their families, and the congregation.

Family and Household Faith Assets

The family and household Faith Assets describe the importance of family faith, adding another influence to the youth-friendly culture of the whole congregation and the effective age-level ministry with youth. The family and household Faith Assets describe faith and faith practices at home, and the role of the congregation in equipping and support parental and family faith. The parents in the study possess a mature, committed Christian faith and this has a profound influence on the lives of young people. Family faith practices—caring conversations, family devotions and prayer, family rituals and traditions, family service—influence the faith lives of young people. Congregations have a important role to play by equipping parents to pass on faith and strengthening family relationships, contributing to the influence of parents and the whole family on the development of youth of vital Christian faith.

Leadership in the Congregation

Effective, competent, faith-filled leadership is what makes congregations and youth ministries work. At the center of leadership in a congregation is the pastor and four assets describe the pastor's specific impact on youth ministry and developing youth of vital Christian faith: spiritual influence, pastoral effectiveness, love for and support of young people, and support of youth ministry leaders. Pastors matter immensely in effective youth ministry! Six Faith Assets express the strength of the primary youth minister in the congregation, while five Faith Assets describe the effectiveness of the youth and adult leadership in youth ministry. The excellence in leadership begins with the pastor and permeates the entire congregation's life and ministry especially as it focuses on young people. No matter what size the congregation, pastors and youth ministers do not do youth ministry alone—it is a team approach. The youth ministry team, adult leaders, parents, and youth leaders work together with the pastor and youth minister.

Ready, Set, Go

It is our hope that *The Spirit and Culture of Youth Ministry* can provide you and your congregation with affirmation for the work you are doing and a renewed sense of purpose and direction in your ministry with young people and their families. We believe that the research-based practices and approaches contained in this book can form the foundation for developing and enhancing your congregation's ministry with young people today. *The Spirit and Culture of Youth Ministry* can be a roadmap for promoting youth of vibrant, committed Christian faith for years to come.

INTRODUCTION

the study of exemplary congregations in youth ministry

I n the past decade there have been a number of excellent studies on the religious beliefs, practices, and attitudes of adolescents. Unique among these research projects is the Study of Exemplary Congregations in Youth Ministry, funded by a generous grant from the Lilly Endowment. The Study of Exemplary Congregations in Youth Ministry (EYM) focused on identifying congregations that consistently establish faith as a vital factor in the lives of their youth and discovering what accounts for their effective approaches to ministry. Seven denominations were involved in the study: Assemblies of God, Evangelical Covenant, Evangelical Lutheran Church in America (ELCA), Presbyterian Church (USA), Roman Catholic, Southern Baptist, and United Methodist Church.

As many researchers have demonstrated, almost all Christian denominations are experiencing a dramatic drop in the percentage of older adolescents and young adults who are involved in worship and ministry. However, some congregations are not only able to keep their youth involved but are effectively equipping young people as leaders to serve in their church, community, and world. Why do some Christian young people mature in faith and become devoted disciples of Jesus Christ? One cannot address this critical question regarding the nature and impact of faith in the lives of youth without asking how congregations and their ministries factor into the faith maturity and devotion in these adolescents.

The EYM Study asked: Do congregations with high percentages of committed Christian youth exist? If so, what is going on in these congregations that might be contributing to vital faith in young people? The study went on to see if a positive relationship between the ministries of these congregations and the Christian faith of their young people could be found. The good news from the research findings is that the study identified congregations with high percentages of devoted youth and observed a positive relationship between the congregation's activities and the faith maturity of its youth.

Questions arise concerning the commonality and transferability of the effective elements of their ministries across congregations in a diversity of denominations. So the EYM Study asked a further question: Might congregations exhibiting effective ministries with devoted Christian youth have anything in common with other such congregations? If common elements of effective youth ministries exist, can these common elements be transferred to other congregations? As you will read, the study found essential elements of congregations and youth ministries that are held in common and that have the potential to influence the work of every Christian church.

The ultimate goal of the Study of Exemplary Congregations in Youth Ministry was to understand why those congregations are succeeding at youth ministry when many are not. The EYM Study was developed to take the first steps toward that goal by learning what successful congregations are like: to identify the combination of factors (behaviors, attitudes, beliefs, programs, processes, policies) that typify congregations found to be effective in establishing faith in the lives of their youth. Specifically the Study of Exemplary Congregations in Youth Ministry was designed to:

- *identify congregations with significant numbers of young people of vital faith;*
- *describe the ministries of these congregations that church leaders and young people identify as faithful and effective; and*
- *discover what accounts for those congregations' effective approaches to ministry with young people of vital Christian faith.*

The Study's Methodology

The Study of Exemplary Congregations in Youth Ministry was designed to use both quantitative and qualitative methodologies. The quantitative part of the study (surveys) was designed to map the domain of exemplary youth ministry as experienced by members of congregations practicing it, including how that domain differs in general from that of "average" congregations. The qualitative part (focus groups and interviews with congregations) was designed to learn in greater depth and detail how specific congregations are doing exemplary youth ministry and if possible identify patterns of approaches that appear to be working. In brief form the full design included the following steps:

General

- *Determine the study definition of exemplary youth ministry.*
- *Identify and secure the participation of a sample of congregations doing exemplary youth ministry.*

Quantitative

- *Develop quantitative instruments (surveys) to measure characteristics of exemplary congregations and their members.*
- *Survey youth, parents, adult youth workers, the senior/lead pastor, and youth ministers in exemplary congregations.*
- *Identify from survey data the reliable item clusters, representing meaningful constructs (behaviors, attitudes, beliefs, programs, processes, policies, and so on).*
- *Determine whether EYM congregations differ from "average" congregations regarding the constructs by comparing EYM results to data from previous studies.*
- *Identify patterns of characteristics from pastors' and youth ministers' responses to open-ended survey questions regarding the important elements of their youth ministry.*

Qualitative

- *Develop structured interviews to get in-depth information from EYM congregations.*
- *Collect interviews and first-hand observations through site visits to twenty-one selected EYM congregations.*
- *Identify patterns of characteristics from the site visit data.*

Utilizing both quantitative and qualitative methods of research, the Study of Exemplary Congregations in Youth Ministry study drew upon three data streams: (1) participant surveys (youth, parents, adult youth workers, pastors, and youth ministers), (2) responses to open-ended questions from pastors and youth ministers, and (3) site visits to twenty-one congregations (three from each denomination) selected from the 131 participating congregations.

First, congregational leaders and participants in youth ministry were surveyed. Youth leaders at many levels of youth ministry in seven denominations (Assemblies of God, Evangelical Covenant, Evangelical Lutheran Church of America (ELCA), Presbyterian Church (USA), Roman Catholic, Southern Baptist, and United Methodist Church) were invited to nominate congregations to be studied. These congregations were chosen on the basis of their perceived capacity to nurture or attract youth of vital faith as described in a "portrait of youth with vital Christian faith" (see chapter 1).

While recognizing the difficulties and limitations of "defining" youth of vital faith, the research team discovered that by modifying a long-standing, well-utilized profile it was able to generate a description of maturing Christian youth that received widespread acceptance among Christian leaders of diverse traditions and worked well in identifying a large number of congregations with exemplary youth ministry throughout the seven denominations.

Once congregations with high percentages of youth of vital, committed Christian faith were identified and validated, quantitative and qualitative research methods were employed to get at the rich complexities of young people of vital faith and the congregations ministering with them (see appendices for a full description of the quantitative and qualitative methodologies utilized in the study). The 131 small, medium, and large congregations represented in the study reflect many regions and contexts in the United States. While most of the congregations were Anglo-American, some had significant populations of or consisted largely of Latino-American, Asian-American, and African-American peoples. Urban, rural, small town, city, and large suburban congregations were included.

The study moved through three stages of research. First, nearly six thousand pastors, youth ministers, adult youth workers, parents and youth from 131 congregations completed extensive surveys. This number included 2252 youth responses, 223 pastors and youth ministers, 1668 parent, and 1452 youth workers. Second, in addition to responding to survey items, 204 pastors and youth ministers from the 131 congregations surveyed submitted responds to four open-ended questions regarding the ministries with youth in their churches. These pastors and youth ministers provided 440 pages of written responses to these four open-ended questions. Third, from the 131 congregations with the highest scores on the surveys, twenty-one small, medium and large congregations, three from each of the seven denominations in the study, were chosen for three day site visits and extensive interviews. During this qualitative phase of the research, interviews, focus groups, and participant observation were conducted at twenty-one locations in all regions of the United States. These site visits generated over two thousand pages of field notes.

Through the combination of quantitative research (surveys of youths, parents, adult youth ministry leaders, and church staff in 131 congregations) and qualitative research (on-site, in-depth interviews in twenty-one congregations selected from the 131 who participated in the survey), the study uncovered important findings that affirm the best in congregational youth ministry and provide direction for enhancing and expanding ministry with youth.

The EYM Team

To coordinate and conduct the study, a twelve-member EYM Advisory Council was formed consisting of a representative from each of the seven participating denominations, a team of research professionals, and additional staff for project coordination and site direction. The project was coordinated by Luther Seminary under the direction of Roland Martinson. The members of the EYM Advisory Council included: Thomas Berkas (EYM researcher, professor at Bethel University); Wesley Black (Southern Baptist Convention, professor at Southwestern Baptist Theological Seminary, book coauthor); Mark Brekke (EYM researcher, Brekke and Associates); Marti Burger (Evangelical Covenant Church, national staff); Susan Hay (representing the United Methodist Church, national staff); Roland Martinson (Evangelical Lutheran Church in America, Academic Dean at Luther Seminary, book coauthor); John Roberto (Catholic Church in America, LifelongFaith Associates, book coauthor); Kenneth Slifer (Presbyterian Church–USA, national staff); Merton Strommen (researcher, founder of the Search Institute); Kristen Venne (EYM project coordinator); Hal Weldin (EYM site director, researcher); Rod Whitlock (Assemblies of God, national staff).

The Spirit and Culture of Youth Ministry Book

This book presents the findings of the Study of Exemplary Congregations in Youth Ministry—what we discovered about the vital Christian faith of young people and the effective congregations and youth ministries in which they worship, learn, and serve. More importantly it lays out the study's implications for more faithful, effective youth ministry in all Christian churches.

We envision this book as a guide for all Christian churches to use in developing, enhancing, and expanding their ministry with young people. We are not prescribing what that should look like, rather we are describing what effective congregations believe and practice so that this may inspire and guide all churches in their ministry with youth. We have learned a great deal about the congregational factors that contribute to developing a vital Christian faith in young people. Our understanding is drawn from our survey research, our interviews, and our onsite focus groups and interviews in twenty-one congregations. This book presents what we have learned and how it can help you and your congregation.

Chapter 1—Youth of Vital Faith presents a description of the seven characteristics of youth of vital Christian that we uncovered through the youth surveys in the 131 congregations participating in the study, and that was confirmed by the findings from the surveys of parents, adult leaders in youth ministry, pastors, and youth ministers. With the knowledge that we had discovered committed Christian youth in these 131 congregations, we move on to explore what these congregations are doing to develop these young people.

Chapter 2—The Importance of Congregational Culture presents the central finding of the Study of Exemplary Congregations in Youth Ministry. Among a great diversity of Christian traditions across the United States, in congregations of every size in all regions of the country, in churches who are deeply influencing the faith and lives of young men and women, the EYM Study discovered that it is the culture of the whole church that is most influential in nurturing youth of vital Christian faith. The genius of these churches seems best described as a systemic mix of theology, values, people, relationships, expectations, and activities. It appears that a culture of the Spirit emerges with its pervasive and distinct dynamics and atmosphere that is more powerful than its component parts. Chapter 3 presents the forty-four Faith Assets that help to describe the congregational culture of churches who nurture youth of vital Christian faith.

Chapters 3 through 6 present the Faith Assets in four categories: Congregational Faith and Qualities, Youth Ministry Qualities, Family and Household Faith, and Leadership in the Congregation. Each chapter is built around the Faith Assets: describing the grounding of the assets in the research findings from the surveys of youth, parents, adult youth workers, pastors, and youth ministers; illustrating the assets through the stories of congregations involved in the onsite visits and interviews; and offering practical ideas and strategies for applying the Faith Assets to ministry in your congregation.

Chapter 7—Embracing the Spirit and Culture of Youth Ministry in Your Congregation presents practical directions, drawn from the most important findings from the Study of Exemplary Congregations in Youth Ministry, that every congregation can use to strengthen its ministry with young people.

Any one of the chapters can stand alone, providing the reader with a small piece of the study to digest and work. It is the whole story, however, that will give you the best sense of the culture of the Spirit and the forty-four Faith Assets and their potential for your congregations and the larger discipline of youth ministry.

CHAPTER ONE

youth of vital christian faith

W hat do youth of vital Christian faith look like? What are the characteristics of a committed, maturing Christian youth? To answer these questions the Study of Exemplary Congregations in Youth Ministry used the research findings from previous studies on the beliefs and practices of committed Christian youth. A profile of thirty-four indicators of committed, maturing Christian youth was developed for identifying congregations with high concentrations of youth with a vibrant faith (see Table 2). This historic portrait, drawn from studies such as the Effectiveness in Christian Education Study, by the Search Institute in 1986, had not only been frequently and thoroughly field tested, it brought together a broad spectrum of indicators regularly associated with the practice of Christian faith as well the reputation of having proven itself as a widely accepted and an easily understood articulation of the beliefs and practices of a committed Christian young person. After extended conversation and significant modification, this "portrait" of youth of vital Christian faith was approved for use in identifying congregations with exemplary youth ministry. The thirty-four indicators are not the product of a particular developmental theory or a specific theology, but a framework for assessing the thinking of committed Christian young people and a great many adults who have been and are in ministry with them.

Once modified this portrait of committed Christian young people was utilized in the study's first stage requesting leaders from the seven participating denominations to nominate congregations where there were high concentrations of maturing youth of vital Christian faith. The project team defined "exemplary congregations in youth ministry" in terms of an observable end product: *exemplary congregations in youth ministry consistently develop youth of vital, maturing Christian faith.* The portrait served the project well. Leaders in the seven denominations identified hundreds of congregations where they observed such young people present. A total of 131 congregations from the seven denominations were selected for the study.

The survey findings from the 2252 young people in the 131 congregations provide strong and detailed evidence of their vital, maturing Christian faith. The teenagers demonstrated significantly higher scores than youth participating in earlier national studies on all seven characteristics of vital faith, especially in the areas of faith maturity, involvement in the activities of the congregation, and positive rating of their congregation.

The survey findings from youth, adult youth workers, pastors and youth ministers, confirmed that the 131 congregations selected for study were in fact nurturing youth of vital faith. Comparisons between these congregations and those of previous studies on eighty-six aspects of faith, congregational life, and youth ministry show that the 131 congregations in the study scored significantly higher on sixty-five of those measures.

Survey findings and interviews with the young people, adult youth workers, youth ministers and pastors in these congregations strongly supported the picture of vital faith in the youth of these exemplary congregations. Indeed what was most impressive in the interviews was the depth and freshness with which these young people give expression to the content of their faith and the manner in which it deeply informed their lives. The data from both the quantitative and qualitative dimensions of the study provides overwhelming evidence that the young people in these congregations are men and women of vital faith.

Understanding the Nomenclature and Structure
of the Quantitative Research

Items: Individual questions or statements in the survey to which youth, parents, adult youth workers, youth ministers, and pastors responded. Over 750 appeared in the questionnaires. **Example:** *How true is each of these statements for* *you? I am keenly aware of the presence of God.* It's one of a cluster of eight items making up the dimension: Personal Christianity.

Dimensions: Clusters of items from the survey that have a strong coherent relationship to a common meaning or action. These clusters of items reveal the patterns of thought of the youth, parents, adult youth workers, youth ministers, and pastors who filled out the surveys. Over ninety emerged in the first round of analysis of the data. **Example: Y48. A Personal Christianity.** Consists of eight items from the survey; one of the twelve dimensions making up the theme: Committed Christian Youth.

Themes: Clusters of dimensions of the findings that have a strong coherent relationship to a common meaning or action. These clusters of dimensions reveal large patterns of thought of the youth, parents, adult youth workers, youth ministers, and pastors who filled out the surveys. Fourteen emerged in the second round of analysis of items and dimensions. **Example: Committed Christian Youth.** Consists of twelve dimensions describing the faith of youth in the exemplary congregations.

Seven Characteristics of Vital Faith in Youth

The Study of Exemplary Congregations in Youth Ministry utilized seven essential characteristics of vital faith in young people, drawn from prior research studies.

CHART 2

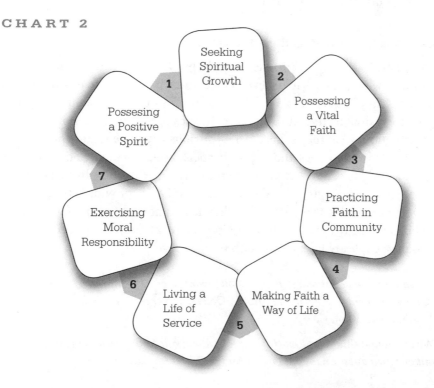

1. *Seeking Spiritual Growth*: Youth are pursuing spiritual growth through conversation, study, reading the Bible, prayer, small groups, retreats.
2. *Possessing a Vital Faith*: Youth are keenly aware of God present and active in their own life, the lives of others, and the life of the world.
3. *Practicing Faith in Community*: Youth actively practice their faith in Jesus Christ, privately and publicly, through participation in the congregation's worship, ministries, and leadership.
4. *Making the Christian Faith a Way of Life*: Youth recognize God's "call" and integrate their beliefs into the conversation, decisions, and actions of daily life.
5. *Living a Life of Service*: Youth are involved in activities caring for others, reaching out to others in need, and addressing injustice.
6. *Exercising Moral Responsibility*: Youth live with integrity utilizing their Christian faith in making moral decisions.
7. *Possessing a Positive Spirit*: Youth reflect loving and hopeful attitudes toward others and life.[1]

These seven essential characteristics of vital faith in young people summarize the survey findings of the 2252 young people in 131 congregations. Drawing upon the research from the Committed Christian Youth Theme, the eleven dimensions (out of a total of thirteen dimensions) in Table 1 describe the most significant qualities of youth of vital Christian faith.

Characteristic 1. Seeking Spiritual Growth

Youth of maturing faith are curious, actively pursuing questions of faith. They want to know what it means to believe in God and what it's like to be a disciple of Jesus Christ. They frequent Bible studies and small group discussions where they can voice their doubts, find answers to their questions, and learn how to speak intelligently about what they believe. These curious young people are open to the activity of God in their lives and regularly speak about seeking God's guidance as well as asking friends what God has recently done in their lives. For these young people, their congregations and youth ministries provide settings where they have relationships through which they learn more about the faith and its implications for daily life. They worship, pray, and study the Bible individually. These young people are integrating faith into their very self.

> We want to talk about real issues; we don't want to be entertained. We want a safe environment to grow in our faith in God and to encounter God. (Youth, Costa Mesa, CA)

> We talk about things that matter. We talk about our faith, world religions, and our own questions about faith. (Youth, Grand Rapids, MI)

TABLE 1

Eleven Dimensions of Committed Christian Youth Linked with the Seven Characteristics of Youth of Vital Faith

11 Dimensions of Committed Christian Youth*	Rating**	Characteristic of Vital Faith
1. A Personal Christianity	7.74	#1 and #2
2. Moral Responsibility	7.37	#6
3. Caring Relationships ("Defends and Supports Friends")	6.86	#7
4. Faith Impact of Church Involvement	6.83	#3
5. Faith Maturity	6.50	#1, #2, and #4
6. Personal Religiousness	6.36	#1
7. Moral Integrity	5.94	#6
8. Seeks Spiritual Growth	5.76	#1
9. God Consciousness	5.38	#2
10. Lives a Life of Service	5.35	#5
11. Speaks Publicly about One's Faith	5.31	#2

See Table 3 for a description of each dimension.

** Mean scores: highest rating is "9," indicating a response of "Always" or "Almost Always True."*

Here we talk about everyday situations, like you can pick out things happening at school and they can help you relate Scripture to everyday life. (Youth, Valparaiso, IN).

Young people in the survey identified the most significant aspects of what it means for them to be "seeking spiritual growth." They rated the following beliefs and activities, drawn from items in dimensions 6 and 8, as being among the most important for them:

I prefer and attend gatherings where I can learn more about the Christian faith.
I join Christian groups to build friendships and learn how to be a friend.
I pray, have devotions, or meditate, either alone or with others.
I like to worship and pray with others.
I accept opportunities to learn how to speak naturally and intelligently about their faith.
I ask sincere and searching questions about the nature of a life of faith in God.
I take advantage of opportunities to study the Bible and our faith tradition
I seek out opportunities to grow spiritually.

Characteristic 2. Possessing a Vital Faith

Youth of maturing faith are keenly aware of God present and active in their lives, the lives of others, and the life of the world. God is experienced as an active presence, a "friend" who contributes to their lives as guide and protector. They talk about God in personal, intimate terms. They not only report that God is active in their lives, but they also see evidence of God's activity in others and the world.

Our pastor always asks for highs and lows in life (on Wednesdays), and one time he asked how God has been active in my life. I hadn't really thought about it much—my upbringing was one of not attending—and it made me think about how much strength God has given me to get through the hardships in life with strength and love. (Youth, Round Top, TX)

God is always there, and He will never fail me even though I fail myself, and I fail Him. I really don't have to worry about it. I think it always comes back to the point where when I think of the Psalms, and know that He's done it before. Even though my life is perfectly unique, it has been sculpted by God, and God knows what's going to happen. (Youth, Terre Haute, IN)

Right now, I feel really close to God. I spend time with Him every day, and I just love to sing, so that's a way that I get closer to Him, is I like to sing to Him. That's when I feel the closest to Him. I guess you could say. I feel like I know Him so much better. (Youth, McKinney, TX)

Young people in the survey identified the most significant aspects of what it means for them to be "possessing a vital faith." They rated the following beliefs and activities, drawn from items in dimensions 1 and 9, as being among the most important for them:

God cares for me in a special way.
God is a close personal friend who guides and protects me.
I see evidence that God is active in the world.
The active presence of God in my life has been a positive influence on my religious faith.
My life is committed to Jesus Christ.
I am keenly aware of the presence of God.
I reassure others that God is active to make things work out all right in the long run.

Characteristic 3. Practicing Faith in Community

Youth of maturing faith actively practice their faith in Jesus Christ through regular attendance at worship, participation in ministry, and leadership in a congregation. In addition to faith's significant role in their day to day existence, these committed young people exercise their faith personally and publicly through communal religious practices. They are eager to worship, pray, and participate in the community with adults throughout the ministries of the congregation. They see their church as an important part of their Christian lives, a place where God is active. Most importantly, they understand the church as more than just their youth ministry. They feel very much a part of the larger life of the congregation.

Sometimes, when I have a stressful day, I can't wait to be with our small group because there I can be around people who talk about God.
(Youth, Portland, OR)

I know our whole church focuses on how your walk is with Jesus. . . . It keeps you very accountable and it's so personal, not just, I'm going to tell you what you need to know, but, where are you with God, and how can we encourage you? (Youth, Rochester, MN)

This church is very welcoming. Like, if you come, they'll just take you under their wing. Or if you're going through a hard time, they'll love you, they take you in for who you are; they don't judge people. . . . They welcome anybody in the whole church. Pretty much everybody knows everybody. It's a good family. (Youth, Grand Prairie, TX)

This youth program uses all these different aspects—building strong community, with advisors and with God—that we're so much like a family (that) if anyone called and said they had an emergency, we'd all be there. This is a safe community (that) we are all a part of. (Youth, Des Moines, WA)

Adult Christians in these congregations, especially those involved in leadership in youth ministry have powerful influence in young peoples' lives. Most importantly, young people's involvement in their church community is not just receiving the support of the adults; they see themselves as active participants in the ministry and vision of the congregation. One gets a larger and perhaps even different picture of an effective ministry with youth from these young people's comments which reflect an inclusive intergenerational understanding of the church, an understanding of the church in which ministry with young people is a congregation-wide commitment, a ministry in which young people become "fully practicing participants."

The really big thing (here) is relationships between youth and adults. (Youth, Fort Dodge, IA)

The adults we have are great. We can depend on them for anything. (Youth, Saint Augustine, FL)

There are a ton of adults in the church that have a strong passion for God. I love everyone in this church. . . . they take time out of their lives to talk to me, make me feel better, get me back on the right track. (Youth, Billerica, MA)

Young people in the survey identified the most significant aspects of what it means for them to be "practicing faith in community." They rated the following beliefs and activities, drawn from items in dimensions 4, 5, and 6, as being among the most important for them:

The youth group at my church has been a positive influence on my religious faith.
My involvement in youth programs have helped me make serious life choices (about my future, my relationships, my values).
I like to worship and pray with others.
Worship services at my church have a positive influence on my religious faith.
The youth group leader at my church has been a positive influence on my religious faith.
Christian education programs at my church (classes, Bible studies) have been a positive influence on my religious faith.
A religion teacher at my church has been a positive influence on my religious faith.

Characteristic 4. Making the Christian Faith a Way of Life

Youth of maturing faith recognize God's call and integrate their beliefs into the conversations, decisions, and actions of daily life. In addition to believing in Jesus Christ, these young people claim that faith makes a difference in their lives and regularly speak about and act out their faith with family, friends, and even strangers. Faith is a driving force in their lives. When speaking about reasons for what they do, they mention faith as a significant impetus for their actions. They also speak about the Christian faith as a necessary force in society that helps them and others develop defined, constructive values and attitudes. For these committed Christian adolescents, faith is not something just to know or to understand or even to believe. Faith is something one lives, something one does, something one is.

> *I have come to know who I am, where I am, and where I stand in my faith, the world around me, and what I have to be thankful for.*
> *(Youth, Terre Haute, IN)*

> *I'm more serious about God now; the leadership makes us hungry for God in worship. It's during worship that we can dance, kneel, pray or cry. We want to serve God and worship Him. (Youth, Louisville, KY)*

Young people in the survey identified the most significant aspects of what it means for them to be "making the Christian faith a way of life." They rated the following beliefs and activities, drawn from items across the ten dimensions, as being among the most important for them:

> *I am a religious person.*
> *My life is committed to Jesus Christ.*
> *My faith shapes how I think and act.*
> *My life is filled with meaning and purpose.*
> *I have a real sense that God is guiding me.*
> *I go out of my way to show love to people I meet.*
> *I talk with other people about my faith.*
> *I feel God's presence in my relationships with other people.*
> *Personal prayer is a positive influence on my faith.*
> *I think Christians must be about the business of creating international understanding and harmony.*
> *I try to apply my faith to political and social issues.*

Characteristic 5. Living a Life of Service

Youth of maturing faith are "turned outward from themselves" toward others and the world. In speech and action they serve others and take public stands on moral issues and advocate for justice. They reach out to neighbors and friends in times of crises with comfort and support. They have friends of diverse socioeconomic, ethnic and religious backgrounds. They are especially concerned about the "shunned" or "difficult" or "losers." These young people get involved in church and community. For them faith is busy, active participation in Gods' mission in the world. The importance of service in their lives is yet another example of the integrative faith of these young people. Their faith is expressed in action for the sake of others.

Service is being Christ-like and we are taught to live a Christ-like walk—it isn't how you achieve it—it is a result of it. (Youth, Forth Worth, TX)

I think mission helps develop your faith. You learn how other people live beside yourself and it just kind of opens your horizons when you realize that you are not the only one in the world who might be suffering."
(Youth, Billings, MT)

One of the good experiences I had was (when we) went to Alamo, near Mexico, on a churchwide missions trip. It wasn't just youth group, but adults and college kids. There were a lot of older people there, got to talk to them and learned stuff about them. It was interesting to see where other people come from. It was an experience you couldn't have if you just stayed in the building. We did a lot of missions work, but we also got to know each other." (Youth, Grand Prairie, TX)

Young people in the survey identified the most significant aspects of what it means for them to be "living a life of service." They rated the following beliefs and activities, drawn from items in dimension 10, as being among the most important for them:

I am involved in activities of service related to church, community, or world.
I give portions of my time and money for helping people.
I assume responsibility for some part of my congregation's youth ministry.
I reach out to lonely and hurting youth.
I speak out publicly against specific social injustices.
I take public stands on moral issues.
I organize or participate in study or action groups to address injustice or immorality.

Characteristic 6. Exercising Moral Responsibility

God is involved in these young peoples' decision-making and direction-setting. Through Bible study, conversation with Christian friends, prayer, and "faith-informed reflection," God helps them determine right or wrong as well as supports them in their decisions. They made statements about the role faith has had in the choices that they make. These adolescents find God calling them to help others. They discourage others from being irresponsible or dishonest, such as speaking out against cheating at school. They know the moral decisions they make now will affect their future. They see hurtful actions taken not only as damaging to other people but also as a sin against God. These young people are known for their honesty, integrity, hospitality, and kindness.

For me, a lot of times it goes beyond what happens on Wednesday night. I think about it at school and I use the experience to help me make decisions. It equips you to deal with situations. When a situation comes along, it gives you options so you don't panic. I think it helps me see God in everyday life and not just at church on Sunday morning." (Youth, Fargo, ND)

When I first started, it is kind of like you are young and coming for friends, but our youth ministry does such a good job of instilling Christian values in you, it becomes part of your life. You go to church to be around all the people you have become really close to, to learn more about God. It is the jump-start for the rest of the week. (Youth, Fort Dodge, IA)

I try to create an open door, and open doors with conversation. I really don't want to scare anyone. I also do it by telling people what I think about what they are doing sometimes, like when people at my school are doing stuff that is ridiculous and stupid. I can show my faith by saying "do you know that what you are doing is not right?" (Youth, McKinney, TX)

Young people in the survey identified the most significant aspects of what it means for them to be "exercising moral responsibility." They rated the following beliefs and activities, drawn from items in dimensions 2, 5, and 7, as being among the most important for them.

My faith helps me know right from wrong.
I want to be the kind of person who helps people.
The kind of moral decisions I make now will affect my future happiness.
God helps me decide what is right or wrong behavior.
When people wrong other people, they sin against God.
I have found a way of life that gives me direction.

Characteristic 7. Possessing a Positive Spirit

These Christian young people are optimistic and full of hope. They are convinced they can make the world a better place. This positive spirit is reflected in their participation in the lives of other Christian youth for whom they have high regard, for whom they regularly care and whom they frequently defend. In a world where adolescent development is consistently disconnected from spirituality, these young people are concrete examples of how spiritual development appears to have generated a hopeful, confident spirit that characterizes their sense of self and their positive stance toward one another and the world.

> *I think we set examples for each other. Like we say we don't do it just for us and the fun; we shape each other's faith. . . . We can see Christ working through our youth group. (Youth, St. Augustine, FL)*

> *The way we share Christ through fun things and little events that people get drawn to is real; kids want to be a part of it. (Youth, Grand Rapids, MI)*

Young people in the survey identified the most significant aspects of what it means for them to be "possessing a positive spirit." They rated the following beliefs and activities, drawn from items in dimension 3, as being among the most important for them.

> *I respect and care about the youth in our youth group.*
> *When my friend or neighbor experiences a death or tragedy, I offer comfort or support.*
> *I am eager, responsive, and cooperative, rather than unresponsive, disinterested, and apathetic.*
> *I defend friends and acquaintances who are being talked about when they aren't there.*
> *I am optimistic, trusting, and I am convinced that I can do much to make the world a better place.*
> *I show a grace, loving attitude toward people not easy to like.*
> *I have friends of diverse socioeconomic, ethnic, and religious backgrounds.*

Adult Perspectives of Vital Faith in Youth

The parent, adult youth worker, youth minister, and pastor surveys asked the adults for their views and experience of the young people in the congregation. Comparing the responses of all three groups (see Table 4) shows that there is a strong shared perspective among the three adult groups about the faith of committed Christian youth, confirming the personal assessment of young people about their own faith lives. In the exemplary congregations in youth ministry, the vital faith of young people is demonstrated in such a way that parents, adult youth workers, youth ministers, and pastors have seen it, experienced it, and share a common perception with the youth of their congregations about what makes for committed Christian faith in youth.

Comparing the findings with the Seven Characteristics of Vital Faith in Youth, the adult survey results present a portrait of committed Christian young people.

Characteristic 1. Seeking Spiritual Growth

- *attending gatherings where they can learn more about the Christian faith*
- *giving portions of time and money for helping people*
- *taking advantage of opportunities to study the Bible and their faith tradition*
- *asking sincere and searching questions about the nature of a life of faith in God*

Characteristic 2. Possessing a Vital Faith

- *coming to know Jesus Christ as their Savior and Lord*
- *witnessing publicly about their faith*

Characteristic 3. Practicing Faith in Community

- *faithfully attending worship services*
- *willing participate in leadership within the congregation (teach Sunday school or vacation Bible school, service on a church task force, and so on)*

Characteristic 5. Living a Life of Service

- *involved in serving others*
- *involved in activities to better their community*
- *reaching out to lonely and hurting peers*
- *involved in activities of service related to church, community, or world*

Characteristic 6. Exercising Moral Responsibility

- *taking public stands on moral issues*
- *not participating in activities such as lying, stealing, substance abuse, and so on; and have a reputation for honesty, integrity, hospitality, and acts of kindness*

Characteristic 7. Possessing a Positive Spirit

- *offering comfort or support to a friend or neighbor in the event of a death or a tragedy either by talking or by action*
- *showing a gracious, loving attitude to people not easy to like*
- *reflecting positive, loving attitudes toward each other*
- *establishing a joyous atmosphere at our youth meetings*
- *known for their general optimism, trust, and conviction that one person can do much to make the world a better place*
- *joining Christian groups to build friendships and learn how to be a friend*
- *enjoying being together as evidenced by their laughing, singing, and conversation*
- *eager, responsive, and cooperative*
- *going out of their way to welcome persons from different ethnic backgrounds*

Conclusion

The young people in the study are typical teens in so many ways, facing the challenges and struggles and joys of growing up in America today. Yet in matters of faith, they possess a desire to know and follow God that defines them, shapes their character, and guides their lives.

It is clear from the study's findings that congregations *can* nurture youth of vital Christian faith. The study found congregations with high percentages of committed, maturing Christian youth. What's going on in these congregations that is contributing to vital faith in young people? What are these congregations doing that is making a difference in the faith lives of young people? What are the qualities and practices of these congregations that can serve as a guide for all congregations? We now turn our attention to these questions.

TABLE 2

Thirty-Four Characteristics of Maturing Christian Youth

Characteristic 1: Seek Spiritual Growth

Youth are pursuing spiritual growth through conversation, study, reading the Bible, prayer, small groups, retreats.

1. Are heard referring to having prayer, devotions, and meditation times.

2. Ask sincere and searching questions about the nature of a life of faith in God.

3. Prefer and attend gatherings where they can learn more about the Christian faith.

4. Accept opportunities for learning how to speak naturally and intelligently about their faith.

5. Are involved in Bible study and/or prayer groups.

6. Join Christian groups to build friendships and learn how to be a friend.

Characteristic 2: Possess a Vital Faith

Youth are keenly aware of God present and active in their own life, the lives of others, and the life of the world.

1. Speak openly about seeking or experiencing God's guidance.

2. Are heard asking each other about what God has recently done in their lives or the lives of others.

3. In times of trouble, reassure others that God is active to make things work out all right in the long run.

4. Occasionally speak of having been keenly aware of the presence of God.

Characteristic 3: Make the Christian Faith a Way of Life

Youth recognize God's "call" and integrate their beliefs into the conversation, decisions, and actions of daily life.

1. Speak publicly about their relationship with Jesus Christ.

2. When providing a rationale for their actions will at times cite specifics of their faith.

3. In conversation with family and friends bring up topics of faith or Christian living.

4. Pray for people especially needing God's help.

Characteristic 4: Practice Faith in Community

Youth actively practice their faith in Jesus Christ, privately and publicly, through participation in the congregation's worship, ministries, and leadership.

1. Regularly attend worship services.

2. Have willingly participated in two or more of the following:

   ° taught Sunday School, Bible class, or Vacation Bible School

   ° served with a group to improve conditions at school or neighborhood

   ° made a presentation before a faith group or in worship

   ° helped in raising money for a Christian project or mission trip

   ° served on a congregational or denominational committee or task force

   ° regularly contribute money to a congregation or faith project.

Characteristic 5: Possess a Positive Spirit

Youth reflect loving and hopeful attitudes toward others and life.

1. Enjoy being together, as evidenced by their laughing, singing, and conversation.

2. Show a gracious, loving attitude to people not easy to like (for example, the difficult, rude, shunned, loser).

3. Have friends of widely diverse socioeconomic, ethnic, and religious background or persuasion.

4. Have been heard describing the Christian faith as a necessary force in society, helping people develop attitudes of understanding, sympathy, and cooperation.

5. Are known for their general optimism, trust, and positive expectation of other people, being convinced that one person can do much to make the world a better place.

6. Are eager, responsive, and cooperative rather than unresponsive, disinterested, and apathetic.

Characteristic 6: Live a Life of Service

Youth are involved in activities caring for others, reaching out to others in need, and addressing injustice.

1. Give portions of time and money for helping people.

2. Attend conferences or workshops that present the challenge of service professions such as the ordained ministry.

3. Speak out publicly against specific social injustices.

4. Try to offer comfort or support to a friend or neighbor in the event of a death or tragedy either by talking or by action (personal presence, help with routine tasks, transportation, visit in hospital, and so on).

5. Defend a friend or acquaintance who is being talked about when he or she isn't there.

6. Organize and participate in study or action groups to address injustice or immorality.

7. Are involved in activities of service related to church, community, or world.

8. Are assuming responsibility for some aspect of their youth ministry.

Characteristic 7: Exercise Moral Responsibility

Youth live with integrity utilizing their Christian faith in making moral decisions.

1. Are heard referring to seeking help from Scripture in deciding what is right and wrong.

2. Actively seek to discourage friends from cheating at school.

3. Have a reputation for not participating in activities such as lying, stealing, substance abuse, etc. and have a reputation for honesty, integrity, hospitality, and acts of kindness.

TABLE 3

YOUTH OF VITAL CHRISTIAN FAITH: YOUTH SURVEY RESULTS

Eleven Dimensions of the Committed Christian Youth Linked with the Seven Characteristics of Youth of Vital Faith

11 Dimensions of Committed Christian Youth*	Rating**	Characteristic of Vital Faith
1. A Personal Christianity	7.74	#1 and #2
2. Moral Responsibility	7.37	#6
3. Caring Relationships ("Defends and Supports Friends")	6.86	#7
4. Faith Impact of Church Involvement	6.83	#3
5. Faith Maturity	6.50	#1, #2, and #4
6. Personal Religiousness	6.36	#1
7. Moral Integrity	5.94	#6
8. Seeks Spiritual Growth	5.76	#1
9. God Consciousness	5.38	#2
10. Lives a Life of Service	5.35	#5
11. Speaks Publicly about One's Faith	5.31	#2

Each Dimension includes items from the survey that show a strong coherent relationship.

** Mean Scores: highest rating is "9," indicating a response of "Always" or "Almost Always True."*

Eleven Dimensions of the Committed Christian
Youth Theme with Survey Items

11 Dimensions of Committed Christian Faith	Rating*

1. A Personal Christianity — 7.74

- God cares for me in a special way. (8.54)
- I know that Jesus Christ is the Son of God who died on a cross and rose again. (8.54)
- I have a sense of being saved in Christ. (8.08)
- God is a close personal friend who guides and protects me. (8.02)
- I see evidence that God is active in the world. (7.27)
- The active presence of God in my life has been a positive influence on my religious faith. (7.22)
- My life is committed to Jesus Christ. (7.17)
- I am keenly aware of the presence of God. (7.03)

2. Moral Responsibility — 7.37

- I want to be the kind of person who helps people. (8.01)
- The kind of moral decisions I make now will affect my future happiness. (7.57)
- God helps me decide what is right or wrong behavior. (7.33)
- When people wrong other people, they sin against God. (7.02)
- I have found a way of life that gives me direction. (6.92)

3. Caring Relationships ("Defends and Supports Friends") — 6.86

- I respect and care about the youth in our youth group. (7.88)
- When my friend or neighbor experiences a death or tragedy, I offer comfort or support. (6.94)
- I am eager, responsive, and cooperative, rather than unresponsive, disinterested, and apathetic. (6.91)
- I defend friends and acquaintances who are being talked about when they aren't there. (6.88)

Mean Scores: highest rating is "9" indicating a response of "Always" or "Almost Always True."

- I am optimistic, trusting, and I am convinced that I can do much to make the world a better place. (6.60)

- I show a grace, loving attitude toward people not easy to like. (6.32)

- I have friends of diverse socioeconomic, ethnic, and religious backgrounds. (6.49)

4. **Faith Impact of Church Involvement**   6.83

- The youth group at my church has been a positive influence on my religious faith. (7.42)

- Worship services at my church have a positive influence on my religious faith. (6.83)

- The youth group leader at my church has been a positive influence on my religious faith. (6.47)

- Christian education programs at my church (classes, Bible studies) have been a positive influence on my religious faith. (6.45)

- A religion teacher at my church has been a positive influence on my religious faith. (6.33)

5. **Faith Maturity**   6.50

- My faith helps me know right from wrong. (7.44)

- My life is filled with meaning and purpose. (7.31)

- I am spiritually moved by the beauty of God's creations. (7.03)

- I like to worship and pray with others. (6.78)

- My faith shapes how I think and act. (6.53)

- I have a real sense that God is guiding me. (6.51)

- I go out of my way to show love to people I meet. (6.37)

- I seek out opportunities to grow spiritually. (6.33)

- I talk with other people about my faith. (6.30)

- I feel God's presence in my relationships with other people. (6.28)

- I think Christians must be about the business of creating international understanding and harmony. (5.92)

- I try to apply my faith to political and social issues. (5.87)

- I take time for periods of prayer or meditation. (5.75)

6. **Personal Religiousness**   6.36

  - I am a religious person. (7.20)

  - My involvement in youth programs has helped me make serious life choices (about my future, my relationships, my values). (7.05)

  - I have prayed privately in the past six months. (6.96)

  - The Bible is a positive influence on my faith. (6.88)

  - Religious faith is important in my life. (6.85)

  - Personal prayer is a positive influence on my faith. (6.18)

7. **Moral Integrity**   5.94

  - I don't participate in activities such as lying, stealing, substance abuse, etc., but known for my honesty, integrity, hospitality, kindness. (6.74)

  - I try to discourage friends from cheating at school. (5.55)

  - I seek help from Scripture in deciding what is right and wrong. (5.49)

8. **Seeks Spiritual Growth**   5.76

  - I prefer and attend gatherings where I can learn more about the Christian faith. (6.19)

  - I join Christian groups to build friendships and learn how to be a friend. (6.07)

  - I pray, have devotions, or meditate, either alone or with others. (6.11)

  - I accept opportunities to learn how to speak naturally and intelligently about my faith. (5.96)

  - I ask sincere and searching questions about the nature of a life of faith in God. (5.94)

  - I take advantage of opportunities to study the Bible and our faith tradition. (5.49)

9. **God Consciousness**   5.38

  - I reassure others that God is active to make things work out all right in the long run. (5.98)

  - I speak openly about seeking or experiencing God's guidance. (5.65)

  - I ask my friends about what God has recently done in their lives or the lives of others. (4.53)

10. Lives a Life of Service   5.35

- I am involved in activities of service related to church, community, or world. (6.51)

- I give portions of my time and money for helping people. (6.12)

- I assume responsibility for some part of my congregation's youth ministry. (6.11)

- I reach out to lonely and hurting youth. (6.07)

- I take public stands on moral issues. (5.15)

- I organize or participate in study or action groups to address injustice or immorality. (4.44)

- I speak out publicly against specific social injustices. (4.31)

11. Speaks Publicly about One's Faith   5.31

- I talk with my family and friends about faith and Christian living. (5.67)

- I speak about the Christian faith as a necessary force in society that helps people develop attitudes of understanding, sympathy, and cooperation. (5.36)

- When giving a reason for my actions, I mention specifics of my faith. (5.35)

- I speak publicly about my relationship with Jesus Christ. (5.12)

- I witness publicly about my faith. (5.04)

TABLE 4

Youth of Vital Christian Faith: Parents, Adult Youth Workers, Pastor and Youth Minister Survey Results

Committed Christian Youth	Pastor and Youth	Parents	Adult Youth Workers*
1. I see youth who are reflecting positive, loving attitudes toward each other.	8.30	7.94	8.05
2. I see youth who are establishing a joyous atmosphere at our youth meetings.	8.22	8.04	8.12
3. I see youth who are involved in serving others.	8.02	7.31	7.47
4. I see youth who are faithfully attending worship services.	7.86	7.92	8.10
5. I see youth who are coming to know Jesus Christ as their Savior and Lord.	7.85	7.83	7.81
6. I see youth who are involved in activities to better their community.	7.39	7.30	7.05
7. Youth enjoy being together as evidenced by their laughing, singing, and conversation.	7.36	6.98	7.36
8. I see youth who are reaching out to lonely and hurting peers.	7.05	6.57	6.62
9. I see youth who are taking advantage of opportunities to study the Bible and their faith tradition.	7.02	6.63	6.59
10. Youth are eager, responsive, and cooperative.	6.58	5.98	5.97
11. I see youth who are involved in witness groups (singing, instrumental, drama).	6.53	7.08	6.96

*Mean scores: highest rating is "9," indicating a response of "Always" or "Almost Always True."

12.	I see youth who are going out of their way to welcome persons from different ethnic backgrounds.	6.52	6.42	6.38
13.	I see youth who are witnessing publicly about their faith.	6.36	6.46	6.33
14.	Youth willingly participate in leadership within the congregation (teach Sunday school/vacation Bible school, service on a church task force, etc.).	6.33	5.91	6.02
15.	I see youth who take public stands on moral issues.	6.20	6.03	6.18
16.	Youth are involved in activities of service related to church, community, or world.	6.12	5.47	5.50
17.	Youth try to offer comfort or support to a friend or neighbor in the event of a death or a tragedy either by talking or by action.	6.08	5.50	5.58
18.	Youth of the congregation regularly attend worship services.	5.96	6.22	6.31
19.	Youth are asking sincere and searching questions about the nature of a life of faith in God.	5.96	5.24	5.27
20.	Youth have a reputation for not participating in activities such as lying, stealing, substance abuse, etc; and have a reputation for honesty, integrity, hospitality, and acts of kindness.	5.85	6.17	6.05
21.	Youth prefer and attend gatherings where they can learn more about the Christian faith.	5.57	5.50	5.40
22.	Youth give portions of time and money for helping people.	5.47	5.08	5.05
23.	Youth show a gracious, loving attitude to people not easy to like.	5.53	5.12	5.29
24.	Youth are known for their general optimism, trust, and conviction that one person can do much to make the world a better place.	5.37	5.18	4.99
25.	Youth join Christian groups to build friendships and learn how to be a friend.	5.26	5.25	5.25

CHAPTER TWO

congregations that promote youth of vital christian faith:

the importance of congregational culture

T here are long-held assumptions in American Christianity that effective youth ministry has to do with adopting the newest techniques, the finest resources, the best training programs, or securing the most dynamic leader. Given such assumptions, one would expect to find these factors to be at the forefront of congregations in the Study of Exemplary Congregations in Youth Ministry.

Indeed good practice, resources, training, and leadership are present in the congregations. However, these factors in themselves are not sufficient to describe the influence these churches have on the faith of their young people. They may not even be at the heart of these faithful and effective ministries with youth. Among a great diversity of Christian traditions across the United States, in congregations of every size in all regions of the country, in churches who are deeply influencing the faith and lives of young men and women, the EYM Study discovered that it is the culture of the whole church that is most influential in nurturing youth of vital Christian faith. The genius of these churches seems best described as a systemic mix of theology, values, people, relationships, expectations, and activities. It appears that a culture of the Spirit emerges with its pervasive and distinct dynamics and atmosphere that is more powerful than its component parts.

What Is Congregational Culture?

A dictionary would define *culture* as the sum of attitudes, customs, and beliefs that distinguish one group of people from another. Its root meaning is shared with the world *agriculture*, referring to the soil that has been tilled and by extension a set of traits that have been plowed into a group's way of life. Culture is transmitted from one generation to the next through language, material objects, ritual, institutions, and art.

In *Culture Shift: Transforming Your Church from the Inside Out*, Robert Lewis and Wayne Cordeiro write, "The idea of church culture is often ignored, in part because so little material is available about it. Yet we believe *culture is to the church what a soul is to the human body.* It is an overall life force that the Holy Spirit uses to give energy, personality, and uniqueness to everything a body of believers says and does."[1] Church culture influences everything you do. It colors the way you choose and introduce programs. It shapes how you select and train leaders. "Your culture is the lens through which you view your life. If you change the lens, you change your outlook. Change the culture, and everything else changes, including the future."[2]

Nancy T. Ammerman, professor of sociology at Boston University, has researched and written extensively about American congregations and the role of congregational culture. In her essay "Culture and Identity in the Congregation," she explains what a congregational culture is:

> Culture is who we are and the world we have created to live in. It is the predictable patterns of who does what and habitual strategies for telling the world about the things held most dear. A culture includes the congregation's history and stories of its heroes. It includes its symbols, rituals, and worldview. It is shaped by the cultures in which its members live (represented by their demographic characteristics), but it takes on its own unique identity and character when those members come together. Understanding a congregation requires understanding that it is a unique gathering of people with a cultural identity all its own.

Congregations draw their culture and identity from their specific religious tradition. What each congregation cooks up, then, is always a mix of local creativity and larger tradition. What we see in a given locale is that group's selective retrieval of their own theological heritage, along with the local inventions that have been necessary to make sense of life in that place. . .

A congregational culture is constructed out of theological and denominational traditions, expectations from the larger culture, patterns of social class and ethnicity, and the like. All those things are carried into the congregation by its members and leaders. Whenever any of those elements changes, the congregational will inevitably change as well. . .

Congregational culture is more than the sum of what people bring with them and more than a mirror image of the theological tradition they represent. It is a unique creation, constructed out of their interaction together over time.[3]

The dynamics of congregational culture at work can be seen in this analysis of the genius of black congregations by Robert Michael Franklin in his essay "The Safest Place on Earth: The Culture of Black Congregations."

In order to understand the genius of black congregations, it is important to understand how the congregation's entire culture does the work of empowering parishioners for mission. Central to that cultural work is the pivotal role of pastoral leadership in its manifestation of theological convictions, rhetorical skills, and practical wisdom. Most portraits of black congregations emphasize the role of clergy. This is understandable, given the elevated office of ministry in most black communities. A more careful examination of black congregational culture, however, requires attention to the array of practices that are sustained by the laity—style of worship, singing, ecstatic rituals (shouting, altar prayer), and politically relevant religious education. Effective congregational mission actually flows from the dynamic interaction between qualified, gifted leadership and an empowering congregational culture. Black clergy are, in the first instance, servants called to nurture and maintain a healthy congregational culture. Once progress in this task has been demonstrated, then they may be authorized in the public arena.[4]

The characteristics of black congregational culture according to Franklin include: (1) full engagement of the senses in worship, (2) intimate prayer, (3) cathartic shouting, (4) triumphant singing, (5) politically relevant religious education, and (6) prophetic, imaginative preaching. Franklin concludes his analysis with these insights:

The entire culture of the black church thus works to create the sensibilities necessary for public mission. Black church culture is a rich and vibrant ensemble

*of practices that offer praise to God and hope to oppressed humanity. Clergy
are expected first to maintain and then to mobilize this culture for Christ's
mission in the world. Maintenance and mobilization are dialectically related.*

*Preaching is the ecclesial practices most central to the sacred oral culture of
African Americans and most essential for mobilizing and sustaining people for
public action. Good black social preaching names and frames crises creatively,
analyzes them in biblical perspective, describes solutions using indigenous
symbols and images, prescribes specific plans, and offers hope via celebration.*[5]

With this understanding of congregational culture we can now examine the most
striking finding in the Study of Exemplary Congregations in Youth Ministry: the
role that congregational culture plays in nurturing the faith of young people and
in the effectiveness of the church's youth ministry. This congregational culture of
the Spirit has distinct features and dynamics that are more powerful than any of
its individual parts.

The Impact of Congregational Culture
on the Faith of Young People

The Study of Exemplary Congregations in Youth Ministry presents a portrait of
the strong impact faith communities can have on the faith and lives of young
people when churches set their minds to fully enfranchise young people in their
life and ministry. When pastors, congregational leaders, parents, and adult youth
leaders work together to promote real commitment to young people as full members of the body of Christ and carry that commitment across the life and mission
of the entire congregation, teenagers mature in faith and grow to respect and love
their church. The EYM Study demonstrates how age-level youth ministry and
ministries with family are dependent upon and greatly enhanced by congregations setting young people and youth ministry as one of its essential priorities. If
a congregation is not willing to make this commitment, youth and youth ministry will always be tangential and second rate. Congregational commitment to
young people is essential for an effective ministry with youth.

While confirming the power of several well known youth ministry practices,
the EYM Study pointed to a congregational culture of the Spirit—something
more basic and central in establishing vital faith in youth. The research points to
the value of a congregation's culture endowed with a palpable sense of the living,
active presence of God at work among (1) the people of the whole congregation,
(2) its ministries with youth, (3) its parents, (4) the ministries of the congregation, and (5) its congregational leaders (pastor, youth minister, youth, and adult

leaders) as providing the most powerful, pervasive influence these congregations have on young people long-term. It is the communal awareness of participation in God's presence and action that permeates the values, relationships, and activities of these congregations, giving rise to an atmosphere, a culture of the Spirit focused on mission and the transformation of life that seems to make them so influential in the lives and faith of young people.

The most convincing evidence of this culture comes from the witness of the young people themselves. The youth interviewed regularly spoke directly about qualities, relationships and practices in the ministries of their congregations that had profoundly shaped their life and their faith. Here are several of their reflections:

> *I experience God at work in the lives of my friends and our adult leaders here; this church is the most real place in my life. I find hope and support for working out my life in a very difficult family situation. Without these people caring and praying for me, I don't know how I would make it. I live off the worship experiences and people here who believe in me.*

> *I know our whole church focuses on how your walk is with Jesus . . . It keeps you very accountable and it's so personal, not just, I'm going to tell you what you need to know, but, where are you with God and how can we encourage you?*

> *This church is very welcoming. Like, if you come, they'll just take you under their wing. Or if you're going through a hard time, they'll love you, they take you in for who you are; they don't judge people . . . They welcome anybody in the whole church. Pretty much everybody knows everybody. It's a good family.*

> *I'm more serious about God now; the leadership makes us hungry for God in worship. It's during worship that we can dance, kneel, pray or cry. We want to serve God and worship him.*

At the heart of this culture of the Spirit is the belief that God is present, active, and alive in everything they do. These are congregations that live their belief that Jesus Christ is present and graciously at work in and through the body of Christ for the sake of the salvation of the world. Their commitment: We, his disciples, his Church are called to pass on faith and call young people to discipleship, witness and service. From these shared beliefs and commitments flow the practices of ministry with youth.

The congregational culture of the Spirit generates four spheres of relationships and practices that intersect and powerfully impact the lives of young people in the EYM congregations. First, these congregations' basic ministries are thoroughly *intergenerational*. Young people are welcomed and expected to participate and lead in church-wide ministries, including worship, education, fellowship, outreach, and decision-making. Second, these congregations have developed *age-level youth ministries* marked by trusted relationships and custom-designed ministry practices and activities within a caring atmosphere of high expectation. There are multiple nurturing relationships and activities intentionally planned to create an atmosphere of respect, growth, and belonging. Third, these congregations educate *parents* in the faith and equip them for at-home caring conversations, prayer, ritual, Bible reading, and service; and parents and the whole family are engaged in faith practices at home. Fourth, these congregations are blessed with competent, faith-filled, *leadership* from the pastor to the youth minister to the youth and adult leaders who are committed to young people and developing their faith lives.

Aligning and integrating the intergenerational ministries of the congregation with adolescent age-level ministries and the families of the young people, supported by competent, faith-filled leaders (pastors, youth ministers, and youth and adult leaders), generates intersecting arenas of influence that seem to make the work of these congregations so significant in the lives of their young people.

CHART 3

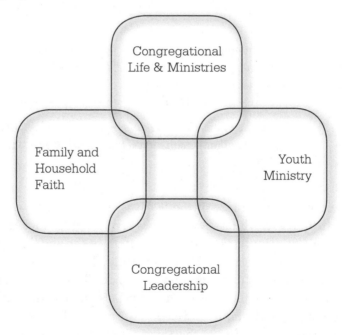

Youth ministries do not exist on the side of or separate from the entire on-going lives and ministries of these congregations. Youth ministries are integrated into and supported by the congregation as a whole. The research indicates that effective youth ministry exists as an integral dimension of youth-friendly, youth-engaging congregations. These congregations are powerful faith- and life-shaping systems. Young people do not grow and flourish in isolation in these congregations. They participate in families, friends, and intergenerational relationships. They move from one age to the next in a journey influenced by peers as well as those older and younger. Young people influence and are profoundly influenced by adults and youth. What is going on with young people in the congregation impacts the whole body and vice versa.

Alignment of Mission: Congregation and Youth Ministry

Congregations in the study dovetailed the ministries of the larger congregation with youth ministry. The research team discovered striking similarities of both identity and mission in the vision statements of congregations and their youth ministries. In part, the power of these congregations and their youth ministries lies in this integration of these visions and missions.

The alignment between the mission of the whole church and the mission of the church's youth ministry can be seen through two examples from the twenty-one congregations selected for onsite visits and interviews: Grace Lutheran Church in Des Moines, WA, and Travis Avenue Baptist Church in Fort Worth, TX.

Grace Lutheran Church

Mission
We, the members of Grace Lutheran Church, have been called together by God's love in Jesus Christ and equipped by the Holy Spirit to proclaim the Gospel. Through Word and Sacraments, our mission is to invite and welcome people into a relationship with Jesus Christ and his church. It is our intention to provide a nurturing environment for everyone to:

Glorify God—Worship
Reach the unchurched —Evangelism
Advance community—Fellowship
Care for those in need—Ministry
Educate God's people—Discipleship

Mission of Youth Ministry
We believe in discipling youth through walking beside them in many aspects of life. Through retreats and missions we expand their knowledge and have real life experiences of God working in their lives and through them to touch the lives of others. Through monthly fellowship events we add fun and excitement and give a time for youth to celebrate the life that God has given. Through weekly study

we educate and grow spiritually and intellectually. Ultimately the youth program is a place for youth to come, bring friends, and have a place to experience God through many different avenues of events and relationships.

Travis Avenue Baptist Church

Mission

We envision a vibrant church composed of passionate followers of Jesus Christ who, having received the gift of eternal life and being transformed by the love of God, are empowered to live out the following

- *Learn and apply the truth of God's Word*
- *Obey God and deny self*
- *Serve God and others*
- *Share Jesus Christ with others*
- *Live by faith in God*
- *Seek God in worship*
- *Build Christ-centered relationships*

Mission of Youth Ministry

Our mission in the Travis Avenue Student Ministry is to lead students to live for Jesus Christ. The student ministry exists for the purpose of teaching students to walk with God on their own. Through our ministry, students will encounter and be introduced to the richness of God's Word as we challenge them to live the life God intended for them.

We have an incredible group of adult and student leaders from the surrounding Fort Worth community who are committed to living a life fully devoted to Christ. Our Student Ministry meets twice each week and we encourage students to be part of our Sunday school hour. We also offer a Wednesday night Bible study—a time of worship and to hear the Word of God. In addition to these weekly programs, we have special events throughout the year such as weekend retreats, student camp, disciple now, and Travis Round-Up.

Supportive congregations make a vital difference to youth ministries. Youth, adult leaders, youth ministers, and parents depend on pastors, funds, facilities, and community for the lifeblood of youth ministry. This may seem like a one-way flow of influence with little return for the congregation. Sometimes adults and leaders of other ministries in the congregation may even resent efforts expended on teenagers who often seem unappreciative of that support.

We learned from the EYM churches that youth ministry flourishes in the context of informed, committed congregation of vital faith. This study confirms the need for pastors to think theologically and strategically about the place and priority of youth ministry in the congregation they are called to lead. The pastor does not have to be directly involved in all the relationships and practices of youth ministry, but the direction of the congregation's youth ministry requires the pastor's advocacy, guidance, and support.

The EYM congregations present a portrait of the strong impact faith communities can have on the faith and lives of young people when churches set their minds to fully enfranchise young people in their life and ministry. When pastors, congregational leaders, parents and adult youth leaders work together to promote real commitment to young people as full members of the body of Christ and carry that commitment across the life and mission of the entire congregation, teenagers mature in faith and grow to respect and love their church. The EYM Study demonstrates how age-level youth ministry and ministries with family are dependent upon and greatly enhanced by congregations setting young people and youth ministry as one of its essential priorities. If a congregation is not willing to make this commitment, youth and youth ministry will always be tangential and second rate. Congregational commitment to young people is at the heart of effective ministry with youth.

Faith Assets: Describing the Culture of Exemplary Congregations in Youth Ministry

One of the most important contributions of the Exemplary Youth Ministry Study is the identification of forty-four Faith Assets that contribute to the development of a vital Christian faith in young people. Developed from the survey results from the 131 "exemplary" congregations and the on-site interviews with twenty-one of these congregations (three in each of the seven denominations), the Faith Assets are elements or building blocks that describe congregational culture and constitute a framework for congregations to use in developing the faith of young people. The study points to these forty-four elements as ways and means through which congregations have over time, with great effort and struggle, built their capacities to influence the faith and lives of young people.

It is important to remember that the forty-four Faith Assets are descriptive, not prescriptive. They are not *the* definitive list. They are part of a growing body of knowledge about faith maturing in youth and the role of the congregation-as-a-whole, the family, and the youth ministry. The Faith Assets are a roadmap for developing congregations and youth ministries that promote youth of vital Christian faith. They are cumulative. They build on each other. The more the better for everyone involved: the congregation, leaders, families, and young people. The key is working toward the "tipping point" when the cumulative effect of the forty-four Faith Assets creates a congregational spirit and culture that maximizes efforts to nurture youth of maturing Christian faith.

CHART 4

Congregational Faith and Qualities

The Congregational Faith Assets describe the values and dynamics of the inter-generational life and ministry of the whole congregation. The Congregational Faith Assets reflect attributes the congregation as a whole brings to its relationships with youth. They describe aspects of the congregation's theological orientation, faith maturity, values, attitudes, and practices that bear directly on its capacity to engage and influence the faith of young people. Each Faith Asset identifies an element of the congregation's overall functioning that contributes to effective ministries with youth.

Congregational Faith

Asset 1. Experiences God's Living Presence: The congregation possesses a sense of God's living presence in community, at worship, through study, and in service.

Asset 2. Makes Faith Central: The congregation recognizes and participates in God's sustaining and transforming life and work.

Asset 3. Emphasizes Prayer: The congregation practices the presence of God as individuals and community through prayer and worship.

Asset 4. Focuses on Discipleship: The congregation is committed to knowing and following Jesus Christ.

Asset 5. Emphasizes Scripture: The congregation values the authority of Scripture in its life and mission.

Asset 6. Makes Mission Central: The congregation consistently witnesses, serves and promotes moral responsibility, and seeks justice.

Congregational Qualities

Asset 7. Supports Youth Ministry: Youth and ministry with young people are high priorities for the congregation.

Asset 8. Demonstrates Hospitality: The congregation values and welcomes all people, especially youth.,

Asset 9. Strives for Excellence: The congregation sets high standards, evaluates, and engages in continuous improvement.

Asset 10. Encourages Thinking: The congregation welcomes questions and reflection on faith and life.

Asset 11. Creates Community: Congregational life reflects high quality personal and group relationships.

Asset 12. Encourages Small Groups: The congregation engages members in study, conversation, and prayer about faith in daily life.

Asset 13. Promotes Worship: The congregation expands and renews spirit-filled, uplifting worship.

Asset 14. Fosters Ethical Responsibility: The congregation encourages individual and social moral responsibility.

Asset 15. Promotes Service: The congregation sponsors outreach, service projects, and cultural immersions both locally and globally.

Asset 16. Demonstrates Effective Practices: The congregation engages in a wide variety of ministry practices and activities.

Asset 17. Participate in the Congregation: Youth are engaged in a wide spectrum of congregational relationships and practices.

Asset 18. Assume Ministry Leadership: Youth are invited, equipped and affirmed for leadership in congregational activities.

Youth Ministry Qualities

The Youth Ministry Faith Assets describe the quality of the congregation's age-level ministries with youth. They indicate the attitudes, expectations and practices of the congregation's age-level ministries with youth within the larger intergenerational culture of quality ministry with young people.

Asset 19. Establishes a Caring Environment: Youth ministry provides multiple nurturing relationships and activities resulting in a welcoming atmosphere of respect, growth, and belonging.

Asset 20. Develops Quality Relationships: Youth ministry develops authentic relationships among youth and adults establishing an environment of presence and life engagement.

Asset 21. Focuses on Jesus Christ: Youth ministry's mission, practices, and relationships are inspired by the life and ministry of Jesus Christ.

Asset 22. Considers Life Issues: Youth ministry values and addresses the full range of young people's lives.

Asset 23. Uses Many Approaches: Youth ministry intentionally and creatively employs multiple activities appropriate to the ministry's mission and context.

Asset 24. Is Well Organized and Planned: Youth ministry engages participants and leaders in long range planning, implementation, evaluation, and innovation in an atmosphere of high expectations.

Family and Household Faith Assets

The Family and Household Faith Assets describe the importance of family faith, adding another influence to the youth-friendly culture of the whole congregation and the effective age-level ministry with youth. The Family and Household Faith Assets describe faith and faith practices at home, and the role of the congregation in equipping and support parental and family faith.

Asset 25. Possesses Strong Parental Faith: Parents possess and practice a vital and informed faith.

Asset 26. Promotes Family Faith Practices: Parents engage youth and the whole family in conversations, prayer, bible reading, and service that nurture faith and life.

Asset 27. Reflects Family Harmony: Family members' expressions of respect and love create an atmosphere promoting faith.

Asset 28. Equips Parents: The congregation offers instruction and guidance that nurture parental faith and equips parents for nurturing faith at home.

Asset 29. Fosters Parent-Youth Relationships: The congregation offers parent-youth activities that strengthen parent-youth relationships.

Leadership

Effective, competent, faith-filled leadership is what makes congregations and youth ministries work. At the center of leadership in a congregation is the pastor and four assets describe the pastor's specific impact on youth ministry and developing youth of vital Christian faith. Six Faith Assets express the strength of the primary youth minister in the congregation, while five Faith Assets describe the effectiveness of the youth and adult leadership in youth ministry.

Pastor

Asset 30. Exercises Spiritual Influence: The pastor knows and models the transforming presence of God in life and ministry.

Asset 31. Demonstrates Interpersonal Competence: The pastor builds a sense of community and relates well with adults and youth.

Asset 32. Supports Youth Ministry: The pastor understands, guides, and advocates for youth ministry.

Asset 33. Supports Leaders: The pastor affirms and mentors youth and adults leading youth ministry.

Youth Minister

Asset 34. Provides Competent Leadership: The youth minister reflects superior theological, theoretical, and practical knowledge and skill in leadership.

Asset 35. Models Faith: The youth minister is a role model reflecting a living faith for youth and adults.

Asset 36. Mentors Faith Life: The youth minister assists adult leaders and youth in their faith life both one-on-one and in groups.

Asset 37. Develops Teams: The youth minister reflects a clear vision and attracts gifted youth and adults into leadership.

Asset 38. Knows Youth: The youth minister knows youth and the changes in youth culture, and utilizes these understandings in ministry.

Asset 39. Establishes Effective Relationships: The youth minister enjoys effective relationships with youth, parents, volunteers, and staff.

Youth and Adult Leaders

Asset 40. Are Equipped for Peer Ministry: Youth practice friendship, care-giving, and outreach and are supported by ministry training and caring adults.

Asset 41. Establish Adult-Youth Mentoring: Adults engage youth in the Christian faith and life supported by informed leadership.

Asset 42. Participate in Training: Youth and adults are equipped for ministry in an atmosphere of high expectations.

Asset 43. Possess Vibrant Faith: Youth and adult leaders possess and practice a vital and informed Christian faith.

Asset 44. Demonstrate Competent Adult Leadership: Adults foster authentic relationships and utilize effective practices in youth ministry with a clear vision strengthened by training and support.

Chapters 3 through 6 present each cluster of Faith Assets: describing the grounding of the assets in the research findings from the surveys of youth, parents, adult youth workers, pastors, and youth ministers; illustrating the assets through the stories of congregations involved in the onsite visits and interviews; and offering practical ideas and strategies for applying the Faith Assets to ministry in your congregation.

Resources for Further Study

Ammerman, Nancy T, Jackson W. Carroll, Carl S. Dudley, and William McKinney, editors. *Studying Congregations: A New Handbook*. Nashville: Abingdon, 1998.

East, Thomas, with Ann Marie Eckert, Dennis Kurtz, and Brian Singer-Towns. *Effective Practices for Dynamic Youth Ministry*. Winona: Saint Mary's, 2004.

Lewis, Robert and Wayne Cordeiro. *Culture Shift: Transforming Your Church from the Inside Out*. San Francisco: Jossey-Bass, 2005.

Lytch, Carol E. *Choosing Church—What Makes a Difference for Teens*. Louisville: Westminster/John Knox, 2004.

Robinson, Anthony B. *Transforming Congregational Culture*. Grand Rapids: Eerdmans, 2003.

CASE STUDY 1

Rochester Covenant Church
Rochester, MN

We desire to be a group of Christians of all ages and backgrounds who seek to follow Jesus and live by the Bible.

Mission and Purposes of Rochester Covenant Church

Our Community

- *We seek spiritual growth.* We seek to balance participation in small groups with the activity of the entire congregation. Periodically, we have special services for prayer and thanksgiving.

- *We're missions minded.* We support missionaries on each of the Covenant's ten international fields and a wide range of local projects, such as a crisis pregnancy center, Habitat for Humanity and prison outreach. Members of our congregation participate in short-term missions projects, and some members have been called to full-time Christian service.

- *We like variety.* We worship through traditional hymns, praise choruses, and contemporary music. We also attempt to balance order and spontaneity in our services.

- *We are a diverse group.* Reflecting the nature of Rochester, our congregation is a mixture of Covenanters and people who come from many other different backgrounds.

- *We enjoy fellowship.* We enjoy Lake Beauty Bible Camp, meals at the church and in one another's homes, and recreational programs. Many of our activities are informal, reflecting the interests of our people, and they change as needed. There's a warm welcome to everyone to participate.

Purpose/Mission

- *First Purpose: Knowing Jesus (Fellowship)*: It is our desire at RCC to have an intimate relationship with Jesus Christ. We do this by making a personal commitment to Jesus. We also meet with other followers of Christ in fellowship.

- *Second Purpose: Following Jesus (Discipleship)*: We want to grow in our relationship with Jesus by reading the Bible, praying, meeting in small groups, and spending time alone with God.

- *Third Purpose: Modeling Jesus (Service)*: Jesus gave us the best example of a life of loving service. We want to use our talents, spiritual gifts, temperaments and life experiences to serve God and others.

- *Fourth Purpose: Honoring Jesus (Worship)*: We want to give thanks for who God is and for what He has done for us in Jesus. With a joyous sense of awe and reverence we sing, pray, listen and share together weekly in weekly worship.

- *Fifth Purpose: Serving Jesus (Stewardship)*: We want to use our time, talents, treasures, and testimonies to serve the loving cause of Christ through the Church. We want to make every aspect of our lives part of God's plan for reconciliation.

- *Sixth Purpose: Sharing Jesus (Evangelism)*: We want to share the Good News of God's love with our friends and with people in need around the world. We believe our message has eternal significance!

Youth Ministry at Rochester Covenant Church

Purpose/Mission

To see students and families experience ongoing transformation by the person of Jesus Christ.

Passion

We desire to see transformed lives by inviting those around us into a community of young people growing as leaders that study the Word of God, engage in worship, serve others, and experience the power of God.

Five Passion Points:

1. Leadership Development
2. Bible Study
3. Worship
4. Service
5. Power

Middle School Growth and Service Opportunities

- *Confirmation*: Confirmation is discipleship training for Middle School students that meets every Sunday during the 9:45 am Christian Education hour.
- *Refuge*: Refuge is a chance for Middle School students to connect, laugh, and learn more about Jesus and meets every Wednesday from 6-7:30 pm.

Senior High Growth and Service Opportunities

- *TRUTH*: A topical study and discussion time for Senior High students on Sunday mornings during the 9:45 am Christian Education hour.
- *X-Cell*: A weekly Bible study for Senior High students that meets every Monday night in various homes from 6-8 pm. We eat from 6-7 pm and then study and discuss from 7-8 pm.
- *Passion!*: Passion! is a group for Senior High girls that meets on Tuesday mornings at 6:30 am at Vintage Light Coffee and Tea House.
- *Men of Action*: Men of Action is a weekly Bible study for Senior High guys that meets weekly before school to study what it means to be a godly man of action.
- *Holy Ground*: Holy Ground is a monthly student led worship service. There are many ways to be involved with Holy Ground such as Open Door (student led worship band), drama team, sound/media, and activity planning.
- *SALT Team*: Student Action Leadership Team (SALT) meets monthly to plan youth activities and develop more as young leaders in our churches, schools, and communities.

Opportunities for All Students

- *Friendship Place*: Friendship Place is an after school program located in the Meadow Park area where teens volunteer there every Tuesday during the school year from 4-5:30 pm to read to elementary students and help students with their homework.
- *Sanctuary Choir*: All sixth through twelfth grade students are invited to sing with the Sanctuary Choir, which practices every Wednesday from 7:30-8:45 pm.
- Listening to the Youth, Parents, and Leadership at Rochester Covenant Church: Reflections from the Onsite Interviews

The mission of Rochester Covenant Church, as reflected in the Six Purposes, is the mission of the youth ministry—"To see students and families experience ongoing transformation by the person of Jesus Christ." This happens in a "community of young people growing as leaders that study the Word of God, engage in worship, serve others, and experience the power of God."

A senior high youth expressed the mission in this way: "It all goes back to God—music and drama and Bible study are all different ways of praising God. It all flows from one's relationship with God." Rochester Covenant's youth minister expressed the mission, vision and purpose as helping kids develop "healthy relationships with Jesus Christ and with each other." "When Jesus becomes the center of their life, they are more interested in what he wants. Our desire is to keep creating an environment that is conducive to live that out."

Rochester Covenant sees God's hand in their youth ministry relationships and practices. The youth minister shared that "unless the Lord builds the house, you labor in vain. We depend on the Lord to give us wisdom, to change hearts. We will risk and reach out to people. They may reject the gospel, but we are willing to reach out anyway." One parent said, "We're not about programs, it's about the evangelism, discipleship, and the love of Jesus. We certainly have great programs going, but the programs have evolved around those purposes."

"We're good at establishing relationships with people who aren't Christians so that eventually we can share our faith with them," said one high school student. "Some non-Christians come to our lock-in and say, 'this wasn't that bad.' It's all about being their friend until they're ready."

The core practices of the Rochester Covenant youth ministry are small group Bible study, large group education, retreats, student worship service (with music, drama, etc.), choir, youth leadership, camp, lock-ins, and mission events. The practices of youth ministry at Rochester Covenant Church focus on relationships with Christ and with each other—activities, classes, and events serve to strengthen those relationships. That doesn't mean that youth ministry is light on substance, said a parent. "They really are challenged. "The bottom line is their walk with 'church,' not just (knowing) some theory, but (learning) practical ways to grow."

As part of a discipling approach to ministry, the youth ministry staff and volunteers work toward safe, trustworthy, faith-filled, deep relationships. "This place is pretty much my home; it's a fun place," said a senior high school student. "I feel adopted by many families in this church." "For me, it keeps me accountable in a way that's not threatening," said another high school student. "I don't have to come in and pretend that I'm perfect. If I'm struggling, I feel OK about coming in and sharing it with the group and I know they will be mature about it. Middle school and high school students need accountability."

The openness and vulnerability of these relationships strikes a deep chord with many of the students. "If no one tells each other what's going on in their life, you won't know that other people are going through it too," said a student. "It's good to know that you're not the only one."

While these relationships are important, so is deepening one's relationship with God and as a Christian in the world. "I know our whole church focuses on 'how is your walk with Jesus and where is it written,'" said a student. "It keeps you very accountable and it's so personal, not just, 'I'm going to tell you what you need to know,' but, 'where are you with God and how can we encourage you?'" "It all goes back to relationship with God," said one teenager. "Music and drama and Bible study are all different ways of praising God . . . it all focuses on how to have relationship with God."

The older adults and volunteers bring a sense of mentorship and accompaniment to their relationships. "We find that the older generation is willing to walk alongside," observed the youth minister. The longevity of the adult volunteers and companions has deepened the youth ministry at Rochester Covenant Church. These long-time disciples bring the whole of their lives to the program even as older students graduate and new students enter. "Every six years we have a new clientele but leaders stick around. There's a sense of refreshment constantly brought in, not dying, there's a sense of real purpose, why do we do what we do. We impress upon people the importance of creating an environment that is safe, with genuine relationships."

When asked about the genius of youth ministry at Rochester Covenant Church, students, leaders and parents voiced a similar refrain. "We try to be obedient to God," said one high school student. The thriving youth ministry program "is something that the Lord has blessed us with," said a parent. "It's not something we're doing; we're watching it happen." "I believe that we are here to facilitate what we know to be true—Jesus' love and sacrifice," said a volunteer. "We are intentional, and we have our own mistakes. But overall, it's not us, it's God." "The genius is a passion for Christ, everything else just falls into place," said another volunteer." "The genius is that it's biblically focused, and relationally based," said a youth staff member.

"Our youth minister would also say relevant," said another staff person. "Who they are, where they are at now." "Hopefully, it's also relevant to what God is trying to do, biblical, relationship-based, relevant—and what we do is always changing, we're always re-evaluating," said a third staff member. "If there is anything good going on here," concluded another staff person, "it's by the grace of God."

APPLICATION
TOOL 1

Faith Assets Assessment

The Faith Assets can provide a common language to involve all members of the congregation in discovering their role in the lives of young people. Use this assessment tool to reflect on the *priority* and *practice* of the Forty-Four Faith Assets in the life of your congregation and youth ministry. The Assessment Tool can be used with church staff, key leadership, and leadership councils to conduct an overall assessment of the congregation's impact on young people. It can be used by the youth ministry team, as well church staff and key leaders, to assess the effectiveness of the youth ministry effort. This tool is best used in group settings where there can be discussion and shared analysis. Begin by giving people time to complete the assessment individually. Then, use the following process to share reflections and analysis, and plan for improvement in each of the four asset groupings.

Assessment Process

1. Select your first Faith Asset grouping for analysis: (1) Congregational Faith and Qualities, (2) Youth Ministry Qualities, (3) Family/Household Faith, or (4) Leadership.

2. Develop a profile of current practices and activities for this Faith Asset grouping: *How does our congregation (as a whole community, as youth ministry, and/or as leaders) promote these Faith Assets?*

3. Develop a composite score of the group's assessment of the *priority* of the Faith Assets in this grouping. (How important is this assets to our congregation?)

4. Discuss the reasons for people's ratings using the following questions: (a) *Is this an accurate picture of our congregation's priorities in this asset area?* (b) *Why do we believe it is accurate or inaccurate?* (c) *Should a particular asset be a higher priority than it currently is?*

5. Develop a composite score of the group's assessment of the *practice* of the Faith Assets in this grouping. (How well are we doing in this area as a congregation?)

6. Discuss the reasons for people's ratings using the following questions: (a) *Is this an accurate rating of our congregation's practices in this asset area?* (b) *Why do we believe our rating is accurate or inaccurate?* (c) *How does our rating compare with the quality and scope of our specific activities for these Faith Assets? Which assets do we need to develop more fully?*

7. Identify the Faith Assets in this grouping that your congregation needs to make a higher priority and/or develop more effective practices.

8. Plan for improvement to strengthen the Faith Assets that you have identified as important areas for growth: (1) brainstorm potential strategies to develop the Faith Asset, (2) select one or more strategies for action, and (3) develop an action plan with implementation steps, budget, leadership, and dates for completion.

Part 1. Congregational Faith and Qualities

Priority of Importance*	Congregational Faith	Practice Effectiveness*
1 2 3 4 5	1. **Experiences God's Living Presence:** The congregation possesses a sense of God's living presence in community, at worship, through study, and in service.	1 2 3 4 5
1 2 3 4 5	2. **Makes Faith Central:** The congregation recognizes and participates in God's sustaining and transforming life and work.	1 2 3 4 5
1 2 3 4 5	3. **Emphasizes Prayer:** The congregation practices the presence of God as individuals and community through prayer and worship.	1 2 3 4 5
1 2 3 4 5	4. **Focus on Discipleship:** The congregation is committed to knowing and following Jesus Christ.	1 2 3 4 5
1 2 3 4 5	5. **Emphasizes Scripture:** The congregation values the authority of Scripture in its life and mission.	1 2 3 4 5
1 2 3 4 5	6. **Makes Mission Central:** The congregation consistently witnesses, serves and promotes moral responsibility, and seeks justice.	1 2 3 4 5

Identify the Practices in Your Church that Promote Assets 1-6:

* 1 = low   5 = high

Priority of Importance	Congregational Qualities	Practice Effectiveness
1 2 3 4 5	7. **Supports Youth Ministry:** Youth and ministry with young people are high priorities for the congregation.	1 2 3 4 5
1 2 3 4 5	8. **Demonstrates Hospitality:** The congregation values and welcomes all people, especially youth.	1 2 3 4 5
1 2 3 4 5	9. **Strives for Excellence:** The congregation sets high standards, evaluates, and engages in continuous improvement.	1 2 3 4 5
1 2 3 4 5	10. **Encourages Thinking:** The congregation welcomes questions and reflection on faith and life.	1 2 3 4 5
1 2 3 4 5	11. **Creates Community:** The congregation reflects high quality personal and group relationships.	1 2 3 4 5
1 2 3 4 5	12. **Encourages Small Groups:** The congregation engages members in study, conversation, and prayer about faith in daily life.	1 2 3 4 5
1 2 3 4 5	13. **Promotes Worship:** The congregation expands and renews spirit-filled, uplifting worship.	1 2 3 4 5
1 2 3 4 5	14. **Fosters Ethical Responsibility:** The congregation encourages individual and social moral responsibility.	1 2 3 4 5
1 2 3 4 5	15. **Promotes Service:** The congregation sponsors outreach, service projects, and cultural immersions both locally and globally.	1 2 3 4 5
1 2 3 4 5	16. **Demonstrates Effective Practices:** The congregation engages in a wide variety of ministry practices and activities.	1 2 3 4 5
1 2 3 4 5	17. **Participate in the Congregation:** Youth are engaged in a wide spectrum of congregational relationships and practices.	1 2 3 4 5
1 2 3 4 5	18. **Assume Ministry Leadership:** Youth are invited, equipped and affirmed for leadership in congregational activities.	1 2 3 4 5

Part 2. Youth Ministry Qualities

Priority of Importance	Youth Ministry Qualities	Practice Effectiveness
1 2 3 4 5	**19. Establishes a Caring Environment:** Youth Ministry provides multiple nurturing relationships and activities resulting in a welcoming atmosphere of respect, growth, and belonging.	1 2 3 4 5
1 2 3 4 5	**20. Develops Quality Relationships:** Youth Ministry develops authentic relationships among youth and adults establishing an environment of presence and life engagement.	1 2 3 4 5
1 2 3 4 5	**21. Focuses on Jesus Christ:** Youth ministry's mission, practices, and relationships are inspired by the life and ministry of Jesus Christ.	1 2 3 4 5
1 2 3 4 5	**22. Considers Life Issues:** Youth ministry is values and addresses the full range of young people's lives.	1 2 3 4 5
1 2 3 4 5	**23. Uses Many Approaches:** Youth ministry intentionally and creatively employs multiple activities appropriate to the ministry's mission and context.	1 2 3 4 5
1 2 3 4 5	**24. Is Well Organized and Planned:** Youth ministry engages participants and leaders in long range planning, implementation, evaluation and innovation in an atmosphere of high expectations.	1 2 3 4 5

Identify the Practices in Your Church that Promote Assets 19–24:

Part 3. Family / Household Faith

Priority of Importance	Family / Household Faith	Practice Effectiveness
1 2 3 4 5	**25. Possesses Strong Parental Faith:** Parents possess and practice a vital and informed faith.	1 2 3 4 5
1 2 3 4 5	**26. Promotes Family Faith Practices:** Parents engage youth and the whole family in conversations, prayer, bible reading, and service that nurture faith and life.	1 2 3 4 5
1 2 3 4 5	**27. Reflects Family Harmony:** Family members' expressions of respect and love create an atmosphere promoting faith.	1 2 3 4 5
1 2 3 4 5	**28. Equips Parents:** The congregation offers instruction and guidance that nurture parental faith and equips parents for nurturing faith at home.	1 2 3 4 5
1 2 3 4 5	**29. Fosters Parent-Youth Relationships:** The congregation offers parent-youth activities that strengthen parent-youth relationships.	1 2 3 4 5

Identify the Practices in Your Church that Promote Assets 25–29:

Part 4. Leadership

Priority of Importance	Leadership of the Pastor	Practice Effectiveness
		1 2 3 4 5
1 2 3 4 5	**30. Exercises Spiritual Influence:** The pastor knows and models the transforming presence of God in life and ministry.	
		1 2 3 4 5
1 2 3 4 5	**31. Demonstrates Interpersonal Competence:** The pastor builds a sense of community and relates well with adults and youth.	

Priority of Importance		Practice Effectiveness
1 2 3 4 5	**32. Supports Youth Ministry:** The pastor understands, guides, and advocates for youth ministry.	1 2 3 4 5
1 2 3 4 5	**33. Supports Leaders:** The pastor affirms and mentors youth and adults leading youth ministry.	1 2 3 4 5

Identify the Practices in Your Church that Promote Assets 30–33:

The Leadership of the Youth Minister

Priority of Importance		Practice Effectiveness
1 2 3 4 5	**34. Provides Competent Leadership:** The youth minister demonstrates superior theological, theoretical, and practical knowledge and skill in leadership.	1 2 3 4 5
1 2 3 4 5	**35. Models Faith:** The youth minister is a role model reflecting a living faith for youth and adults.	1 2 3 4 5
1 2 3 4 5	**36. Mentors Faith Life:** The youth minister assists adult leaders and youth in their faith life both one-on-one and in groups.	1 2 3 4 5
1 2 3 4 5	**37. Develops Teams:** The youth minister reflects a clear vision and attracts gifted youth and adults into leadership	1 2 3 4 5
1 2 3 4 5	**38. Knows Youth:** The youth minister knows youth and the changes in youth culture and utilizes these understandings in ministry.	1 2 3 4 5
1 2 3 4 5	**39. Establishes Effective Relationships:** The youth minister enjoys effective relationships with youth, parents, volunteers, and staff.	1 2 3 4 5

Identify the Practices in Your Church that Promote Assets 34–39:

Priority of Importance	Youth and Adult Leadership	Practice Effectiveness
1 2 3 4 5	**40. Are Equipped for Peer Ministry:** Youth practice friendship, care-giving, and outreach supported by training and caring adults.	1 2 3 4 5
1 2 3 4 5	**41. Establish Adult-Youth Mentoring:** Adults engage youth in the Christian faith and life supported by informed leadership.	1 2 3 4 5
1 2 3 4 5	**42. Participate in Training:** Youth and adults are equipped for ministry in an atmosphere of high expectations.	1 2 3 4 5
1 2 3 4 5	**43. Posses Vibrant Faith:** Youth and adult leaders possess and practice a vital and informed faith.	1 2 3 4 5
1 2 3 4 5	**44. Demonstrate Competent Adult Leadership:** Adults foster authentic relationships and effective practices in youth ministry with a clear vision strengthen by training and support.	1 2 3 4 5

Identify the Practices in Your Church that Promote Assets 25–29:

Planning for Improvement

Identify the Faith Assets that your congregation had decided to make a *higher priority* and/or develop more *effective practices*. Use this planning form to help you generate ideas for improvement and develop an action plan for implementing your improvement.

Faith Asset: _____

1. Brainstorm potential strategies to develop this Faith Asset.

2. Select one or more strategies and develop an action plan.

Strategy:

Implementation Steps	Budget	Leadership	Completion Date

APPLICATION
TOOL 2

Identifying Your Church's Culture*

Viewing Your Church as an Outsider

Begin by analyzing your church's culture through the eyes of an outsider. Imagine that in the last month people from your community participated in your church's worship services, sat in on church programs, met several core people, and learned a bit of the history of your church. The goal in this first set of questions is to describe your church's invisible cultural "megaphone" as it is perceived by an observer.

1. What values are communicated most strongly when someone approaches your church from the outside?

2. What would an outsider, after sitting through several worship services, say your church values most?

3. What are outsiders' two to three leading perceptions of your church, after they have participated for a month in a variety of your church's programs and ministries.

4. How would an outsider describe the spirit (or attitudes) most prevalent at your church?

5. Read over your impressions, and sum them up. List a handful of values that the church seems to be broadcasting. How surprised are you by how they compare to what you want to be known for?

---

* *Adapted from* Culture Shift: Transforming Your Church from the Inside Out, *Robert Lewis and Wayne Cordeiro (San Francisco: Jossey-Bass, 2005).*

Analyzing Your Church's Current Culture

Consider each of these ingredients carefully, and write your assessment of it.

1. Look at leadership and values.
   - Who are the culture setters in your church (pastor, church staff, volunteer ministry leaders, community members)?
   - What are the primary values exhibited by those who lead (pastor, church staff, volunteer ministry leaders boards/councils, influential members of the church)?
   - What are the real values coming from each major leadership group? How much unity exists between these groups? In what ways do they clasp?

2. Look at the mission statement of your church. Write your assessment of your mission statement, and how you are or aren't living it out.
   - Is your mission expressed in a serious written document that leaders and the congregation know and embrace?
   - Does your mission statement communicate what you really believe and live?
   - If it does, what are the cultural values it clearly spells out? If not, where are the gaps?
   - If you don't have a written mission statement, what is the implied or assumed mission.

3. Look at your symbols, ceremonies, and celebrations. Write your assessment.
   - What symbols do you see when you look around your church facility? What do these things say about what you really value? What do they communicate about your culture?
   - What ceremonies and traditions does your church honor? How popular are they with the congregation?
   - Who are the heroes in your church—the members who are most celebrated, honored, and emulated? What cultural values do those heroes represent?

4. Look at yourself as a leader.
   - What do I really value?
   - What am I really trying to do and build here at this church?
   - Is it my passion to build a kingdom culture that honors and serves God, or a culture that rewards me?
   - What are my measurements of success as a leader? Do they match up with what I say my real values are?

The Bottom Line

Answer the following questions with some short, highly descriptive phrases.

1. How would I describe our church's current culture?

2. Now it's time to boil it down. As I look over the list I just made, what two or three phrases stand out as the key values that presently *drive* the culture of our church? Are these the values I am passionate about and the ones our leadership team believes that God wants for our church?

APPLICATION TOOL 3

Investigating the Life of a Congregation

Theological Commitments

The first area of investigation focuses on the theological commitments of the congregation. This set of questions enable congregational leaders to delve deeply into the core beliefs, language, and actions that define the congregations' theology, mission and vision.

- Identify the primary names, images and metaphors utilized to describe God.
- Who is the subject of sentences when church leaders and members speak about ministry or actions taken or when they speak about God?
- How are God's presence and actions evidenced and expressed?
- How are "life in Christ," "discipleship" and "call/vocation" understood and practiced?
- What "urgency," "role" and "form(s)" does God's mission have in the life of the church and its ministry?
- What theological commitments are contained in the mission/vision statement of the congregation and of the youth ministry?

Qualities of Ministry

The second area of investigation focuses on the qualities of the congregation and ministry. This set of questions enable congregational leaders to delve deeply into the manner in which the people and congregation value youth ministry, the quality of their relationships, and the commitment and competence of their leadership.

- Search for indications of youth and youth ministry being a high priority in the congregation. For example, pay attention to facility, budget, leadership, leadership development, schedules, relationships, value placed on youth, the gifts youth bring to ministry, and so on.
- Investigate the role of the pastor(s) in developing and sustaining youth ministry in the congregation. Are there indications that the pastor(s) understand, value and support youth ministry through their particular role in the leadership of the church?

- Describe the qualities, types and dynamics of the relationships among the members of the congregation including the relationships with and among youth.

- Look for evidence regarding the congregation's or the youth ministry's sense of community. Develop a description of the values, practices and tone that shape the congregation's and youth ministry's sense of belonging and care for one another.

- Identify the cast of leadership involved in youth ministry. Include both clergy and lay, paid and volunteer, adult and youth. In each case chronicle the nature, length and quality of their leadership. Make note of any indications as to their education and training. Do they work as a team?

Contextualized Ministry Practices

The third area of investigation focuses on the contextualized ministry practices of the congregation. This set of questions enable congregational leaders to delve deeply into the particular ministry activities in each setting, with attention given to the way these activities have been adapted to their context and integrated with each other.

- Find any connections the youth ministry has with parents and families. Describe the ways in which the congregation and household work together to develop the faith and life of young people.

- Identify all the ministry practices utilized in the youth ministry. Consider any activity that engages youth and the congregation in relationships, study, prayer, mission, and so on. Look also, for those activities that seem to develop or support the youth ministry itself.

- Pay attention to the manner in which the ministry practices in the congregation are put together. Does there seem to be a pattern and purpose to their timing and relationship with one another? Are the adapted in any way that you can tell to the peculiar setting of the congregation and its people?

- How is your prayer life today? Consider the following questions:
  - When do you pray?
  - Where do you pray?
  - What do you do during your prayer time—e.g., read the Bible, contemplate, listen to music, be silent, or recite traditional prayers?
  - What do you pray *for* or pray *about*?

- How has your prayer life changed or grown or evolved over the course of your life? What was your prayer life like when you were a child? a teenager? a young adult? a midlife adult? an older adult? (Answer as many as apply to you.)

- Which prayer traditions have been helpful to you? How? When? Why, or why not?

- What new ways of praying have you tried? Have they been helpful? How? Why? Or why not?

- Has there ever been a time when you made no effort to pray and "gave things a rest," either inadvertently or on purpose, in your prayer life? Why? What was this like? Looking back, can you see any benefits from this experience?

- Have you ever felt "stuck" in your prayer? When? How? What do you do about it?

- Has they ever been a time when you couldn't pray, but felt sustained by the prayers offered on your behalf?

- Have you experienced any change in God's faithfulness to you?

- Have you experienced any change in your faithfulness to God?

- When were the prayer times when you felt closest to God? Why?

- Would you say that prayer is an integral part of your everyday life today? Why or why not? If not, how could it be?

congregational faith and qualities

W hat kind of congregational faith and life nurtures youth of maturing Christian faith? A surprising discovery emerges from the findings of the EYM Study—the entire congregation makes a difference in youth ministry. The congregations in the study are powerful faith- and life-shaping systems. The study found two distinct features of congregational life that directly influence the development of a vital Christian faith in young people: the theological commitments of the congregation (congregational faith) and the quality of community life within the congregation (congregational qualities).

Congregational Faith

The theme of "congregational faith" is described in six dimensions that reflect findings from almost six thousand youth, parents, adult youth workers, pastors, and youth ministers. Each of the six dimensions are clusters of items (survey questions) that have a strong coherent relationship to a common meaning or action: biblical emphasis, core Christian concepts, moral concepts, worship, service, and mission. The six dimensions of congregational faith were the most significant findings giving evidence of the theological and faith commitments of the exemplary congregations in youth ministry. There is a high degree of shared perceptions about the key characteristics of congregational faith among the youth, parents, and adult leaders in the study. Dimensions 1 and 2 are similar in content—one reflects the youth's responses, the other parent's responses.

Combining the survey findings (the six dimensions) with the reports from the onsite interviews and focus groups in the twenty-one exemplary congregations produces a number of common themes that point to theological and faith commitments that have a direct influence on developing youth of vital Christian faith. Even though the congregations in the study represent seven denominations with diverse theologies, the following common themes emerged:

- *Scripture and most especially the gospel are understood as prime "bearers" of God's presence.*
- *Bible study and biblical literacy are extensive and substantive. Bible study and biblical knowledge are pursued as opportunities to "encounter God speaking to people today."*
- *Congregational faith, life, and ministry are grounded in Jesus Christ— present and active within individuals and the whole community.*
- *Worship within the life of the community is understood as participation in the life and presence of God in the world.*
- *Prayer is a pervasive, core activity attached to every dimension of the congregation's relationships, decisions, and activities.*
- *God's presence is named and celebrated in the everyday life and work of youth and adults.*
- *Service to those in need and outreach to the community is seen as essential to living the Christian faith as individuals and communities.*

The research shows that the theological commitments of the congregation as a whole become the theological commitments of the congregation's youth ministry. For example, because of the centrality of the Gospel and discipleship in congregational life, knowing Jesus Christ and following him in discipleship are at the core of these congregations' youth ministries. A second example of this dynamic at work is the alignment of the mission/vision statements of the congregation and

TABLE 5

Six Dimensions of Congregational Faith

Theme: Congregational Faith	Youth	Parents	Adult Leaders
1. Congregation's Biblical Emphasis	7.16	-	-
2. Teaches Core Christian Concepts	-	6.95	
3. Congregation's Moral Guidance	6.60	6.81	6.96
4. Worship Services' Positive Characteristics	6.29	6.27	6.40
5. Congregation Promotes Service	6.40	6.42	6.43
6. Congregation's Mission Effectiveness	6.71	-	6.04

*Mean scores: highest rating is "9," indicating a response of "Always" or "Almost Always True."

its youth ministry, reflecting striking similarities of both identity and mission. In part, the power of these congregations and their youth ministries lies in the integration of vision and mission. This dynamic can be seen in the life of Thornapple Covenant Church, one of the twenty-one congregations selected for an onsite visit. Their theological and faith commitments, as reflected in the mission statement, is directly reflected in the mission and activities of their youth ministry.

Thornapple Covenant Church

Mission
Thornapple Covenant Church is a community sharing a journey of faith, a church family that encourages and cares, and a place of belonging in a world of change. Our mission statement is "helping people find and follow Jesus Christ."
"For the son of Man came to seek and to save what was lost" (Luke 19:10).
"Come, follow me" (Mark 1:17). Our purpose is:

- *To love God with all that we are in all of life*
- *To love each other through community and ministry*
- *To love our neighbors through evangelism and outreach*

Mission of Youth Ministry
Our youth ministry exists to reach non-believing students, to connect them with other Christians, to help them grow in their faith, and to challenge them to serve others and honor God with their life. We offer opportunities to learn, grow, and build relationships on Sunday mornings, Wednesday evenings, and other times throughout the week. We also offer retreats, mission trips, service projects, bike trips, and other activities.

Although each congregation in the study emphasizes varied aspects of Christ and his work, it is Christ's life, teachings, death, and resurrection present then and present now around which they center their ministries. It is Jesus Christ they trust with their salvation. It is Jesus Christ they seek to follow as disciples. As one youth minister reflected in her interview, "It is my deep desire to help kids know Jesus. . . and that they have a strong sense of God's presence and God's love for them."

Faith Assets: Congregational Faith

From the analysis of the dimensions of congregational faith, six Faith Assets were developed to describe the congregations' theological and faith commitments and the patterns of ministry that flow from those commitments.

Asset 1. Experiencing God's Living Presence: The congregation possesses a sense of God's living presence in community, at worship, through study, and in service.

Asset 2. Makes Faith Central: The congregation recognizes and participates in God's sustaining and transforming life and work.

Asset 3. Emphasizes Prayer: The congregation practices the presence of God as individuals and community through prayer and worship.

Asset 4. Focuses on Discipleship: The congregation is committed to knowing and following Jesus Christ.

Asset 5. Emphasizes Scripture: The congregation values the authority of Scripture in its life and mission.

Asset 6. Makes Mission Central: The congregation consistently witnesses, serves and promotes moral responsibility, and seeks justice.

The specifics of the six Faith Assets can be seen in the most highly rated items in the six dimensions of congregational faith. Youth, parents, and adult leaders in youth ministry rated the following congregational activities as most significant in expressing and living the congregation's faith. (See Table 7 for complete results for each of the six dimensions.)

Dimensions 1 and 2. Biblical Emphasis and Core Christian Concepts

Congregations help people learn who God is and come to know Jesus personally. They teach people how to be a Christian, how to discover the meaning of the Bible for their lives, and how to pray.

Dimension 3. Congregation's Moral Guidance

Congregations teach people about Christian perspectives on moral questions and help people helps people learn how to apply their faith to decisions about what's right and wrong.

Dimension 4. Worship Services' Positive Characteristics

Congregations provide spiritually uplifting worship experiences that are enlightening, fulfilling, inspiring, interesting, easy to understand, and relevant in daily life.

Dimension 5. Congregation Promotes Service

Congregations involve people in helping others through community service. They make use of each member's talents and abilities within the congregation and in the community and world.

Dimension 6. Congregation's Mission Effectiveness

Congregations makes mission and evangelism, i.e., bringing the Gospel to people outside the church, important in church life.

Congregational Qualities

The impact of the congregations' integration of young people into the fabric of their lives and ministries is evident in the attitudes of their youth. The overall culture and climate of these congregations deeply impacts their young people as evidenced in the eight dimensions of congregational qualities. Young people's responses to questions regarding the life of their congregation demonstrate the content and force of their churches' influence in their lives. Notice how youth's perceptions are also reinforced by the parents and adult leaders. Dimensions 1 and 2 reflect similar content.

Faith Assets

Ten Faith Assets describe congregational values, expectations, and practices that develop the faith life of young people and promote respect for youth and their inclusion in congregational life. These congregational qualities describe how the life and ministry of the congregation can engage youth and make a substantive contribution to their maturing faith.

Asset 7. Supports Youth Ministry: Youth and ministry with young people are high priorities for the congregation.

Asset 8. Demonstrates Hospitality: The congregation values and welcomes all people, especially youth.

Asset 9. Strives for Excellence: The congregation sets high standards, evaluates, and engages in continuous improvement.

Asset 10. Encourages Thinking: The congregation welcomes questions and reflection on faith and life.

Asset 11. Creates Community: Congregational life reflects high quality personal and group relationships.

Asset 12. Encourages Small Groups: The congregation engages members in study, conversation, and prayer about faith in daily life.

Asset 13. Promotes Worship: The congregation expands and renews spirit-filled, uplifting worship.

Asset 14. Fosters Ethical Responsibility: The congregation encourages individual and social moral responsibility.

Asset 15. Promotes Service: The congregation sponsors outreach, service projects, and cultural immersions both locally and globally.

Asset 16. Demonstrates Effective Practices: The congregation engages in a wide variety of ministry practices and activities.

Asset 17. Participate in the Congregation: Youth are engaged in a wide spectrum of congregational relationships and practices.

Asset 18. Assume Ministry Leadership: Youth are invited, equipped and affirmed for leadership in congregational activities.

TABLE 6

Eight Dimensions of Congregational Qualities

Theme: Congregational Qualities	Youth	Parents	Adult Leaders*
1. Warm, Challenging Congregational Climate	7.05	-	-
2. Welcoming Atmosphere	-	6.96	7.21
3. Satisfied with the Congregation	6.93	-	-
4. Importance of this Church to Me	-	7.73	7.96
5. Congregation's Moral Guidance	6.60	6.81	6.96
6. Congregation's Social Interaction	6.55	5.18	5.22
7. Congregation's Openness to Change	6.35	6.25	6.31
8. Members Experience Love and Support	-	6.92	-

*Mean scores: highest rating is "9," indicating a response of "Always" or "Almost Always True."

Integrating the most highly rated items of the eight dimensions of congregational qualities with the Faith Assets provides a picture of people's experience of community life and of the activities that congregations provide. Youth, parents, and adult leaders in youth ministry rated each of the following congregational activities as most significant in expressing their experience of congregational life. (See Table 8 for complete results.)

Asset 7. Supports Youth Ministry and Asset 17. Participate in the Congregation
(Reflected in Dimension 1. Warm, Challenging Congregational Climate; Dimension 2. Welcoming Atmosphere; Dimension 4. Satisfaction with the Congregation; Dimension 5. Congregation's Social Interaction, and Dimension 8. Members Experience Love and Support)
Congregations place a priority on youth ministry. There is a consistent vision. It is a purpose-driven vision. Youth feel loved and respected, cared for, and supported by their congregation. Congregations value youth as a vibrant part of the family of faith and support youth activities.

Asset 8. Demonstrates Hospitality and Asset 11. Creates Community
(Reflected in Dimension 1. Warm, Challenging Congregational Climate; Dimension 2. Welcoming Atmosphere; and Dimension 8. Members Experience Love and Support)
Congregations are friendly and feel warm; they help members make friends at church and feel at home. They puts an emphasis on providing love, support, and friendship to members, especially those who are experiencing hardships. Congregations accept people who are different and make them feel welcome.

Asset 9. Strives for Excellence
(Reflected in Dimension 7. Congregation's Openness to Change)
Congregations are willing to change the way things are done to increase involvement with the church. They are innovative, demonstrating openness to suggestions from members and the freedom to try new ideas.

Asset 10. Encourages Thinking
(Reflected in Dimension 1. Warm, Challenging Congregational Climate)
Congregations challenge people to think about religious issues and ideas and encourage them to ask questions and say what they think on religious issues.

Asset 13. Promotes Worship
(Reflected in Dimension 3. Satisfied with the Congregation)
Congregations provide spiritually uplifting worship experiences that are enlightening, fulfilling, inspiring, interesting, easy to understand, and relevant in daily life.

Asset 14. Fosters Ethical Responsibility
(Reflected in Dimension 5. Congregation's Moral Guidance)
Congregations teach people about Christian perspectives on moral questions and help people learn how to apply their faith to ethical decisions.

Asset 15. Promotes Service
(Reflected in Dimension 5. Congregation's Moral Guidance and Dimension 5. Congregation's Social Interaction)
Congregations involve people in helping others through community service. They make use of each member's talents and abilities within the congregation and in the community and world.

Congregational Life and Intergenerational Relationships

The hospitality afforded young people was palpable in the EYM congregations. At Sunday worship adults and youth greet each other and groups of adults gather for informal conversation with young people before and after the services. Young people bring their friends to worship because they are valued and the worship services engage them. An adult leader in youth ministry described her church as "a place where every student can come and feel loved and be free to express themselves in worship."

Parents, adult youth leaders, and youth consistently reported that their congregations were hospitable to teenagers. They indicated that youth felt at home in these safe and nurturing communities where young people's questions are sought out and taken seriously. The church is a "safe place" where youth value being together with adults and each other. Pastors and youth ministers praised the way members of their congregation support young people. One pastor said that youth feel that "this is my church, and I am a part of this congregation." The result is hospitality toward, valuing of, and support for individual teenagers.

The results of the EYM Study indicate that intergenerational, in-depth relationships surround young people involved in their youth ministries. One church has a grand-parenting ministry that matches high school youth with surrogate grandparents with whom they build relationships, share life stories, and work together. These youth and elders have developed relationships in which they each feel secure, cared for, and accountable to one another. In another congregation, prayer bracelets with the names of young people are distributed throughout the congregation before every major youth event. Members pray individually for a young person on their prayer bracelet and look forward to hearing about their experiences in ministry. In a third congregation, each youth, beginning in fifth grade is matched with an adult who prays for them daily. These adults send cards and gifts to young people at significant life passages throughout their teenage years. These youth communicate anonymously with their adult prayer partners through a coordinator at church. Young people often send prayer requests to these committed, caring adults. Some youth ask for advice. In a moment filled with anticipation and gratitude, the adult prayer partner is identified at a breakfast just before the young person graduates from high school.

Acceptance and care generate trust and vulnerability among youth and adults in the EYM congregations. Young people frequently reported that they could turn to adults in the congregations for guidance and care, including their friend's parents, adult youth workers, and youth staff. One young person summarized this intergenerational climate: "Everybody's really cool. We have good relationships. We can always talk to them (adults) and they don't criticize, they never look down on you."

Youth thrive in these positive relationships that generate openness and place a high priority on young people exploring their faith questions and beliefs. These congregations welcome youth and encourage them to learn about their faith while challenging them to think. In the EYM congregations, constructive relationships go deeper than "friendliness" with young people; there is substance, content, and commitment in these strong bonds.

What becomes clear from this profile of the qualities of congregational life is that getting to know a personal and present God involves more than learning dogma or obeying a particular set of rules. In addition to learning about God through excellent Bible teaching (see section 1. Congregational Faith), young people come to know a living and active God through relationships in the community. Certainly, young people learn the gospel, the story of Christ, his teachings, and the rich and substantive Christian traditions. The young people in these congregations get to know Jesus Christ through the witness of believers and ongoing relationships with persons and communities who know Him. The power of faithful, multi-generational Christian relationships ("sociality") is at the heart of effective youth ministry.

Youth Involvement in the Congregation

Two Faith Assets describe young people as full participants in the body of Christ who are given spiritual gifts necessary for the life of the congregation. The gifts of young people are identified, developed, and utilized as youth are invited into leadership and equipped for full ministry in the church and the world. Young people are encouraged to participate in all aspects of the congregation's life and ministry.

Asset 21. Participate in the Congregation: Youth are engaged in a wide spectrum of congregational relationships and practices.

Asset 22. Assume Ministry Leadership: Youth are invited, equipped and affirmed for leadership in congregational activities.

The survey responses (individual items) provide insights on the ways that youth in EYM congregations are involved in the life of the church and in leadership roles. (The highest score is a "9" indicating survey responses of "Always" or "Almost Always True.")

Leadership

- *I have participated in two or more of the following: a) teach Sunday school, Bible, vacation Bible school; b) improve school/neighborhood; c) make a presentation before faith group/worship; d) raise money; and e) church task force. (7.94)*
- *My youth program emphasizes leadership training and experience. (7.06)*
- *My involvement in youth programs has helped me to develop my leadership skills. (6.66)*
- *I am involved in witness groups (e.g., singing, instrumental, drama). (5.01)*

Participation

- *My youth program emphasizes participation in congregational life. (7.36)*
- *My youth program emphasizes weekly worship service geared to youth. (7.34)*
- *My youth program emphasizes community service. (6.77)*
- *There is much informal interaction among youth and adults. (6.37)*
- *My congregation helps me get to know adults in my church. (6.34)*
- *My congregation involves youth in congregational decision-making. (6.17)*
- *My congregation gets me involved in helping people in your town or city. (5.99)*

The findings from the survey confirm youth's positive experience of involvement in congregational life and leadership in ministries. In contrast to many congregations who build youth ministries separate from the larger congregation, the youth ministries of the EYM congregations welcome young people into the center of the congregation's life together. The same relational qualities present in their youth ministries are evident in the life of these congregations as a whole.

Conclusion

Young people's responses to these closely related items of congregational faith and life demonstrate that youth in these exemplary congregations have a keen perception of and appreciation for their churches' substantive faithfulness and effectiveness in the lives of their members, including themselves. The ministry of the entire congregation is a major factor in young people's faith development and their eagerness to be a part of the community's relationships and practices. The study presents a picture of welcoming congregations who respect and value young people and their youth ministries. These congregations involve youth and adults in genuinely integrated relationships and activities. The mission and vision of their youth ministries are aligned with the mission and vision of the church, indeed, their youth ministries often lead the way. Their worship styles reflect an awareness of the sensibilities of their youth; the worship life of the young people often inspires adults to worship in fresh ways.

Anyone acquainted with youth ministry would expect quality relationships to be at the heart of youth ministry. The EYM Study affirmed such expectations and more. What was pervasive and unique in the EYM congregations was the presence and power of quality *intergenerational relationships and a deeply bonded intergenerational faith community* and their impact on the faith and lives of young people. These youth were surrounded by multiple, reinforcing spheres of relational Christian influence. They were immersed in a larger, multi-generational community of quality relationships informed by faith in Jesus Christ.

The EYM Study presents a picture of welcoming congregations who respect and value young people and their youth ministries. These congregations involve youth and adults in genuinely integrated relationships and activities. The mission and vision of their youth ministries are aligned with the mission and vision of the church, indeed, their youth ministries often lead the way. Their worship styles reflect an awareness of the sensibilities of their youth; the worship life of the young people often inspires adults to worship in fresh ways. The essential message from this data points to youth ministry as a valued, critical element of these congregation's mission and vision. Youth ministry matters in these congregations and the ministries of the entire congregation contribute substantively to faithful and effective ministry with young people.

Resources for Further Study

Dean, Kenda Creasy, with Dayle Gillespie Rounds, Roland Martinson, Any Scott Vaughn, and Don C. Richter. *OMG: A Youth Ministry Handbook*. Nashville: Abingdon, 2010.

Dean, Kenda Creasy, Chap Clark, and Dave Rahn. *Starting Right—Thinking Theologically about Youth Ministry*. Grand Rapids: Zondervan, 2001.

Dean, Kenda Creasy, and Ron Foster. *The Godbearing Life—The Art of Soul Tending for Youth Ministry*. Nashville: Upper Room, 1998.

DeVries, Mark. *Sustainable Youth Ministry*. Downers Grove: InterVarsity, 2008.

East, Thomas, editor. *Leadership for Catholic Youth Ministry—A Comprehensive Resource*. New London: Twenty-Third, 2009.

East, Thomas with Ann Marie Eckert, Dennis Kurtz, and Brian Singer-Towns. *Effective Practices for Dynamic Youth Ministry*. Winona: Saint Mary's, 2005.

Kimball-Baker, Kathleen. *Tag, You're It!—50 Easy Ways to Connect with Young People*. Minneapolis: Search Institute, 2003.

Martineau, Mariette, Joan Weber, and Leif Kehrwald. *Intergenerational Faith Formation*. New London: Twenty-Third, 2008.

Ratliff, Mike. *Sacred Bridges—Making Lasting Connections between Older Youth and the Church*. Nashville: Abingdon, 2002.

CASE STUDY 2

Thornapple Covenant Church
Grand Rapids, MI

Helping people find and follow Jesus Christ.

Mission of Thornapple Covenant Church

Mission

Thornapple Covenant Church is a community sharing a journey of faith, a church family that encourages and cares, and a place of belonging in a world of change. Our mission statement is "helping people find and follow Jesus Christ."

"For the son of Man came to seek and to save what was lost." (Luke 19:10)

"Come, follow me . . ." (Mark 1:17)

Statement of Purpose

- *To love God with all that we are in all of life*: The Greatest Commandment calls us to love God with all our heart, soul, strength, and mind (Luke 10:27). We express our love for God by believing in his Son, Jesus Christ, keeping his commandments, and loving others through the power of his indwelling Spirit (1 John 3:21-24).

- *To love each other through community and ministry*: The New Commandment calls us to love the members of God's family the way Christ loved us (John 13:34). We do this by laying down our lives for each other in sacrificial acts of service (1 John 3:16-17). When we love each other in this way, we demonstrate the reality of Jesus Christ to our neighbors (John 17:20-23).

- *To love our neighbors through evangelism and outreach*: The Second Commandment calls us to love our neighbor the way we love ourselves (Matthew 22:39). We do this by sharing the gospel, our lives, and our resources with those around us (Luke 10:29-37).

Core Values

- *Outreach*: serving the needs in our community and world.

- *Hospitality*: welcoming the stranger to our fellowship.

- *Community*: incorporating every person into the church family.

- *Freedom/Diversity*: seeking unity in the essentials of Christian belief without requiring uniformity in other areas.

- *Faithfulness to Scripture*: affirming the authority of God's word as the basis for belief and conduct.

- *Worship*: celebrating with awe the character of God and what he has done through proclamation, praise, and the sacraments

Sunday Worship

There are two Sunday morning worship gatherings at 9:00 am and 10:30 am. In both worship hours we create the time and space for us to respond to God with all that we are, both individually and corporately. We strive to tell God's story through new and classic songs; visual and creative arts; new and ancient prayers; strong Biblical and practical teaching; and times of meditation and reflection. We seek to create a worship environment that reaches into the spiritual depth of the past while embracing the new expressions of the present. The two worship hours have a different musical flavor and educational offerings:

- Our 9:00 am worship gathering is our contemporary hour using a full band with a variety of instruments. In addition to worship at 9:00 there is: an adult education class, children's worship for ages 4 through 3rd grade, a class for children with special needs, and nursery care.

- Our 10:30 am worship gathering is our blended hour merging organ, choir, an acoustic band, and piano. In addition to worship at 10:30 there is: an adult education class, children and student classes (three-year-olds through high school), a class for children with special needs, and nursery care.

Service

Thornapple Covenant Church is committed to serving both inside and outside of the church.

- *Global*: Thornapple Covenant Church is committed to the ministry of world missions. We support over thirty individual missionaries who serve around the globe. In addition we support various missions organizations and sponsor adult short term mission trips. In recent years we have sent small groups of adults on short term missions trips to the Dominican Republic, Jamaica and Mexico. We are open to sending more as God leads our people to serve around the world.

- *Urban Ministry*: Thornapple Covenant Church encourages and enables the family of God at TECC to make serving the "poor" a lifestyle. By living out the Gospel of Jesus Christ we hope to help needy people find and follow Jesus Christ in the city of Grand Rapids. Here is a sampling of the organizations that we work with are: Kid's Food Basket, Habitat for Humanity, Degage Ministries, and The Glenn Vannoord Short-Term Urban Missions Program.

Youth Ministry at Thornapple Covenant Church

Mission of Youth Ministry

Our youth ministry exists to reach non-believing students, to connect them with other Christians, to help them grow in their faith, and to challenge them to serve others and honor God with their life. We offer opportunities to learn, grow, and build relationships on Sunday mornings, Wednesday evenings, and other times throughout the week. We also offer retreats, mission trips, service projects, bike trips, and other activities.

Middle School Ministries

- *Sunday Mornings Christian Foundations* (10:30 am): This is a two-year program that guides students on an exploration of the basic beliefs of Christianity to provide a solid foundation for our them as they make decisions in the present and the future. Yearly focus rotates between Old and New Testaments. Students keep a daily journal, meet in small groups weekly on Sunday Morning, write a paper, and interview with a pastor.
- *Wednesday Evenings J.A.M.* (Jesus And Me) (6:30 pm): J.A.M. is a midweek meeting for students and gives students an opportunity to use their enthusiasm and high energy in: 1) outreach to their friends, 2) service to others, and 3) personal growth in faith. Each week focuses on something different.
- Middle School Winter Retreat
- Summer Adventure Week

Senior High Ministries

- *The CORE* (Sunday Mornings 10:30 am): Study, discuss, and learn about Biblical topics such as the Trinity, atonement, grace and mercy, forgiveness and more theology (study of God). Learn it then apply to your world.
- *REFUEL* (Wednesday Evenings 7:30 pm): A midweek meeting for High School students. REFUEL provides a relaxed environment for students to explore and grow their faith. Includes music, relevant discussions, hanging out and making new friends—a great break during the week.
- *Radiant* is for students committed to making the student ministry "a light on the hill" by letting Jesus' light shine through them in service to others. Radiant meets the first

Sunday of each month at 11:45 and is open to all high school students. Lunch is provided.

- *Breakfast Clubs*: This is our small group ministry for High School students. Four to eight students meet with one "mentor" to walk through life together. These groups meet twice a month to study the Bible or a specific topic, pray together, and talk about issues relating to their life.
- High School Winter Retreat
- Summer Mission trip to Saltillo Mexico
- Summer Colorado Adventure Trip

Listening to the Youth, Parents, and Leadership at Thornapple Covenant Church: Selections from the Onsite Interviews

Relationships connect the mission, vision, and purpose of the congregation and its youth ministry program. "Our ministry is about relationships," said the minister to students. "We do a lot of programs, but they are all about relationships either horizontally or vertically. We don't do things just to do them; there is intentionality to everything we do."

The mission statement for youth ministry emphasizes the impact of authentic, faith-filled relationships: "Our youth ministry exists to reach non-believing students, to connect them with other Christians, to help them grow in their faith, and to challenge them to serve others and honor God with their life."

The middle school ministry program is also integrated into the congregation's vision. "Our vision is that kids know and hear the Gospel," the middle school minister said. "For those who have accepted Christ, our vision is that they are growing and that they get connected to the others."

"The youth pastor reaches the kids and has a heart for the ministry and the kids love him," said a parent. "He meets them at their level and challenges them." "Relational is so key, it takes time and if you think about Christ, it is all about being in relationships and growing," said another parent. "At the previous church we attended it doesn't jump out like it does here; we are modeling Christ."

"We have a strong commitment to youth ministry," said the pastor. "We want to be a church that provides for our youth but is also reaching out to the unchurched."

"We have great families and great volunteers who have great hearts and love Jesus," said the minister to students. "They are willing to share their struggles and look at themselves and see that if they are going to share it with kids they need to live it themselves. Being here a long time has had its benefits."

The practices of youth ministry at TECC serve to create a culture of relationships in which young people can learn about and grow in their faith. Through these relationships, they come to own their own faith and lives as Christian believers.

The high school program really begins in middle school and earlier, said one parent. "The program is building," the parent said. "I see the middle school program as providing the building blocks of faith, the basics. Senior high challenges them to live out their faith and own their own faith."

"We challenge them and get them to think about their faith," said an adult volunteer. "We ask them what questions of faith they have. We are willing to talk faith issues with them and let them come to their own conclusions with some guidance."

• • •

The practices of youth ministry at Thornapple have a theme of being fed and feeding; discipleship and mission.

"From middle school and younger there is an expectation of growth. You are in the Bible and you grow and you are also expected to reach out to others," said an adult volunteer. "The expectation is to grow and to reach out. Our youth pastor tells them they are here to be fed and to then feed others."

The middle school program picks up on this theme through its small group time that is woven in between the larger group sessions of confirmation and faith development. The students who come to Thornapple to chew on faith and life appreciate that the ingredients are sometimes raw. "We talk about things that matter," said one student. "We talk about how to talk about your faith, world religions, and our own questions about faith." "The questions are deep," added another student. "It is always a God thing when you go in to talk to an adult."

While being fed strengthens these young people, being the ones who feed others is often a whole different experience, as one freshman student posted to the church's blog about his service in Washington, D.C. "On the day of today, my group went to DC Central Kitchen," he wrote. "They prepare meals for homeless people. While I was there, I washed dishes and put them back on shelves. It was hard work, but once I think about the cause and what I was doing it for, it wasn't that bad. At the end we ate the fruits of our labor including macaroni and cheese and beef stroganoff. It was a fun and rewarding experience."

The relationships at Thornapple can be described as "real food," the kind that is planted, tended, watered, weeded, fertilized, prayed over, and enjoyed. "Authentic is an important word—with the pluses and flaws," said a parent. "God is definitely here." "We plant the seeds and God makes them grow," said another parent. "We are reaching out, and there are kids that will fall through the cracks, and that is the nature of the body of Christ. Hopefully the seeds will grow later."

A major part of youth ministry is "building the relationships with the kids so they know we care about them," said the middle school ministry director. These relationships may begin with adults, but students are doing their own inviting and mentoring. "The kids reached out to my oldest when we moved here in sixth grade and now he is doing it to the kids that are behind him," said a parent who is also a volunteer with the youth ministry program. "The kids are reaching out to others and making them feel at home. This is a real blessing."

Students in the TECC youth ministry program say that because the church and its leaders accept and respect them, they find that they can accept, respect and invite others. "Acceptance is encouraging," said one student. "The adults know we exist." "We can bring friends and they are accepted and they fit in right away," added another student.

These relationships, with adults, with the youth minister, with each other, and with God nurture the students in their faith and their Christian lives. "Since we are really good friends, we don't talk about random stuff. We can talk about the deep stuff, like God," said one high school student. "It is easy to talk to our friends and we can talk about what is going on in our lives."

How does one create a culture of being fed by God and by others so that you can feed others in the name of God? How does an exemplary youth ministry program grow, develop, harvest and replant among students, parents, families and others in a congregation?

The longevity and the respectful relationship between the senior pastor and the minister to students is certainly one factor. The core of committed volunteers who invest in students' lives also contributes to the effectiveness of the youth ministry.

The youth ministry program's intentional focus on relationships is another factor. The minister to students carries and communicates this focus, letting relationship-building drive events and programs and using the open doors that trust brings to build faith.

A third factor is the culture of feeding and being fed through small groups, Bible study, and high-impact events. The high-impact events, such as the mission trip and the bike trip, carry high expectations that the youth seem motivated to meet, such as donating their time, raising money and physical training. These achievements seem to provide a spirit that energizes the daily bread of ordinary time.

The ongoing commitment of this congregation to a youth ministry program and staff is another key factor.

TABLE 7

Six Dimensions of Congregational Faith (expanded)

Theme: Congregational Faith	Youth	Parents	Adult Leaders*
Dimension 1. Congregation's Biblical Emphasis (Youth)	**7.16**	-	-
Dimension 2. Teaches Core Christian Concepts (Parents)	-	**6.95**	-
• Our congregation teaches members about the Bible.	7.09		
• Our congregation helps you learn about the Bible and its meaning for your life.	6.86	6.86	-
• Our congregation helps you learn who God is.	7.47	7.33	-
• Our congregation helps members to know Jesus personally.	7.13	-	-
• Our congregation puts an emphasis on teaching the Bible.	7.29	-	-
• Our congregation teaches one how to be a Christian.	-	7.15	-
• Our congregation helps people learn how to pray.		6.46	-

*Mean scores: highest rating is "9," indicating a response of "Always" or "Almost Always True."

Dimension 3. Congregation's Moral Guidance	6.60	6.81	6.96
• Our congregation helps you make decisions about what's right and wrong.	7.03	6.71	6.94
• Our congregation helps you learn how to resist pressure from other kids to do things you know are wrong.	6.52	-	-
• Our congregations helps you develop concern for people.	6.75	-	-
• Our congregation teaches members about Christian perspectives on moral questions.	6.88	6.79	6.91
• Our congregation helps you learn how to be a peacemaker.	6.31	-	-
• Our congregation helps you develop responsible values and behaviors in the area of sexuality.	6.12	-	-
• Our congregation helps you learn how to apply your faith to everyday decisions.	-	6.95	7.05

Dimension 4. Worship Services' Positive Characteristics	6.29	6.27	6.40
• Our weekly worship service is enlightening.	6.21	6.00	6.04
• Our weekly worship service is fulfilling.	6.27	6.25	6.39
• Our weekly worship service is inspiring.	6.32	-	-
• Our weekly worship service is interesting.	5.93	-	-
• Our weekly worship service is useful in daily life (relevant).	6.40	6.49	6.70
• Our weekly worship service is easy to understand.	6.62	-	-
• Our weekly worship service is comforting.	-	6.33	6.47

Dimension 5. Congregation Promotes Service	6.40	6.42	6.43
• Our congregation involves many members in helping people in our town or city.	6.52	-	-
• Our congregations has many members share responsibility for carrying out the ministry of the congregation.	6.98	-	-

• Our congregation gets you involved in helping people in our town or city.	5.99	6.28	6.23
• Our congregation helps you to know adults in the church.	6.32	-	-
• Our congregation involves youth in congregational decision-making.	6.17	-	-
• Our congregation gets you involved in community service projects.	-	6.37	6.26
• Our congregation gets you involved in helping to improve the lives of people who are poor or hungry.	-	6.36	6.41
• Our congregation helps you develop concern for other people.	-	6.74	6.91
• Our congregation makes use of each member's talents and abilities.	-	6.33	6.35

Dimension 6. Congregation's Mission Effectiveness	**6.71**	**5.82**	**6.04**
• Our congregation is making missions and evangelism important in congregational life.	6.95	6.30	6.50
• Our congregation is bringing the Gospel to people outside the congregation.	6.29	5.38	5.60
• Our congregation is offering outstanding Bible study programs.	6.76	-	-
• Our congregation is reaching out to the poor and hungry in our community.	6.87	-	-
• Our congregation makes Scripture come alive for each member.	-	5.79	6.01

TABLE 8

Eight Dimensions of Congregational Qualities (expanded)

Theme: Congregational Qualities	Youth	Parents	Adult Leaders	Pastor and Youth Minister*
Dimension 1. Warm, Challenging Congregational Climate	**7.05**	**6.36**	**6.68**	-
Climate of Warmth and Openness	-	-	-	**6.63**
• I learn a lot.	6.88	-	-	-
• It feels warm.	7.38	-	-	7.24
• It accepts people who are different.	7.28	-	-	6.50
• Strangers feel welcome.	7.29	-	-	-
• It challenges my thinking.	6.53	6.35	6.71	-
• It is friendly.	7.63	-	-	7.38
• It encourages me to ask questions.	6.37	6.13	6.48	-
• It expects people to learn and think.	7.00	6.59	6.83	-
• Members want to be challenged to think about religious issues and ideas.	-	-	-	6.55
• Our congregation helps members become more loving and compassionate.	-	-	-	6.68
• Members of this church are willing to change the way things are done to increase involvement with the church.	-	-	-	5.32
• My congregation is innovative.	-	-	-	6.74

Mean scores: highest rating is "9," indicating a response of "Always" or "Almost Always True."

Dimension 2. Welcoming Atmosphere	-	6.96	7.21	-
• Our congregation is friendly.	-	7.27	7.47	-
• Our congregation feels warm.	-	6.96	7.28	-
• Our congregation welcomes strangers.	-	6.65	6.87	-
Dimension 3. Satisfaction with the Congregation	6.93	-	7.05	-
• I am excited about my congregation.	6.74	-	-	-
• I am satisfied with the way things are going in my congregation.	6.93	-	-	-
• Our congregation has a clearly defined mission statement.	7.02	-	-	7.21
• Our congregation provides spiritually uplifting worship experiences.	7.00	-	7.38	-
• Our congregation helps members become more loving and compassionate.	-	-	6.98	6.68
• Our congregation helps you get to know adults in the church.	-	-	6.34	-
• I am challenged by how my congregation is living out a sense of mission.	-	-	6.93	-
• Our congregation is making use of members' talents and gifts.	-	-	6.46	-
• Our congregation is intent on some aspect of making the world a better place.	-	-	7.16	-
• I feel at home in this church.	-	-	8.09	-
Dimension 4. Importance of this Church to Me	-	7.33	7.96	-
• If had to change churches, I would feel a great sense of loss.	-	7.50	7.72	-
• The church I attend matters a great deal to me.	-	7.96	8.20	-

	Col1	Col2	Col3	Col4
Dimension 5. Congregation's Social Interaction	6.55	5.18	5.22	-
• Nearly everyone is involved in some way in helping out at church.	5.95	-	4.42	-
• The pastor knows the names of most teenagers and adults.	7.23	6.94	6.80	-
• If one of our families needs help, word quickly spreads throughout our church.	6.69	-	-	-
• There is much informal interaction among youth and adults.	6.37	-	-	-
• In our church, everyone knows each other.	-	-	4.43	-
Dimension 6. Congregation's Moral Guidance	6.60	6.81	6.96	-
• Our congregation helps you make decisions about what's right and wrong.	7.03	6.71	6.94	-
• Our congregation helps you learn how to resist pressure from other kids to do things you know are wrong.	6.52	-	-	-
• Our congregations helps you develop concern for people.	6.75	-	-	-
• Our congregation teaches members about Christian perspectives on moral questions.	6.88	6.79	6.91	-
• Our congregation helps you learn how to be a peacemaker.	6.31	-	-	-
• Our congregation helps you develop responsible values and behaviors in the area of sexuality.	6.12	-	-	-
• Our congregation helps you learn how to apply your faith to everyday decisions.	-	6.95	7.05	-
Dimension 7. Congregation's Openness to Change	6.35	6.25	6.31	-
• We have considerable freedom in our congregation to try out new ideas.	6.62	-	6.29	-
• Members are willing to share and listen to different points of view.	6.07	5.50	-	6.64

My congregation is ready and willing to change things when a good new idea comes along.	-	6.19	6.33	-
Members are encouraged to say what they think on religious issues.	-	5.27	5.80	6.20
Members listen to each other.	-	6.78	6.75	-
Member have a lot of say when important decisions are made.	-	6.62	6.71	7.43
Making independent decisions is highly valued here.	-	6.43	5.95	-
Our congregation is open to the suggestions of these we serve.	-	-	6.82	-
Our congregation's administrative procedures are quite flexible.	-	-	5.98	-
Church groups have freedom to innovate even when funding is involved.	-	-	5.97	-
Members of this church are willing to change the way things are done to increase involvement with the church.	-	-	-	5.32
My congregation is innovative.	-	-	-	6.74

Dimension 8. Members Experience Love and Support	-	6.92	-	-
• Our congregation helps members make friends at church.	-	6.25	-	-
• Our congregation provides support and love to members experiencing hardship.	-	7.31	-	-
• Our congregation puts an emphasis on providing love, support, and friendship to members.	-	7.21	-	-

APPLICATION TOOL 4

Evaluating Faith Assets: Congregational Faith

Use this worksheet as a guide to reflect on the practice of the Congregation Faith assets in your congregation. First, rate your congregation on each of the items in the second column. Then, list in the third column things you already do to strengthen each quality. Finally, identify other things you could do to strengthen the Congregation Faith assets.

Assets	Rating Your Congregation *
1. Experiencing God's Living Presence	_____ People experience God's presence in the community.
	_____ People experience God's presence in worship.
	_____ People experience God's presence through study.
	_____ People experience God's presence in service and mission.

What We Do Now:

What We Could Do Better:

* Rating Scale: ★ = *Needs Work*   ★ ★ = *Okay*   ★ ★ ★ = *Great*

Assets	Rating Your Congregation

2. Makes Faith Central

_____ The congregation helps people learn who God is.

_____ The congregation helps people to know Jesus personally.

_____ The congregation teaches people how to be a Christian.

4. Focuses on Discipleship

_____ The congregation helps people learn about the Bible and its meaning for their lives.

5. Emphasizes Scripture

_____ The congregation makes Scripture come alive for each member.

What We Do Now:

What We Could Do Better:

3. Emphasizes Prayer

_____ The congregation practices the presence of God through prayer and worship.

_____ The congregation helps people learn how to pray.

What We Do Now:

What We Could Do Better:

Assets	Rating Your Congregation

6. Makes Mission Central

_____ The congregation gets people involved in community service projects.

_____ The congregation gets people involved in helping to improve the lives of people who are poor or hungry.

_____ The congregation makes use of each member's talents and abilities.

_____ The congregation makes missions and evangelism important in congregational life.

_____ The congregation brings the gospel to people outside the congregation.

What We Do Now:

What We Could Do Better:

APPLICATION
TOOL 5

Evaluating Faith Assets: Congregational Qualities

Use this worksheet as a guide to reflect on the practice of the Congregation Qualities assets in your congregation. First, rate your congregation on each of the items in the second column. Then, list in the third column things you already do to strengthen each quality. Finally, identify other things you could do to strengthen the Congregation Quality assets.

Assets	Rating Your Congregation *
7. Supports Youth Ministry	_____ Youth feel loved and respected by the congregation.
	_____ The congregation is very caring and supportive of youth.
	_____ The congregation values youth as a vibrant part of the family of faith.
	_____ There is a good spirit and a willingness to get involved with youth.
	_____ The congregation places a high priority on youth and youth ministry.

What We Do Now:

What We Could Do Better:

* ★ = *Needs Work*   ★★ = *Okay*   ★★★ = *Great*

Assets	Rating Your Congregation

8. Demonstrates Hospitality

_____ The congregation values and welcomes all people, especially youth.

11. Creates Community

_____ The congregation feels warm and friendly; makes me feel at home.

_____ The congregation helps members make friends at church

_____ The congregation accepts people who are different; makes strangers feel welcome.

_____ The congregation helps members become more loving and compassionate.

_____ The congregation puts an emphasis on providing love, support, and friendship to members, especially those experiencing hardship.

What We Do Now:

What We Could Do Better:

9. Strives for Excellence

_____ The congregation sets high standards, evaluates, and engages in continuous improvement.

_____ The congregation is innovative.

_____ The congregation is willing to change the way things are done to increase involvement with the church and/or when a good new idea comes along.

_____ The congregation is open to the suggestions from members and involves members in making important decisions.

_____ The congregation gives freedom to try out new ideas

What We Do Now:

What We Could Do Better:

10. Encourages
    Thinking

_____ The congregation challenges people to think about religious issues and ideas.

_____ The congregation encourages people to ask questions.

_____ The congregation encourages people to say what they think on religious issues.

What We Do Now:

What We Could Do Better:

12. Encourages
    Small Groups

_____ The congregation engages members in small groups for study, conversation, and prayer about faith in daily life.

What We Do Now:

What We Could Do Better:

Assets	Rating Your Congregation

13. Promotes Worship

_____ The congregation provides spiritually uplifting worship experiences.

_____ The congregation provides worship that is: enlightening, fulfilling, and inspiring,

_____ The congregation provides worship that is easy to understanding, interesting, useful in daily life (relevant).

What We Do Now:

What We Could Do Better:

14. Fosters Ethical Responsibility

_____ The congregation helps people make decisions about what's right and wrong.

_____ The congregation teaches members about Christian perspectives on moral questions.

_____ The congregation helps people learn how to apply your faith to everyday decisions.

What We Do Now:

What We Could Do Better:

15. Promotes Service   _____ The congregation sponsors outreach, service projects, and cultural immersions **locally**.

_____ The congregation sponsors outreach, service projects, and cultural immersions **globally**.

What We Do Now:

What We Could Do Better:

17. Participate in the   _____ Youth are engaged in a wide spectrum of congregational life
Congregation   and ministries.

What We Do Now:

What We Could Do Better:

Assets	Rating Your Congregation

18. Assume Ministry Leadership

_____ Youth are invited, equipped and affirmed for leadership in congregational activities.

_____ Youth receive training for ministry leadership.

What We Do Now:

What We Could Do Better:

APPLICATION
TOOL 6

Developing a Youth-Friendly and Youth-Involving Congregation

Assessment

How would you rate your efforts in developing a youth-friendly and youth-involving congregation, building intergenerational connections between youth and the congregation?

	Rating *			
1. Our congregation knows and values young people, and this is communicated by church leadership and the whole community.	1	2	3	4
2. Our congregation is knowledgeable about the vision and activities of youth ministry, and places a priority on ministry with young people.	1	2	3	4
3. Our congregation invites and welcomes young people at Sunday worship.	1	2	3	4
4. Our congregation encourages young people to participate with other generations in church-wide ministries and programs.	1	2	3	4
5. Our congregation integrates young people into leadership roles within the church.	1	2	3	4
6. Our congregation involves young people in leading programs, activities, and ministries for the whole church community	1	2	3	4
7. Our youth ministry regularly offers programs that connect youth with the other generations in the church.	1	2	3	4

* 1 = low or not present   4 = high or a strong feature

	Rating

8. Our congregation offers intergenerational programs and activities that connects all of the generations for learning, worship, prayer, building relationships, and service. 1 2 3 4

9. Our youth ministry offers programming that prepares young people to participate in the life of the church throughout the year (worship, service, outreach, and so on). 1 2 3 4

Reflection

Reflect on the results of your assessment with the church staff and youth ministry team.

* What strengths did you identify? What areas of improvement did you identify?
* How "youth-friendly" is your congregation today? How connected to the church community do you think young people feel today?
* What barriers do you face when it comes to connecting youth with the community and building intergenerational relationships? What steps can you take to overcome these barriers?
* What are the one or two priorities that you need to act on now?

Strategies for Becoming More Intergenerational

There is no one way to connect youth with the whole church community. Each congregation is a very specific community with its own unique identity, history, traditions, people, and geography. Customize these ideas for your community. Use them to spark your own creativity. There are many ways to build a youth-friendly and youth-involving congregation.

* **Build a youth-friendly congregation culture where young people are valued and intentionally included in all of congregation life.**

  1. Raise the profile of young people in the congregation community by making them more visible at gatherings, recognizing their presence, and affirming their contributions.
  2. Cultivate a widespread, strong expectation for engagement of the congregation with young people. Develop a consistent expectation that all members should be engaged positively with young people and that positive engagement will be encouraged and appreciated.
  3. Educate the congregation to the "real" picture of young people, confronting the popular stereotypes of youth that they may see in the media. Presenting research

and actual stories of young people that will help the congregation understand and become comfortable with young people.

4. Examine your church's activities—from worship to education to social events—to determine if they are welcoming to all generations, especially young people. Explore whether these activities offer opportunities for more relationship building across generations.

5. Involve the congregation in praying for youth and their events, such as service trips or retreats, and milestones in the life of young people, such as graduations and other accomplishments.

6. Offer simple, one-time opportunities for adults and young people to get to know each other, such as social events, service projects, or educational experiences.

7. Link young people with adults in the congregation who have insights and life experiences that may be helpful to the particular young person, such as discerning life choices, planning for a career, managing money.

8. Create communication strategies for promoting the good news about young people and their role in the church and wider community, such as photo displays in the church building, newsletters, photos/video/stories on the church website, and presentations at church meetings and gatherings.

- **Infuse intergenerational relationships and programming into the existing youth ministry program and activities.**

1. Integrate intergenerational programming into the youth ministry plan and calendar, for example, quarterly intergenerational nights.

2. Intergenerationalize youth programs—take a youth-only program and redesign it to include other generations, for example, intergenerational service.

3. Structure youth programs with an intergenerational connection, for example, include interviews with church members of different ages or a invite a panel of congregation members into a youth program.

4. Incorporate intergenerational dialogues into programming—provide opportunities for youth to access the wisdom, experience, knowledge, and interests of older adults through presentations, performances, and discussions and provide seniors with an opportunity for recognition.

5. Develop mentoring relationships between youth and adults, such as prayer partners, learning-to-pray spiritual direction, service involvement, and Confirmation mentors.

- **Incorporate youth into the ministries and leadership roles of the congregation.**

1. Identify ways to integrate youth into leadership roles in the life of the congregation: (a) Identify all of the possibilities for leadership in the ministries, programs, and

activities of the congregation. (b) Identify specific roles for youth and work with leaders to connect young people with leadership roles. (c) Provide training for adults on how to work with youth and for youth on how to work with adults.

2. Organize a leadership or ministry apprenticeship for youth to serve in ministry leadership positions or on committees and councils.

3. Create new church leadership roles that are led by young people and which draw upon some of their unique and special gifts that can benefit the entire parish community, such as online and website strategies, video production, drama productions, music concerns (instrumental and voice), youth choir for Sunday worship, and art for worship.

4. Create a youth program or task form to analyze youth involvement in the congregation. Working in teams, take a month to explore the life and ministries of the church. Create a report on youth involvement in church life and present it to the young people, the church staff and church leadership groups, and the whole congregation.

- **Create models of intergenerational programming for all the generations in the congregation.**

1. *Intergenerational service/mission opportunities*: Offer a variety of service/ mission projects for all ages where people can choose from different levels of commitment from beginner experiences to advanced projects that are local, regional, national, and international. Each mission/service project includes a learning component that focuses on understanding the issue being addressed, exploring the teachings of Scripture and tradition, developing the skills for mission and service, and then, upon completion of the project, reflecting upon the involvement. Service/mission projects can be "developmental" with projects geared to different levels of involvement and challenge including:

   - local mission projects lasting anywhere from a few hours to one day in length.

   - short-term mission trips lasting anywhere from two to five days and requiring an overnight stay on location

   - weeklong mission trips within the United States as well as to foreign countries, designed for those who are ready to take the next big step in service.

   - global expedition trips of ten to fourteen days that provide the opportunity to be immersed for a longer period in the targeted community and culture

2. *Intergenerational retreat experiences*: Develop a congregation-wide retreat over several days with weekend and/or evening sessions. Organize the retreat experience by conducting intergenerational sessions, rather than sessions for

individual groups. Develop a focus for the mission, such as following Jesus, or growing in prayer, or what we believe as Christians. Select individual topics for each session of the retreat and provide participants with materials to continue the retreat at home.

3. Intergenerational learning programs: Develop learning programs that involve all ages in the congregation, such as:

    - monthly large group intergenerational learning programs (that can replace age-group programs once a month)
    - intergenerational workshops throughout the year focused on all-ages content, such as faith practices, church year seasons, and/or current social issues
    - intergenerational small group learning programs, such as Bible study or lectionary-based Scripture reflection (at the church or in homes)
    - intergenerational family retreats and camps

    One model for intergenerational learning that is being used in thousands of churches incorporates the following elements:

    - Welcome, community building, and opening prayer
    - Part 1: An All-Ages Learning Experience for the whole assembly that introduces the theme or topic for the program.
    - Part 2: In-Depth Learning Experiences that probe the theme or topic, organized for all ages (intergenerational) or for specific age-groups (families with children or children-only, adolescents, young adults, and adults), and conducted in one of three formats:

        - *Whole Group Format*: learning in small groups with the whole group assembled in one room (age-specific or all ages small groups);
        - *Age Group Format*: learning in separate, parallel groups organized by ages;
        - *Learning Activity Center Format*: learning at self-directed or facilitated activity centers (age-specific and/or all ages learning centers).

    - Part 3. An All-Ages Contributive Learning experience in which each generation teaches the other generations.
    - Part 4. Reflection on the learning experience and interactive group sharing.
    - Closing Prayer

Source: See Intergenerational Faith Formation, *Mariette Martineau, Joan Weber, and Leif Kehrwald (New London: Twenty-Third, 2008).*

CHAPTER FOUR

youth ministry qualities

The Impact of Youth Ministry on the Lives of Young People

One of the perennial questions asked about youth ministry by pastors, church staff, and members of the congregation is pretty direct: Is youth ministry making a difference in the lives of young people? Is our congregation's investment of time, energy, and money producing results? The Study of Exemplary Congregations in Youth Ministry certainly provides plenty of rich information to answer these questions.

We know that the true test of a youth ministry's effectiveness is the impact that it is has on the faith and practice of young people. Based on responses of survey responses of 2252 youth and the interviews at the onsite visits in twenty-one congregations, we can clearly see the impact of youth ministry on the lives of young people. When youth were specifically asked about the impact that their involvement in youth activities had on their religious faith, they responded *very positively*. Their involvement deepened their relationship with Jesus and their understanding of the Christian faith, and helped them apply faith to their daily lives. Here are their responses (highest rating 9):

My involvement in youth programs has helped me . . .

- *deepen my relationship with Jesus (7.56)*
- *understand my Christian faith better (7.52)*
- *apply my faith to daily life (7.20)*
- *make serious life choices (about my future, my relationships, my values) (7.05)*
- *share my faith (6.83)*

To what extent have the following been a positive influence on your religious faith . . .

- *a youth group leader at my church (7.47)*
- *the youth group at my church (7.42)*
- *worship services at my church (6.47)*
- *Christian education programs (e.g., Sunday school, classes, Bible studies) (6.45)*
- *a religion teacher at my church (6.33)*

Young people's involvement in youth programs has also helped them address a variety of important life issues.

My involvement in youth programs has help me to . . .

- *help other youth deal with problems (6.90)*
- *respect other ethnic or racial groups (6.25)*
- *address issues of conflict and violence. (6.24)*
- *address issues of drugs and alcohol (6.16)*
- *raise my awareness of church vocations (6.13)*
- *understand sexuality and its role in life (6.13)*
- *improve my family relationships (5.75)*
- *better understand parents/teachers/adults (5.68)*
- *raise my awareness about social justice (5.51)*

Youth ministry *does* make a difference in the lives of young people—it promotes their growth in faith and the application of their faith to daily life, while also helping them respond to the personal, family, and social issues they face daily. But how does youth ministry do this? This chapter will explore the findings from the research about the qualities of effective youth ministries in the exemplary congregations we studied.

Faith Assets: Youth Ministry Qualities

Building on the survey findings and the results of the onsite congregational visits, six Faith Assets describe the qualities—attitudes, expectations, and practices—of the congregation's age-level ministries with youth. Woven through the six Faith Assets is the use of a variety of ministry practices that are "custom-designed" to address the real lives of young people in a particular congregation.

Asset 19. Establishes a Caring Environment: Youth ministry provides multiple nurturing relationships and activities resulting in a welcoming atmosphere of respect, growth, and belonging.

Asset 20. Develops Quality Relationships: Youth ministry develops authentic relationships among youth and adults establishing an environment of presence and life engagement.

Asset 21. Focuses on Jesus Christ: Youth ministry's mission, practices, and relationships are inspired by the life and ministry of Jesus Christ

Asset 22. Considers Life Issues: Youth ministry values and addresses the full range of young people's lives.

Asset 23. Uses Many Approaches: Youth ministry intentionally and creatively employs multiple activities appropriate to the ministry's mission and context.

Asset 24. Is Well Organized and Planned: Youth ministry engages participants and leaders in long range planning, implementation, evaluation, and innovation in an atmosphere of high expectations.

Focusing on Jesus Christ and Discipleship

Asset 21. Focuses on Jesus Christ: Youth ministry's mission, practices, and relationships are inspired by the life and ministry of Jesus Christ.

One could sum up the purpose of the EYM congregations' youth ministries in a single goal: making disciples of Jesus Christ These congregations focus their youth ministries on Jesus Christ and engage young people in discipleship, witness, and service that transforms their lives. As we have already seen, effective youth ministries make a significant impact on the personal of faith of young people by deepening their relationship with Jesus, helping them understand the Christian faith better, applying their faith to daily life and serious life choices, and sharing their faith with others.

A strong evangelical emphasis in the youth ministry program was one of the five most important factors cited by pastors and youth ministers in their written responses to the question: Why do you think your congregation's youth ministry is able to accomplish this while so many other congregations struggle at it? They described the strong evangelical emphasis of their youth ministry in these words:

- *Our goal is that they know Christ and make Him known.*
- *We go beyond knowing the faith to living it.*
- *Out teens are enthusiastic about their Lord.*
- *We are conscious of our need for God's intervention.*
- *Our focus is on Jesus Christ and the Gospel.*
- *We disciple our youth to walk with God.*
- *We feature small, weekly Bible study fellowship groups.*
- *We are equipping them for a life of faith.*
- *Ours is Bible-based, Christ-centered teaching and preaching.*
- *Ours is a commitment to long term spiritual goals.*
- *We encourage spiritual renewal and commitment.*
- *We ask a high commitment of our youth.*
- *We have established a strong prayer base.*

Several "marks and means" of discipleship emerge in the study. These elements describe the core attributes of the congregations, their youth ministries, and their young people.

1. **Disciples Know Jesus Christ:** Discipleship is grounded in the teachings, life, death, resurrection, and lordship of Jesus Christ alive and present. Disciples are in relationship with Christ, learn about Christ, and follow Christ's leading. In the vast majority of congregations in the study, youth ministry is consciously designed to cultivate a relationship with Jesus Christ through worship, prayer, community-building, study, retreats, and service.

2. **Disciples Know the Bible:** Discipleship is anchored in Bible study. It is in the Bible that youth learn the story, the truth that shapes the life of faith. Bible studies take many shapes and forms. Most popular are small group conversational explorations of the Scripture texts in which youth and their leaders hear God speaking truth to their lives. Bible studies are a constitutive exercise in discipleship.

3. **Disciples Know the Christian Faith:** Discipleship is learning the Christian faith. The Christian faith has a history, traditions, beliefs, and values that are critical to its shaping and transforming power. Congregations are committed to teaching young people the content of the Christian faith through a variety

of ministry experiences. Adult leaders guide young people in exploring the long and rich life of the people of God, creating more sturdy beliefs, engaging the tough questions, and assisting youth in finding their own "faith voice."

4. **Disciples Make Faith a Way of Life:** Discipleship is the "knowledge of faith" becoming a way of life. Discipleship is regularly described as much in languages of the "heart" and the "hands" as of the "head." For the congregations in the study, it was not enough for young people to know the content of Scripture or to understand the richness of Christian beliefs. Whether small or large these churches developed expansive ministries with youth for the purpose of participating in faith as a way of life. The adults and youth in these ministries seemed to be "living into" faith that is simultaneously centered in God yet genuinely their own. They spoke about what they believed with conviction and in fresh language. Compassion, honesty, respect, integrity, service to others, and justice were evident in their speech, life styles, and relationships with others. All this was carried on with an eye on both tradition and experience; text and context; faith and life.

5. **Disciples Are Mentored:** Discipleship is formed in relationships with mentoring individuals and communities. Even though discipleship is primarily a faith-relationship in which Christ is at the center, adolescent disciples are formed in relationship with other Christians. Whole congregations become intergenerational crucibles in which conversation, relationships, and practices wrap youth in a culture of "knowing and doing God." Within these congregations, people walk intentionally and directly alongside young people providing diverse, concrete "snapshots" of following Jesus Christ as these mentors encourage and teach through their presence, speech, and action.

6. **Disciples Are Equipped:** A young person's strengths and gifts of the Spirit are integral to discipleship. To follow Christ involves a call to witness and to serve others. To make disciples is to identify a teenager's spiritual gifts and equip that teenager for service in the church and the world. Congregations combine study, fellowship, personal strengths and spiritual gifts discovery with service to equip young disciples to follow Jesus Christ in the church and into the world.

Discipleship at Travis Avenue Baptist Church

Travis Avenue Baptist Church in Fort Worth, Texas, one of the twenty-one exemplary congregations selected for an onsite visit, has created a culture of youth ministry in which relationships with God, with each other, and with the world are at the heart of the practices that move young people through a matrix of faith maturation and discipleship. This youth ministry is developed around the dynamic that relationships begin with God, generate community, and radiate into the world. These relationships are nurtured through Bible study, small groups, leadership training, and serving others.

Travis Avenue Baptist youth ministry's mission statement reflects is emphasis on discipleship: "Our mission in the Travis Avenue Student Ministry is lead students to live for Jesus Christ The student ministry exists for the purpose of teaching students to walk with God on their own. Through our ministry, students will encounter and be introduced to the richness of God's Word as we challenge them to live the life God intended for them."

The youth ministry is led by a team of adult and student leaders who are committed to living a life fully devoted to Christ Mentoring plays a significant role in "discipling" young people at Travis Avenue Baptist Adult volunteers of vital faith meet youth individually several times a month for encouragement, prayer, "faith talk," and accountability.

Travis Avenue Baptist's focus on discipleship permeates every aspect of their youth ministry.

1. *Backstage* is the weekly mid-week gathering focused on diving into God's word, engaging in authentic worship, and pursuing genuine relationships.
2. *Epic* is the weekly Sunday evening gathering where youth are practically learning to walk with God on their own as they are placed in small groups led by other students for the purpose of learning to read, interpret, and obey the Scriptures for themselves.
3. *Choir* takes place every Sunday evening before *Epic* and is an exciting time for youth as they practice musical excellence within the context of glorifying God through the fine arts. Each week youth gather for a time of praise and worship as they unify their hearts in glorifying Christ through son.
4. *Parent Connection* equips parents to the primary discipler of their son or daughter.
5. *Sunday School* is a time of Bible study and fellowship.
6. *Special Events* are offered throughout the year: mission trips, weekend retreats, student camp, *Disciple Now* weekend, and the *Travis Round-Up*.

A teenager at Travis Avenue Baptist described her experience at Travis Avenue Baptist in this way: "I think they basically invited me in and helped me grow and then equipped me to help others grow." Through Disciple Now, a weekend event, she experienced worship, Bible study, small group conversation, prayer, and leadership training for young people who are eager to follow Christ and be equipped for ministry. She was a participant in small groups that meet every Sunday evening for discipleship, Bible study, and accountability. Adults accompany the group, but youth are responsible for leadership. These groups reinforce effective Sunday morning Bible teaching led by adult volunteers. They profoundly influenced this young woman who began her journey with Travis Avenue as an unchurched teenager.

Travis Avenue's youth ministry team understands that discipleship means not only an invitation to know and follow Jesus Christ, but also a "call to invest in the lives of God's people and the world." The minister to students referenced Ephesians 4:11-12 as the heart of his work: "The gifts he gave were that some would be apostles, some prophets some evangelists, some pastors and teachers, to equip the saints for the work of ministry, for building up the body of Christ" "My job is to teach the students and adults and parents. I teach them how to do ministry and I let them do ministry. The goal is to get them to teach themselves. They need to ask: How do I make this true? I have to live it—to think and grow to lead to maturity. It is our goal to help them live the life of a Christian."

Travis Avenue's intention is personally to invite people by name, claim them in the name of God, bring them into the church to be equipped in the Word, and send them out into the world to spread the good news of Jesus Christ. The marks of discipleship are not only learned from Scripture and not only embedded in youth ministry activities and modeled by adult and youth leaders. They are reflected in the expectations of all aspects of their youth ministry. Like the other EYM congregations, the youth ministry at Travis Avenue Baptist is consciously designed to cultivate a relationship with Jesus Christ through worship, prayer, community-building, study, retreats, outreach, and service.

Developing a Caring Environment and Quality Relationships

Asset 19. Establishes a Caring Environment: Youth ministry provides multiple nurturing relationships and activities resulting in a welcoming atmosphere of respect, growth, and belonging.
Asset 20. Develops Quality Relationships: Youth ministry develops authentic relationships among youth and adults establishing an environment of presence and life engagement.

Youth ministries in the EYM Study work from a foundation of authentic relationships and a caring environment. Throughout the interviews, the most common description of the relationship of young people with their youth ministries and congregations was "we are a close community" or "we are a family." And this is affirmed by the very positive results from the youth surveys reporting that youth gatherings have a warm and welcoming climate which is friendly, makes strangers feel welcome, and accepts people who are different.

EYM congregations provide youth with a variety of settings and environments where their love of Jesus Christ becomes a relational lived experience. A caring environment and quality relationships undergird worship, Bible study, classes, faith and life groups, music ministries, mission trips, and a multitude of other youth ministry practices. Pastors, youth ministers, and adult leaders facilitate the development of genuine relationships among adults and youth in these faith communities. Small groups are present everywhere in these youth ministries. Small groups encourage youth to speak out on issues and address concerns in their everyday lives. Small groups focus on Scripture and the discussion of young people's questions. They regularly include meditation, prayer, silence, rituals, and spiritual reflection.

One of highest scoring dimensions in the twelve dimensions of Youth Ministry Qualities is young people's very positive responses to "spiritual support group" (8.39 out of 9.0). The young people in EYM congregations reported that they belong to at least one church group in which others will pray with me and for me as needed (8.64), they talk about spiritual issues (8.50), and it is possible to talk about personal problems (8.02). (See Table 9, Dimension 1)

A hallmark of effective youth ministries in the study is providing and then involving youth in a variety of spiritual support groups. This certainly seems to be a key component of all the youth ministries. Virtually all of the young people in EYM congregations have found a spiritual support group in which they belong and are accepted, pray, share their faith and personal issues, and receive support.

Peer Relationships

EYM congregations find ways to involve young people in peer relationships throughout the life and ministry of the congregation. These church friends are a positive influence on each other's faith and significant contributors to each others' vitality and resiliency. Young people report that they have three or more Christian friends in their congregation whom they see often (7.91 out of 9.0) and that when they are troubled they have friends in their congregation who they can call to discuss problems (7.08). Young people consistently said that their church's youth ministry supported their faith through friends in their congregation with whom they can be open and honest. One teenager captured the importance of peer relationships: "We are free to share our concerns and struggles; our friends hold us accountable for the decisions that we make."

The EYM congregations also incorporated the power of peer relationships in small, intimate circles of youth in which community and strong relationships thrived. These groups were described as safe and welcoming environments by the participants of the study and consistently included engaging Bible study, prayer, and service. A number of EYM congregations engaged youth in ministering with their peers in church, civic, and school settings. These ministries included equipping youth to be care givers with their friends.

Adult-Youth Relationships and Mentoring

EYM congregations develop healthy adult-youth relationships and bring adults and youth together through mentoring. The survey results from parents, adult leaders in youth ministry, pastors, and youth ministers emphasize the importance of adult-youth mentoring in their youth ministries:

- *Youth in our church have an adult mentor.*
- *Mentors in our church feel honored to work with youth.*
- *Mentors in our church have helped youth grow in their faith.*
- *Youth in our church enjoy working with a mentor.*
- *Our congregation trains adult mentors to work one-on-one with youth.*
- *I hear of adults in our congregation who have significantly changed the life and direction of a youth who is not their child.*
  (See Table 9 for more information.)

The youth ministries in the EYM Study recruit mature Christian adults who invest in young people. Youth in these churches report that these experiences help them grow in their faith. Adults sense the value of the mentoring and are honored to work with youth. These positive experiences with mentoring are communicated throughout the congregations, which "fuels" the recruitment of new mentors. Several congregations reported "relationship-based" ministries with adult-youth mentoring as the "centerpieces" of their work. In these ministries relationships are fostered through carefully designed practices that support adult-youth faith-mentoring conversations.

Adult leaders in youth ministry interviewed did not see their responsibilities confined to Sunday morning, youth events, or the church building. These mentors often visit young people during the week, in their homes, at their schools, wherever teenagers "hang out." Many of the adult leaders invite their classes to their homes for Bible study or conversation. Most often this did not occur as a result of formal programming; it happened because of the adult leader's commitment to the young people.

The development of caring adult youth leaders was essential to the substance of the youth ministries in the EYM congregations. Adults invested themselves in the lives of adolescents with patience and unconditional love, becoming bearers and receptors of God's presence in the lives of teenagers. These trusting relationships between youth and adults provided both content and example for young people. These Christian adults became a source of Christian knowledge and wisdom. Youth learned about God and discipleship from their experience with these seasoned Christians.

Using a Variety of Custom-Designed Practices and Approaches

Asset 23. Uses Many Approaches: Youth ministry intentionally and creatively employs multiple activities appropriate to the ministry's mission and context.

Asset 24. Is Well Organized and Planned: Youth ministry engages participants and leaders in long range planning, implementation, evaluation, and innovation in an atmosphere of high expectations.

One of the five most important factors cited by pastors and youth ministers for the effectiveness of their youth ministries was the wide variety and nature of youth programs. They described an impressive diversity of events and program features that characterize the youth ministries of their congregations. They referred to each of these programs or activities as making a significant impact on the spiritual development of their youth.

- *Peer ministry*
- *Youth involvement in leadership positions*
- *Youth involvement in all aspects of church life*
- *A focus on intergenerational participation*
- *Annual retreats and summer mission trips*
- *Youth involvement in service projects*
- *A strong, innovative faith formation and/or confirmation program with an emphasis on disciple-making*
- *A strong emphasis on being a part of the church family*
- *A safe, loving environment where youth can explore their faith*
- *A strong biblical, educational program; a weekly Bible study that uses Scripture to provide answers to youth's questions*
- *Ownership of the youth ministry given to youth, parents, and adult leaders in youth ministry*
- *Freedom and trust to be creative and take risks*
- *Cooperation with neighboring congregations on youth activities*
- *Early involvement of children, preparing them for later participation in youth ministry*

These programs and activities are confirmed by the survey results. First, they are reflected in the top five responses by the young people to the major emphases of their congregation's youth program: faith relationship with Jesus Christ (8.09), prayer (7.92), a safe and caring place (7.91), leadership training and experience (7.06), and Bible study (6.78). (See Table 9, Dimension 2)

Second, when youth, parents, adult leaders, pastors, and youth ministers were asked about their youth ministry's effectiveness (See Table 9, Dimension 8-Achievement of Desired Outcomes), they identified a similar list of highly rated programs and activities, including the following:

- *Helping youth recognize that God is at work changing their lives*
- *Guiding youth in developing a personal relationship with Jesus Christ*
- *Helping youth make a commitment to Jesus Christ*
- *Creating an atmosphere (physical and emotional) where youth are accepted and have a sense of belonging; creating an environment which nurtures meaningful relationships.*
- *Inviting and welcoming youth in the faith community; helping youth feel loved and respected by their congregation*
- *Helping youth connect their involvement in service projects with their Christian faith; helping youth understand justice issues and Christian responses*
- *Helping youth learn how to pray; providing a variety of prayer experiences for youth*
- *Engaging youth to spread the Gospel to other young people*
- *Teaching Christian concepts of right and wrong*
- *Enabling youth to be involved in ministry*

From the responses of youth, parents, adult leaders, pastors and youth ministers, we can discern common youth ministry practices and approaches in the 131 congregations.

CHART 5

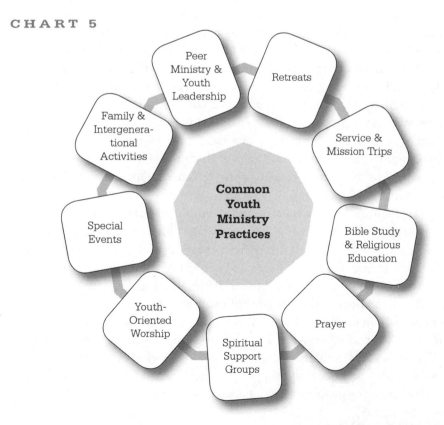

The findings from youth, parents, adults leaders, pastors, and youth ministers in EYM congregations provide us with important insights into how effective youth ministries make a significant impact on the faith of young people. What is surprising about the list of practices and approaches is how "ordinary" it is. You can probably find many of these practices in churches all across the country. Youth ministry in EYM congregations might well be characterized as "ordinary practices done extraordinarily well" in response to the needs of youth in their communities. As we have said throughout this book, it is the whole culture—the congregation, the youth ministry, family and household, and leadership—that makes for effective youth ministry. These youth ministry approaches and practices do not stand alone. They are important, but they are part of an interconnected congregational culture that develops youth of vital Christian faith.

EYM congregations take the ordinary practices and approaches of youth ministry and developed custom-designed, innovative ways to address the particular needs of youth, their families, and the congregation. Innovative and unique approaches to custom-designed youth ministries flow from the congregations' pastoral and youth ministry leadership teams. Over 85% of the youth ministers surveyed agreed or strongly agreed with the statement, "Doing things in new and creative ways is appreciated by my senior/lead pastor or supervisor." Nearly 70% of the ministers described their congregations as being "willing to change the way things are done to increase involvement in the church." Over half of the ministers (58.5%) either agreed or strongly agreed that their congregation is innovative. The creative and innovative EYM youth ministries take place in the context of congregations that are willing to take risks and accept change.

These findings are supported by the survey results from youth, parents, adult leaders in youth ministry, and the pastors and youth ministers. They describe the characteristics of congregations that are open to change and innovation: openness to new ideas, freedom to try out new ideas, a willingness to share and listen to different points of view, and a readiness to change things when a good new idea comes along. (For more details, see Chapter 3, Table 8, Dimension 7. Congregation's Openness to Change.)

The exploration into custom-designed youth ministry practices and approaches reveals that developing a contextually unique expression of a long-standing, common practice can bring fresh meaning and impact to youth ministry. By considering the unique needs and context of youth, leaders can contextualize common practices, making them distinctive and fresh. Second, it also reveals that the variety and scope of youth ministry practices is important. No one strategy will fit everyone. To reach and minister to a larger audience of youth means that the type of events, functions, and opportunities must be varied. Third, it is important to balance congregational integration of young people with age-level ministry practices, and support for their families. Effective youth ministry addresses young people's developmental, social, and spiritual needs through "age-level oriented" practices, as well as intergenerational experiences and activities within the larger body of believers and their families.

To get a glimpse at the variety of custom-designed practices and approaches among the congregations in the EYM Study, read the case studies at the end of each chapter. The case studies were developed by the research team based on the visits and interviews with the twenty-one exemplary congregations.

- *Case Study 1. Rochester Covenant Church (Chapter 2)*
- *Case Study 2. Thornapple Evangelical Covenant Church (Chapter 3)*
- *Case Study 3. Newport Mesa Christian Center (Chapter 4)*
- *Case Study 4. Tri-Parish Youth Ministry of Sacred Heart, Saint Benedict, and Saint Ann Parishes (Chapter 4)*
- *Case Study 5. Service and Mission at Myers Park United Methodist Church (Chapter 4)*
- *Case Study 6. Faith Formation and Confirmation at Hope Lutheran Church (Chapter 4)*

An Emerging Pattern of Youth Ministry

In the EYM congregations, it was not enough for young people to know the content of Scripture or to understand the richness of Christian beliefs. Whether small or large these churches developed expansive ministries with youth for the purpose of participating in faith as a way of life. The adults and youth in these ministries seemed to be "living into" faith that is simultaneously centered in God yet genuinely their own. They spoke about what they believed with conviction and in fresh language. Compassion, honesty, respect, integrity, service to others, and justice were evident in their speech, life styles, and relationships with others. All this was carried on with an eye on both tradition and experience; text and context; faith and life.

A "pattern" in the youth ministries of exemplary congregations emerges out the research findings. We can discern a process in these youth ministries that seems to move through the following elements:

1. Focus on ministry with youth "outside as well as within" the faith community.
2. Make contact with those who do not belong to a congregation or who don't know Christ or who are different or in need.
3. Speak with outsiders about faith and Jesus Christ and serve them at their point of need.
4. Invite those outside the congregation to experience Jesus Christ through participation in his "body," the community of faith.

5. When new people come, welcome them into the faith community and encourage them to stay and become participants in its life.
6. Through worship, prayer, Bible study, discipleship groups, and ongoing faith relationships (for example, mentoring) nurture young people's life and faith.
7. Identify young people's strengths and gifts and invite them into leadership utilizing their "giftedness" to build up the body of Christ.
8. Equip young people both for leadership within the congregation and for following Christ in the world.
9. Send young people out into the world to serve others and bear witness to Jesus Christ.

While not every congregation articulated all of these elements, and each congregation worked at the elements of the pattern differently, one could see a flow of "welcoming, instructing, equipping and sending" at work in the congregation's mission statements and strategies of ministry. What's more, "sending into the world" seemed to be integral to the congregation's understanding of a young person's relationship with God. For these ministries with youth, the life of faith includes following Christ into witness and service in the world. Doing Christ's mission in the world, these young Christians meet God in new ways, are drawn outside their egocentricity, and come to understand more fully the creative, restorative and transformative work of God, Jesus Christ, and the Holy Spirit. A young woman spoke for hundreds of young people we interviewed as she summed up the impact of their youth ministry: "We meet in our houses once a week. That is where I feel I learn the most about myself and my relationship with God. On the mission trips I feel it. . . . Every day I wake up and I say, 'God, how can I serve you today?' I'm really feeling it and living it. . .living the Christian life."

Applying the Insights from the Youth Ministry Qualities
Faith Assets to Your Congregation

The six Youth Ministry Faith Assets and in particular the common youth ministry practices discovered in the EYM congregations are basic, significant building blocks in the spiritual life of a young person. Pastors, church staff, youth ministers, and youth ministry teams can use the research to reflect on how many of the common practices found in the EYM congregations are present in their ministries. How well are these being done in our congregation? Are they faithful? Are they effective? What can we do to provide a local expression of this practice that will better engage young people in this community?

They EYM Study provides a number of directions for developing and enhancing the effectiveness of a congregation's youth ministry.

1. Bring fresh meaning and impact to youth ministry by developing a contextually unique expression of a long-standing, common practice.
2. Utilize a variety of youth ministry practices because no one strategy will fit everyone. To reach and minister to a larger audience of youth means the type of events, functions, and opportunities must be varied.
3. Engage youth in leadership. Youth leadership has multiple impacts and value. The best practices involve youth in planning and leading. Adult leaders become mentors and guides providing leadership and wisdom with youth who are growing as leaders.
4. Saturate and frame all youth ministry practices with authentic, affirming relationships. Relational approaches to youth ministry impart a sense of God's presence, consistency and action. Youth ministers build relationships with the broader audience of church members so as to interpret with them the world of teenagers.
5. Plan all individual practices within the context of a long-term purposeful strategy of youth ministry.
6. Consider the unique features of the context or locale of your congregation, and use those insights to contextualize common practices, making them distinctive to your setting.
7. Don't try to plan, schedule, or organize all youth ministry practices. Expressions of care by adults and ministerial staff cannot be programmed, yet play a major role in well-executed youth ministry.
8. Don't evaluate the effectiveness of your youth ministry according to the number of events or activities. Full youth calendars do not equal effective youth ministry. Youth ministry practices are best chosen with purpose framed by vision.
9. Balance congregational integration of young people with age-level ministry practices and support of their families. Youth have specific developmental, social, and spiritual needs. These needs are best addressed by "age-level oriented" practices. Youth are greatly influenced by positive intergenerational experiences among the larger body of believers and within their families.

Resources for Further Study

Arzolo Jr., Fernando. *Toward Prophetic Youth Ministry: Theory and Praxis in Urban Context.* Downers Grove: InterVarsity, 2008.

Burns, Jim. *Uncommon Youth Ministry.* Ventura: Gospel Light, 2001.

Clark, Chap, and Kara E. Powell. *Deep Justice in a Broken World: Helping Your Kids Serve Others and Right the Wrongs around Them.* Grand Rapids: Zondervan, 2007.

Dean, Kenda Creasy, with Dayle Gillespie Rounds, Roland Martinson, Any Scott Vaughn, and Don C. Richter. *OMG: A Youth Ministry Handbook*. Nashville: Abingdon, 2010.

Dean, Kenda Creasy, Chap Clark, and Dave Rahn. *Starting Right—Thinking Theologically about Youth Ministry*. Grand Rapids: Zondervan, 2001.

Dean, Kenda Creasy, and Ron Foster. *The Godbearing Life—The Art of Soul Tending for Youth Ministry*. Nashville: Upper Room, 1998.

DeVries, Mark. *Sustainable Youth Ministry*. Downers Grove: InterVarsity, 2008.

East, Thomas, editor. *Leadership for Catholic Youth Ministry—A Comprehensive Resource*. New London: Twenty-Third, 2009.

East, Thomas with Ann Marie Eckert, Dennis Kurtz, and Brian Singer-Towns. *Effective Practices for Dynamic Youth Ministry*. Winona: Saint Mary's, 2005.

Edie, Fred. *Book, Bath, Table and Time: Christian Worship as Source and Resource for Youth Ministry*. Cleveland: Pilgrim, 2007.

Fashbaugh II, Edward M. *Creating an Authentic Youth Ministry*. Nashville: Discipleship Resources, 2005.

Mahan, Brian, Michael Warren, and David White. *Awakening Youth Discipleship*. Eugene: Cascade, 2008.

Oestreicher, Mark and Scott Rubin. *Middle School Ministry: A Comprehensive Guide to Working with Early Adolescents*. Grand Rapids: Zondervan, 2009.

Powell, Kara and the Fuller Youth Institute. *Essential Leadership: Ministry Team Meetings that Work*. Grand Rapids: Zondervan, 2009. (Leader's Guide and Participant's Guide)

Richter, Don. *Mission Trips That Matter: Embodied Faith for the Sake of the World*. Nashville: Upper Room, 2008.

Root, Andrew. *Relationships Unfiltered*. Grand Rapids: Zondervan, 2009.

Root, Andrew. *Revisiting Relational Youth Ministry: From a Strategy of Influence to a Theology of Incarnate*. Downers Grove: InterVarsity, 2007.

White. David F. *Practicing Discernment with Youth*. Cleveland: Pilgrim, 2005

Yaconelli, Mark. *Growing Souls: Experiments in Contemplative Youth Ministry*. Grand Rapids: Zondervan, 2007.

Yaconelli, Mark. *Contemplative Youth Ministry: Practicing the Presence of Jesus*. Grand Rapids: Zondervan, 2006.

CASE STUDY 3:
YOUTH MINISTRY

Newport Mesa Christian Center
Assemblies of God
Costa Mesa, CA

Mission of Newport Mesa Christian Assembly

Our Mission

We seek to reach the people within our community through irresistible lifestyles, influential works of service, and through God's unconditional love.

Wherever you are in your spiritual journey—just starting out or well on your way—we want to be a safe place where anyone can come to discover who Jesus is, ask questions, learn more, connect with others and be a vital, dynamic part of God's loving family.

Our Values

- Teach God's Word
- Be God's loving family
- Be innovation in our ministry and relevant to our community
- Be contagious followers of Jesus Christ
- Every believer is a minister with a ministry

Our 5 Purposes

- Belong – We exist to incorporate people into God's family.
- Grow – We exist to equip people to reflect the character of Christ
- Serve – We exist to equip people to use their spiritual gifts to serve others.
- Reach – We exist to reach out in love to our world.
- Celebrate – We exist to celebrate God's greatness.

Youth Ministry at Newport Mesa Christian Assembly

Mission

"The desire of Solid Rock leadership is to take students spiritually where they have never been and to teach them to "Go into all the world and preach the good news," Mark 16:15. We want them to experience God in a real way. We have seen so many teens' lives changed as they begin to experience God personally."

"Solid Rock is a place where youth can begin to learn what the Lord has from them and how they can better serve him. It is a place where teens come together without shame and feel confident in their choice to serve God."

Junior High Ministries

To create a safe and relevant place for students to take ownership of their choices and their walk; to explore and develop a relationship with God and help them understand what it means to follow Christ.

By creating a relational ministry that is led by example and focused on listening to each student. We will arrive at our vision by focusing on reaching each student, helping them fell that they belong within our ministry, assisting them in their spiritual growth, serving them and serving with them, as well as joining them in the celebration of Jesus Christ.

- *SML* (Sunday Morning Live): SML is a the weekly Sunday morning service. At 9 am all students from fifth through eighth grade take part in a morning of fellowship, worship, and diving into God's word. Our services are geared toward helping each student find their own path towards God. Whether it is through worshipping, playing games, talking to others or taking part in a message, we strive to create moments for each student to grow in their relationship with Jesus.
- *W7* (Wednesdays @ 7): W7 is the midweek service specifically for seventh and eighth grade students. During this time students are divided into small groups to allow for deeper and more focused study into the Word of God, and to talk about life and how God can be a part of it.
- *Worship Band*
- *Special Events*: summer camp programs, Transition Sunday (into the fifth grade), overnight experiences

Senior High Ministries

Sunday Nights

- *Rock Groups* (6-7:30 pm): Beginning in October and running through May, Rock Groups help our students grow closer to God in a small group setting.
- 7:30-9:30 pm Solid Rock Fellowship

Sundays

- 9-10:30 am High School Church
- 11 am Worship Service
- From 9-9:30 am we enjoy a time of fellowship. At 9:30 we begin our service with worship followed by relevant Bible teaching concluding at 10:30 am. At 11 am, students and leaders proceed to the sanctuary for the Worship Service.

Tuesdays

Each week we get together to fellowship with great friends, worship to great music, and get challenged by great speakers or discussions in a small group setting. It is a time for teens to be with their peers in a Christ-centered environment to praise and worship God and learn more about His presence in their lives, schools, and communities.

- *Special Events*: youth convention, winter camp program, mission trips, summer splash, High School Rock Theater

Listening to the Youth, Parents, and Leadership at Newport Mesa Christian Assembly: Reflections from the Onsite Interviews

What's different about youth ministry at Newport Mesa Christian Assembly? What keeps it real in mission, vision and purpose? According to one student, the word is "purpose." "Other youth groups exist just for kids to have a place to go and not get into trouble," the student said. "Our youth minister always makes it apparent to us that our purpose is to get closer to God. We're not here to hang out. If people here to hang out, then this isn't the place to be."

Newport Mesa Christian Assembly's youth ministry program's vision, mission and purpose flows in, with, through, and under the church's overall mission, vision and purpose. They are about creating environments to develop more followers of Jesus and closer followers of Jesus. The youth pastor shared, "We want to raise students to be active participants in the body of Christ."

"We're just all people in need of God really needing to love each other in this love-starved world," said one of the pastors. "We're doing it real and authentic just telling me the story. We want people to be authentic. Pretense sucks. Most people don't live real pretentiously in their living rooms. That's what we want to offer. This is our family. We talk about things honestly. We address this biblical perspective."

Leadership

Longevity is an important element in building a successful youth ministry program because relationships and leadership development take time. The youth pastor observed: "One thing longevity contributes is stability. Teens really need stability in their life and it's a plus for parents. Parents are entrusting their prized possession in to your care and I take that extremely seriously. and that's important to me and that's important to parents. After twenty years (in youth ministry) I feel like I'm just getting started. I've learned adolescent behavior, how to see patterns in youth ministry, and how to not take certain things personally in youth ministry. Only age and experience can give you that."

Young people and their parents respect and admire the youth ministers—not only for their leadership, but for empowering others to develop their gifts. Creating strong leaders multiplies the efforts and vision of the youth program. "We see other people (leaders) and how close they are to God and we realize we can do it too," a young person said.

The volunteer youth ministry leaders are about half college students and half adults in the church. Solid Rock, the name of both the Junior and Senior High youth programs, also has a student council leadership team for the high school youth. This is a leadership team made up of high school students who are nominated by other students and/or adults.

Solid Rock

Here's how NMCC structures its youth ministry, which is called "Solid Rock":

- Tuesday evening youth service
- Sunday morning Youth Church and Youth Discipleship groups (Rock Groups), most of which meet on Sunday mornings following Youth Church or on Sunday evening.
- Missions trips, camps, fun outings
- Worship/prayer

The Tuesday night education and worship gatherings follow a theme and often include guest speakers. The high school students have a Bible study and worship service, which also includes time with small groups. "And most of our topics are how to live life," said a young person. "It just makes us want to live more. I've never had a service I can't apply."

Occasionally a Tuesday night youth service will be devoted to an entire night of worship. The students will worship for a while, there's time for communion and also physically nailing notes, with their sins written on them, to a cross. "I love our worship nights. How often can you just spend an hour-and-a-half worshiping God." one student said.

About ten small groups, called Rock Groups, led by youth leaders, meet mostly on Sunday mornings or evenings. Each has about one adult for every four to five students, who stay. Many students may have the same Rock group leader throughout high school. "I'm a real believer in small group ministry. Relational ministry is where it's at," said the youth pastor.

The youth ministry strives for quality, not just in the production of worship or other program events, but in the authenticity of relationships with people and with God. The practices at Newport Mesa Christian Center aim to create authentic, deep relationships. "You'll find we don't do a lot of programs," the youth minister reports. "We found out that less is more for us. In our demographics, students are constantly bombarded by stuff, way more than most kids. All of our kids have a Disneyland pass. Also, our church isn't at the hub of the community. In Orange County, everyone doesn't flock out when your church does something. There are also sixteen to eighteen high schools represented by our youth group. You can only really target about six of them, so we focus on building a caring place."

Among the core practices are advance planning, leadership development and empowerment, powerful worship and good communication.

Relationships

Relationships are at the heart of youth ministry at NMCC, relationships that are strong, deep, authentic and positive in a world filled with hype, hypocrisy and highs. Between the mentoring relationships, the friendly and casual approach of the congregation to giving youth their own space at NMCC, the church has created an alternative culture in which authentic bonds can form. "For me, (NMCC) is kind of a home away from home," said a student. "My parents are not Christian. This is a place for me to seek God. I'm really close to a lot of people here." "This church is like another family," said another young person. "It's family, not just friends. It's that strong."

One parent says that she's seen lives changed through the relationships developed at NMCC. "I remember one boy who was following one girl around school and she invited him to come here," the parent said. "He wasn't a believer and he was really quiet, but now he has given his heart to the Lord. He's absolutely at peace and he's confident and he's got good friends even though he has a horrible family life. He found this place to be home for him. This place is a place to be safe and secure. This place is a place to be loved."

As they develop relationships with people, students also develop a stronger, deeper, more mature relationship with God. "We're encouraged to be Christ-like, to be truly Christian, to live that life and not just slap a title on ourselves," said one young person.

Making It All Work

Parents at Newport Mesa say one of the key elements is in the passion of the leaders, especially the youth pastor, their longevity and experience, and in their intentional approach to building relationships.

"The genius behind it is that they're intentional about going deep and they've replicated with others who can share the burden with them," said a parent. "They've purposely done that instead of being biggest, flashiest showiest. The purpose here is going deep." This shows itself in the quality and attraction of worship, in the desire for retreats and small groups, and in the opportunities to lead and serve, others say.

Another is the forward thinking, evaluation and planning the youth pastor practices and teaches to the leadership teams. Most events, services, and speakers are planned a year in advance.

The web of relationships, which are woven within a safe, creative environment, are tended so that they remain healthy and positive. Young people in particular say a key element of the program lies in its family atmosphere. This web of relationships and church family culture may be the encouragement, reinforcement and recognition that happen even before students are old enough for the junior and senior high programs. Youth ministry leaders know the names of many younger children. They take the time to tell each child how much they are looking forward to the time when that child is old enough for the youth ministry program.

Youth leaders also reach out to new and visiting students. "If we don't touch people during their first visit, we may never see them again," said the youth pastor. "We must touch every student that comes in."

At a time when pre-teens and teen-agers are among the most targeted consumer groups in the nation; in a place where hype and fantasy and affluence create unusual pressures, Newport Mesa Christian Center has created an alternative culture, grounded and gifted with the grace of God, that invites and catches young people in a web of real relationships relevant to real faith and real lives.

CASE STUDY 4:
YOUTH MINISTRY

Tri-Parish Youth Ministry:
The Catholic Parishes of Sacred Heart,
Saint Benedict, and Saint Ann
Terre Haute, IN

Youth Ministry at Sacred Heart, Saint Benedict, and Saint Ann

Mission of the Tri-Parish Youth Ministry

We, the Youth Ministry Commission of Saint Ann, Saint Benedict, and Sacred Heart of Jesus, are called to serve as advocates for our youth and their families in our parish communities.

We will ensure total Youth Ministry through:

- Maintaining a professional Youth Ministry Coordinator position
- Guiding, directing and supporting our Youth Ministry Coordinator
- Planning that recognizes the needs of our youth and families, Youth Ministry Coordinator, and parishes
- Praying continually for the well-being of the young people in our parishes and for the Pastoral Ministry to them

We commit ourselves to the responsible use of our spiritual and material resources. This tri-parish youth ministry in Terre Haute, IN is over twenty years old. A cooperative venture between three parishes, Saint Benedict, Saint Ann and Sacred Heart, this youth ministry has attracted almost all of the high school students in the three parishes—involving young people from three high schools and even attracting families from as far as twenty-five miles away.

Senior High Youth Ministry

- Grade 9 and 10 Religious Education (twice monthly): Topics include prayer, sacraments, morality, and Scripture.

- Grade 11 and 12 Religious Education (twice monthly): Topics include prayer, Scripture, Trinity, Eucharist, and Confirmation preparation
- Journey with the Holy Spirit Confirmation Retreat
- Retreat programs sponsored by the Archdiocese of Indianapolis CYO Retreat Center
- Drama: Passion Mime on Palm Sunday and Good Friday
- Social activities
- Summer mission trip and service projects throughout the year

Listening to the Youth, Parents, and Leadership at Sacred Heart, Saint Benedict, and Saint Ann: Reflections from the Onsite Interviews

Faith and social justice are two strong elements in the mission and vision statements of these congregations. The youth ministry program holds a vision that focuses on community, Catholic identity, faith and service.

The pastoral leaders, youth coordinator, parents, adult leaders and young people in this co-operative youth program hope that the Saint Benedict/Saint Ann/Sacred Heart youth ministry will help young people:

- belong to an accepting, supportive community
- have a significant relationship with God
- develop their Catholic identity
- have a variety of spiritual experiences
- make prayer a daily part of their lives
- express their faith in service and witness to others
- have adult role models on their faith journeys

"I just want our young people to be, to develop, to be plugged in to the Catholic Church, to find support, love, and to experience community here. "I want them to have that relationship with God," said the long-time youth ministry coordinator, "(so that when they graduate,) their faith has matured and they have matured, and there is an excitement in them that they wanted to share it with others."

Through this vision in action, "(we hope that they will) have developed a real and tangible set of values, that they will be able to express their faith in loving action," said of the parish life coordinator at one of the parishes. "We hope that they would be men and women who will express their faith in worship and who have learned that they need spiritual nourishment," she said. "We hope that they will find new ways to service the poor and that they will not forget they have a loving community here so they feel their connected to their roots."

This vision animates everything that happens in youth ministry here. The vision has become practice for the parish, especially those who work with young people, as they strive to "walk the talk."

Leadership

The three parishes run on lean budgets, which mean that most of its leaders—clergy and lay—perform multiple roles.

The leadership style of the youth ministry coordinator is that of naming gifts and allowing them to emerge and soar. There are a group of twenty-five or more adult leaders in youth ministry. They admire and respect the youth ministry coordinator's enthusiasm, spiritual devotion and genuine love for young people and the privilege of passing on the faith. "Her "can do" attitude is contagious," said one adult volunteer leader. "She has a magic way of lessening the burden and to get the people feeling comfortable—she never intimidates people," added another leader.

Student leaders are also an important part of the youth ministry program. The youth ministry coordinator invites them to be up from the start. She slowly encourages them so by the time they are seniors, being in front of groups is comfortable for them. They are more apt to share that with other people and stand up and say what they believe," said a parent. "When I go to church, it feels good inside the church and I think kids feel that. In Mass you will realize how comfortable the kids are. They are as if they were in their front room at home."

The youth ministry coordinator embeds leadership training into the way volunteers serve, and encourages mentoring between adults and adults and adults and students. "As a leader, I am only who I am because of who our youth minister is," said another parent.

"A youth minister needs to be open," one of the parish pastors said. "I think there needs to be a willingness to be open to service, a willingness to lay yourself down, a humility, a healthy sense of self that is not egotistic. I have seen youth programs built on ego. Also, I think a youth minister needs to be able to enable and empower youth leaders. So in many ways, an effective youth minister is minister to the ministers." "The youth minister is the ground of it," said the parish life coordinator. "That person should be a person with a deep spirituality, because they have the privilege of passing on the faith."

Practices

The youth minister's catch phrase is "walk the talk." Living a right life, or orthopraxis, is a key element of Catholic faith and life. Therefore, daily prayer, worship, the Sacraments, community, service to others and other elements of living a faithful life are built into the practices of this youth ministry program.

"We believe that faith is caught, not taught," said a pastor. "So we work to elicit spiritual opportunities. We work on tools of discernment, teaching our faith and Scripture and building faith in community. If they experience their faith, learning the facts and figure will come alongside. All of those questions (about God, about faith) will come forward and if they have relationships with trusted youth ministers and leaders."

One of the two "program pillars" of this youth ministry is retreats. There are retreats for each of the four years of high school. All of the young people participate in retreat programs. These intensive weekend spiritual experiences are an opportunity for young people to experience, embrace, and express their faith.

"Our biggest strength is the retreat," said one adult leader. "They begin with a young faith as ninth graders and leave with a much more mature faith as twelfth graders. The spirituality they learn and experience helps to develop them."

"Through this program, we've come to realize we are all part of a community," said one student. "This program offers a way for kids to grow in their faith. Some parishes just have classes, but our youth group does a good job of offering service and retreats. Some kids might not like to come to the classes, but they can do other things."

The second pillar of this youth ministry is service programming. All of the young people participate in multiple service projects. There is a wide variety of service programming from indirect service (raising funds for groups, food collections) to direct service (helping the poor, working at a soup kitchen). There is also a weeklong summer service project at Nazareth Farm in a nearby state.

Service projects "have a positive influence on youth's lives," said a teen-ager. "They're the kind of venue where kids can learn valuable life lessons. You feel good about yourself and help people."

"They give you a different taste of trouble that other people go through in life," said another student. "When we deliver food to people, you realize how lucky you really are and how blessed you really are."

It is important to note that between the two "program pillars" are the "ordinary" youth programming during the month—confirmation classes, social events, etc. These weekly programs provide the continuity in the midst of the more intensive experiences of retreats, trips, and service programming. There is a conscious effort in all programming to be interactive, participatory, and fun while addressing serious things.

Another key practice is prayer. "We have them experience different prayer forms, and we not only talk about prayer, we pray for them," said the youth ministry coordinator. "Prayer is essential for what we do. A lot of our meetings get started with prayer requests. The youth commission prays daily for our youth and their parents." Students and adults involved in the youth ministry program can be on an electronic prayer chain. "We e-mail prayer requests to all the leaders and all the kids, so that keeps it going through the week," she said. It's a practice that makes a difference, said a parent. "At the candlelight service, the kids hear prayers about troubles that they are having, or their family is having, they may never mention it, but they know in the heart and they are all touched by it," she said.

Youth ministry isn't just a program or a series of events, it is about trustworthy, safe relationships. "It is all relational. I don't think kids have a hard time believing, but belonging," the youth ministry coordinator said. "They are amazed if you remember their name."

Within this environment of trust, of longevity, of practicing the Catholic life, there is something holy that happens to relationships, said an adult leader. "There is spiritual energy," said a parent.

"Being a kid is so tough, they have to work so hard at being accepted, when you are at a retreat you are accepted from the start, you are accepted just as you are," said a parent.

"I am from the south and I didn't have anyone from my school going there, but they were friendly and caring and it was easier as time went on," said one student.

"When you leave youth group, you leave feeling better about being there," said a high school student. "I don't think you can go without feeling better."

"This place has helped me to talk to God more. I am not afraid to show my faults," said another young person.

Walking the talk with God and attending to being examples of faith and service in one's life are experiences that the graduating seniors in this group say will take with them into the rest of their lives. "I have come to know who I am, where I am, where I stand in my faith, the world around me, and what I have to be thankful for," said a high school student.

"That is where God happens," reflects the youth minister. "It could be on a retreat or on Sunday night. We give them space to explore issues, we give them tools to live out and talk about that faith."

CASE STUDY 5:
SERVICE AND MISSION

Myers Park United Methodist Church
Charlotte, NC

Service and outreach is a distinctive strength of the EYM congregations and their youth ministries. Pastors, youth ministers, parents, adult youth workers, and youth are seriously emphasizing, equipping for, and engaging in service and outreach. They their congregations as valuing "Mission Outreach," "Social Responsibility," and "Service Activities." They see their congregations preparing young people and adults for mission. Second, young people are becoming and doing what the congregations are equipping them to do. They are involved in service and active in public witness and ministry.

Myers Park United Methodist Church in Charlotte, North Carolina, has developed a variety of service and mission projects—locally and globally—to engage young people. Locally, they are involved in service projects which include tutoring children in grades 1–5 and participation in Charlotte urban ministry projects such as home repair for elderly residents and a weeklong camp for children.

Each summer there are a variety of mission trips sponsored by the youth ministry of Myers Park United Methodist Church. Each mission trip has a theme, a biblical basis, and months of pre-planning. Students and adults have to apply and interview for a place on the mission team. On each trip, there are daily check-ins and nightly devotions which enhance and allow the participants to go deeper with their servant experience. In the summer of 2010, they offered the following mission trips:

- *Charlotte Urban Plunge*: two full days of local missions opportunities designed specifically for those completing fifth grade (rising sixth graders). It is an opportunity for young people to learn about their spiritual gifts, spend time helping out at several local missions (emerging housing, urban ministry center), learn about poverty firsthand and talk about what God tells us to do about poverty.

- *Pilgrimage of Hope*: a two-week mission trip to Rio de Janeiro, Brazil designed to be a capstone experience for youth, preparing to leave their youth ministry years and go in to the world. Youth have the opportunity to not only serve alongside others but to truly form relationships with people in other parts of the world who have hope in Christ in the direst of situations. Youth lend a hand at the Instituto Central de Povo (People's

Central Institute), a United Methodist ministry located at the base of Rio's oldest favela (hillside slum). In addition to the service activities, the focus is looking into the ways God is working through Methodists in Rio to meet the needs of the favela residents and asking how God is calling the youth to respond.

- *Hinton Rural Life Center*: a one-week trip to Hayesville, North Carolina, for youth completing sixth grade. Many families who reside in Hayesville live below the national poverty level and struggle to maintain their homes. Youth paint and clean to help bring the beauty of the mountains back to their homes.

- *Group Workcamp*: a one-week trip to Charleston, South Carolina, for youth being confirmed. Over 30% of the residents in North Charleston live at or below the poverty level. Youth help people with projects in their homes, assist the elderly, tutor struggling kinds, conduct a backyard Bible club, serve at a local food bank, staff an activities camp for disabled children, and other community projects.

- *Service Over Self*: a one-week trip to Memphis, Tennessee, for youth completing eighth grade. Service Over Self is an organization that provides much needed home repairs to low-income families in the urban areas of Memphis. Youth paint, clean, and provide hope by revitalizing economically disadvantaged neighborhoods.

- *Ministerio de Fe*: a one-week trip to Reynosa, Mexico for youth completing ninth, tenth, eleventh, and twelfth grades. Just over the border from McAllen, Texas, are third world conditions unlike anywhere else in North America. Youth build four cinderblock homes and put a roof on two others for the poorest of the poor in the colonias surrounding Reynosa. There are not fancy concrete mixers to do the mixing; youth are the concrete mixers.

Ideas for Developing Service and Mission

Develop Service and Mission Trips in Youth Ministry

Service programming combines hands-on action with preparation for service and reflection upon the service experience. Each mission trip/service project needs to incorporate a learning component that focuses on 1) understanding and analyzing the social issue being addressed, 2) exploring the teachings of Scripture and the Christian tradition on that issue, 3) developing the skills for mission and service, and then, upon completion of the project, 4) reflecting upon the involvement.

Service and mission opportunities include both works of service and works of justice.

- *Works of service*, locally and globally, respond to people and communities in need by engaging young people in feeding people, housing people, collecting food and clothing, repairing homes, cleaning neighborhoods, visiting prisoners, tutoring children, and so on.

- *Works of justice*, locally and globally, address the root causes of social issue engaging youth in analyzing justice issues and addressing the underlying causes through social change. Working for justice often means partnering with groups and organization that address justice issues, such as Bread for the World (hunger), the Children's Defense

Fund (children's issues), the ONE Campaign (poverty), and the social justice/relief agencies of each Christian denomination.

Service and mission projects are best organized "developmentally" with projects geared to different levels of involvement and challenge:

- Local mission projects lasting anywhere from a few hours to one day in length
- Short-term mission trips lasting anywhere from two to five days and requiring an overnight stay on location
- Weeklong mission trips within the United States as well as to foreign countries, designed for those who are ready to take the next big step in service
- Global expedition trips of ten to fourteen days that provide the opportunity to be immersed for a longer period in the targeted community and culture
- Personalized small group mission trips, organized around the interests and time of the group

Case Study 5, Myers Park United Methodist Church is a good example of this "developmental approach" to service programming, offering projects for young people completing fifth grade through those graduating twelfth grade.

Incorporate Justice Themes in Youth Ministry

There are a variety of ways to incorporate justice themes throughout the year in youth ministry programming and provide continuous formation of young people for service and mission. Here are several examples:

- Include education and/or discussion of justice topics that are "in the news" as a regular feature of youth gatherings.
- Invite speakers, in the congregation and wider community, who are involved in the works of service and justice, locally or globally, to share their faith and work with young people.
- Model just living as a congregation and youth community by developing and practicing respect for creation (recycling, reusing, and avoiding wasteful conveniences), polices and procedures for just purchasing (e.g., no t-shirts or clothes from sweatshops, buying locally-grown food for meals), etc.
- Practice peace-making by using non-violent communication skills for resolving conflicts.
- Teach peace-making skills and take time to pray for peace locally and around the world.
- Provide retreats on justice issues and the response of the Bible and Christian tradition and on developing a spirituality for justice and service.
- Incorporate global concerns and justice issues in the prayer life of youth gatherings and programs.

Resources

Clark, Chap, and Kara E. Powell. *Deep Justice in a Broken World: Helping Your Kids Serve Others and Right the Wrongs around Them.* Grand Rapids: Zondervan, 2007.

Lansing, Sean. "Justice and Service with Youth." *Leadership for Catholic Youth Ministry—A Comprehensive Resource.* Thomas East, editor. New London: Twenty-Third, 2009.

Richter, Don. *Mission Trips That Matter: Embodied Faith for the Sake of the World.* Nashville: Upper Room, 2008.

CASE STUDY 6:
FAITH FORMATION AND CONFIRMATION

Hope Lutheran Church
Fargo, ND

The core of Hope Lutheran Church's youth ministry is confirmation. *PowerLife Confirmation* is a relational style confirmation program for sixth, seventh, eighth, and ninth graders on Wednesday nights from 7:00-8:00 pm. Weekly sessions alternate between small group and large group experiences. The Wednesday evening program alternates between large group experiences (music, faith presentation, skits, prayer, etc.) and small group experiences (faith and life discussion, mission activities, peer and adult relationship building and mutual care giving). Retreats, summer camp, travel trips and lively Sunday morning worship augment these Wednesday evenings. This creates a sense of the living presence of God among the kids and a community of high quality peer and adult relationships that significantly influence the kids and the adults who work with them.

- Grades 7 and 8 focus on two years of Bible study.

- Grade 9 uses *Luther's Small Catechism* and the Bible to focus on life application of faith as students prepare for their Affirmation of Baptism and to live their lives in faithful witness to Jesus Christ.

- Wednesday Night Learning Events

    - 7:00-8:00 pm: large group one week, small group the next week

    - Large group time uses video, skits, characters, and quality Christian thought with theological integrity to present the lesson for the night; taught be staff

    - Small groups: 5-6 students, grade and gender specific, co-guided (mentored) by a team of parents of students in the group

    - Small group time is for prayer, Bible study, discussion, and planning

- Ninth Grade Confirmation Mission Retreat weekend: a concluding confirmation experience providing an urban immersion in Minneapolis—a hands-on experience of serving others by serving meals at area homeless shelters, working at battered women's centers, restocking groceries at food shelves, and rehabbing low-income housing.

- Fellowship Events and Service Activities/Mission Trips
  - Done independently by each small group
  - At church or out in the community
  - Agreed upon by the group
  - Contribute to building unity, friendship, and trust
  - Each grade does three Fellowship/Service Events

Worship notes, home devotions, fellowship/service events are a part of the PowerLife Confirmation experience.

TABLE 9

Twelve Dimensions of Youth Ministry Qualities

Overview

	Youth Ministry Qualities	Youth	Parents	Adult Leaders	Pastor and Youth Minister*
1.	Spiritual Support Group	8.39	-	-	-
2.	Emphasis on Prayer, Faith Study, Leadership, Safe and Caring Place	7.55	-	-	-
3.	Youth Gatherings Have a Warm, Welcoming Climate	7.44	-	-	-
4.	Youth Ministry's Structural Core (and Youth Ministry Characteristics)	7.36	-	7.25	-
5.	Impact on Personal Faith	7.28	-	-	-
6.	Emphasis on Participation in Congregation	7.16	-	-	-
7.	Peer Ministry	7.14	6.44	6.55	5.80
8.	Achievement of Youth Ministry's Desired Outcomes (and Youth Ministry Effectiveness)	6.75	6.52	6.60	6.08
9.	Teaching Moral Values	-	6.60	-	-
10.	Adult-Youth Mentoring	-	6.56	6.31	-
11.	Adult-Youth Involvement Together	-	5.28	5.02	-
12.	Help with Life Issues	5.82	-	-	-

*Mean scores: highest rating is "9," indicating a response of "Always" or "Almost Always True."

Twelve Dimensions with Items

Youth Ministry Qualities	Youth	Parents	Adult Leaders	Pastor and Youth Minister
1. Spiritual Support Group	**8.39**	-	-	
• I belong to at least one church group in which we talk about spiritual issues.	8.50	-	-	-
• I belong to at least one church group in which others will pray with me and for me as needed.	8.64	-	-	-
• I belong to at least one church group in which it is possible to talk about personal problems.	8.02	-	-	-
2. Emphasis on Prayer, Faith Study, Leadership, Safe and Caring Place	**7.55**	-	-	-
• Our congregation's youth program emphasizes faith relationship with Jesus Christ.	8.09	-	-	-
• Our congregation's youth program emphasizes prayer.	7.92	-	-	-
• Our congregation's youth program emphasizes providing a safe and caring place.	7.91	-	-	-
• Our congregation's youth program emphasizes Bible study.	6.78	-	-	-
• Our congregation's youth program emphasizes leadership training and experience.	7.06	-	-	-
3. Youth Gatherings Have a Warm, Welcoming Climate	**7.44**	-	-	-
• Our youth gatherings feel warm.	7.67	-	-	-
• Our youth gatherings make strangers feel welcome.	7.33	-	-	-

• Our youth gatherings accepts people who are different.	7.62	-	-	-
• Our youth gatherings try out new ideas.	7.47	-	-	-
• Our youth gatherings are friendly.	7.92	-	-	-
• Our youth gatherings encourage me to ask questions.	7.00	-	-	-
• Our youth gatherings challenge my thinking.	6.97	-	-	-
• I am satisfied with the way things are going in my congregation's youth ministry.	7.27	-	-	-
• Our congregation's youth ministry is fun.	7.38	-	-	-
• Our congregations classes and events for teenagers feel warm and inviting.	7.82	-	-	-

4. Youth Ministry's Structural Core / Youth Ministry Characteristics

4. Youth Ministry's Structural Core / Youth Ministry Characteristics	**7.36**	-	**7.25**	-
• Our congregation's youth ministry is well run.	7.31	-		-
• Our congregation's youth ministry is fun.		-	7.51	-
• Our congregation's youth ministry is creative.	-	-	7.12	-
• Our congregation's youth ministry is meaningful.	-	-	7.29	-
• Our congregation's youth ministry has qualified adult youth workers.	7.69	-	7.10	-
• Our congregation's youth ministry is well-organized.	6.61	-	6.69	-
• Our congregation's youth ministry is Christ-centered.	7.68	-	7.77	-
• My involvement in youth programs has helped me to have a safe and caring place to go.	7.50	-	-	-

5. Impact on Personal Faith	**7.28**	-	-	-
• My involvement in youth programs has helped me to deepen my relationship with Jesus.	7.56	-	-	-
• My involvement in youth programs has helped me to apply my faith to daily life.	7.20	-	-	-
• My involvement in youth programs has helped me to understanding my Christian faith better.	7.52	-	-	-
• My involvement in youth programs has helped me to share my faith.	6.83	-	-	-
6. Emphasis on Participation in Congregation/ Community	**7.16**	-	-	-
• My youth program emphasizes participation in congregational life.	7.36	-	-	-
• My youth program emphasizes community service.	6.77	-	-	-
• My youth program emphasizes a weekly worship service or Mass geared to youth.	7.34	-	-	-
7. Peer Ministry	**7.14**	**6.44**	**6.55**	**5.80**
• Our peer ministry youth have intentionally established friendships with other youth who need help.	7.28	6.64	6.63	5.89
• Our peer ministers are likely to stick-up for someone who is laughed at or mocked.	7.51	7.17	7.03	6.38
• Adult mentors guide peer ministers' efforts to do ministry work.	7.40	6.80	6.63	-
• Our youth have had peer ministry training in how to reach others needing help or friendship.	7.50	6.78	6.60	5.66
• Troubled youth at school have sought help from our peer ministers.	6.44	5.69	5.83	5.05

8. Achievement of Youth Ministry's Desired Outcomes & Youth Ministry Effectiveness	6.75	6.52	6.60	6.08
Effectiveness of Involving and Training	-	-	5.85	-

Our congregation's youth ministry. . .

• helps youth recognize that God is at work changing their lives.	-	6.38	6.71	6.20
• guides youth in developing a personal relationship with Jesus Christ.	7.04	-	-	5.96
• helps youth make a commitment to Jesus Christ.	-	6.54	6.74	6.28
• creates an atmosphere (physical and emotional) where youth are accepted and have a sense of belonging.	7.11	6.99	7.02	7.06
• creates an environment which nurtures meaningful relationships.	7.02	-	-	6.95
• invites and welcomes youth in the faith community.	7.12	-	6.17	5.78
• helps youth feel love and respected by their congregation.	-	6.54	6.70	-
• helps youth understand justice issues and Christian responses.	6.28	5.80	5.66	5.07
• helps youth learn how to pray.	6.20	-	6.23	5.85
• provides a variety of prayer experiences for youth.	-	-	-	5.58
• engages youth to spread the Gospel to other young people.	6.39	-	-	-
• provides help for teaching Christian concepts of right and wrong.	6.88	-	-	-
• helps youth connect their involvement in service projects with their Christian faith.	6.75	6.47	6.44	6.13
• involves youth in preparing prayer and worship services.	6.50	-	6.01	4.74
• helps youth develop friendship-making and friendship-maintaining skills.	-	6.26	6.09	6.25
• enables youth to be involved in ministry.	-	6.56	6.87	6.26

• gives ownership of the youth ministry to youth.	-	6.34	6.42	-
• equips adult youth workers who lead small groups.	-	5.96	5.89	-
• gains church support for youth activities	-	6.99	7.04	-
• has a clearly defined mission statement.	-	5.95	6.68	-
• utilize a variety of learning methods and activities to engage youth in learning.	-	-	6.70	6.66
• teaches one's faith tradition: history, beliefs, and practices.	-	-	6.06	5.34
• creates networks of care and support for youth and their families.	-	-	5.46	-
• engages youth to spread the Gospel to other young people.	-	-	5.35	-
• reaches out inactive and non-believing youth.	-	-	4.86	-
• helps parents become more involved in the lives of their youth.	-	-	5.46	-
• I am satisfied with the way things are going in my congregation's youth ministry.	-	7.68	7.52	-

9. Help with Life Issues   5.82   -   -   -

My involvement in youth programs has helped me to:

• address issues of conflict and violence.	6.24	-	-	-
• address issues of drugs and alcohol	6.16	-	-	-
• better understand parents/teachers/adults	5.68	-	-	-
• improve my family relationships	5.75	-	-	-
• respect other ethnic or racial groups	6.25	-	-	-
• help other youth deal with problems	6.90	-	-	-
• raise my awareness of church vocations	6.13	-	-	-
• understanding sexuality and its role in life	6.13	-	-	-
• raise my awareness about social justice	5.51	-	-	-

10. Teaching Moral Values   6.60   -   -

- Adults are made conscious of how important it is that they model life-affirming values.   -   6.81   -   -

- Adult use discussion to teach the reasonableness of a moral teaching.   -   6.37   -   -

- Youth are helped to know why they should say "no" to certain at-risk behaviors.   -   7.08   -   -

- A congenial relationship between youth and adults is encouraged as a factor in communicating moral values.   -   6.80   -   -

- The congregation has identified the moral values it wishes to encourage.   -   6.05   -   -

- Traditional values are consciously taught in our congregation (e.g., keep promises, show generosity, do good to others, care for family).   -   7.34   -   -

- Parents are shown how they can foster the development of moral values in their children.   -   5.70   -   -

11. Adult-Youth Mentoring   6.56   6.31   6.26

- Mentors in our church have helped youth grow in their faith.   -   6.83   6.68   6.48

- Youth in our church enjoy working with a mentor.   -   6.67   6.46   6.47

- Mentors in our church feel honored to work with youth.   -   7.16   6.91   7.03

- Our congregation trains adult mentors to work one-on-one with youth.   -   5.98   5.47   -

- I hear of adults in our congregation who have significantly changed the life and direction of a youth who is not their child.   -   5.34   5.51   -

- Youth in our church have an adult mentor.   -   -   6.17   5.94

12. Adult-Youth Involvement Together	-	5.28	5.02	-
• Our congregation provides opportunities for adults and youth to spend quality time with each other.	-	5.77	5.88	-
• Our congregation's youth ministry recruits adults for one-to-one mentoring with youth.	-	4.65	4.49	-
• Our congregation's youth ministry encourages families to teach service as a way of life through their involvement in helping activities.	-	5.83	5.09	-
• Our congregation involves youth in congregational decision-making.	-	4.89	4.73	-
• Our congregation's youth ministry develops a systematic plan for training adult youth workers.	-	5.14	4.87	-

APPLICATION
TOOL 7

Evaluating Faith Assets: Youth Ministry Qualities

Use this worksheet as a guide to reflect on the practice of the Youth Ministry assets in your congregation. First, rate your congregation on each of the items in the second column. Then, list in the third column things you already do to strengthen each quality. Finally, identify other things you could do to strengthen the Youth Ministry Qualities assets.

Assets	Rating Your Congregation *
19. Establishes a Caring Environment	_____ Our youth ministry offers youth the experience of spiritual support groups.
	_____ Our youth gatherings are warm and friendly.
20. Develops Quality Relationships	_____ Our youth gatherings are safe and make all people feel welcome, especially strangers.
	_____ Our youth ministry provides youth with adult mentors who help them grow in faith.

What We Do Now:

What We Could Do Better:

* ★ = *Needs Work*   ★★ = *Okay*   ★★★ = *Great*

21. Focuses on Jesus Christ

Our youth ministry helps youth become disciples by:

_____ Knowing Jesus Christ

_____ Knowing the Bible

_____ Knowing the Christian faith

_____ Making faith a way of life

_____ Mentoring them

_____ Equipping them for witness and service

What We Do Now:

What We Could Do Better:

22. Considers Life Issues

Our youth ministry helps youth address life issues such as:

_____ drugs and alcohol

_____ understanding parents/adults

_____ family relationships

_____ sexuality and its role in life

_____ social issue and social justice

_____ conflict and violence

_____ respect for people of other ethnic or racial groups

What We Do Now:

What We Could Do Better:

Assets	Rating Your Congregation

23. Uses Many Approaches

24. Is Well Organized and Planned

_____ Our youth ministry offers youth a variety of activities that address a diversity of youth needs.

- retreats
- service and mission trips
- Bible study and religious education
- prayer
- spiritual support groups
- youth-oriented worship
- family and intergenerational activities
- peer ministry and youth leadership
- special events

_____ Our youth ministry involves adult and youth leaders in planning, implementation, and evaluation.

What We Do Now:

What We Could Do Better:

APPLICATION
TOOL 8

Evaluating Your Programming Mix

One of the five most important factors cited by pastors and youth ministers for the effectiveness of their youth ministries was the *wide variety and nature of youth programs*. They described an impressive diversity of events and program features that characterize the youth ministries of their congregations. No one program made the difference, rather it was the diversity of programs and activities that offered young people ways to growing religiously and spiritually. The most common youth ministry practices in the EYM Study included:

1. Spiritual support groups
2. Bible study and religious education
3. Service and mission trips
4. Retreats
5. Prayer and spiritual formation
6. Peer ministry and youth leadership
7. Youth-oriented worship
8. Family and intergenerational activities
9. Special events

Use the following questions to evaluate the overall programming mix of your youth ministry.

Balance of Youth Ministry Practices

Use the nine most common youth ministry practices identified in the EYM Study to reflect on the balance of programming in your congregation's youth ministry.

- What are your strongest youth ministry practices (programs, activities)? Use the nine most common practices as a guide to identifying your strengths.

- Do you have a good balance and variety among the different types of youth ministry practices in your congregation?

- Is your programming mix too oriented toward one or two major programs, neglecting other youth ministry practices and programs?

- How can you begin to expand your congregation's youth ministry practices?

Diversity of Youth Ministry Settings

As the EYM Study found, effective ministry with youth happens in the life of the whole congregation, in the programs and activities of youth ministry, and at home. Use the following questions to reflect on the diversity of settings in your congregation's ministry with youth.

- Where is the primary focus and energy for your congregation's youth ministry—in the whole congregation, in the youth ministry programs, or in the family and household?

- Does your congregation's youth ministry have a good balance among the three settings? Do you overemphasize one setting (e.g., youth programming) to the neglect of the other settings? What are the consequences of an overemphasis on one setting or the neglect of the other settings?

- How can you transform some of your youth programming into family and whole church programs or activities (e.g., developing family or parent-teen service projects, or church-wide mission trips)? (See Chapter 3 for congregational ideas and Chapter 5 for family and household ideas.)

Types of Programming

There are three fundamental types of programs: 1) large group, gathered programs, 2) small group programs, and 3) individualized or one-on-one programs. Use the following questions to reflect on the different types of programming in your congregation's youth ministry.

- What is the current balance among the three types of programming? If you had to assign percentages to each type of programming, what would your profile look like?

- Does your congregation's youth ministry have a good balance among the three types of programming? Does your youth ministry overuse one type of program and underutilize the other two (e.g., too many large group gathered programs and an underutilization of small group or individualized and one-on-one programs)?

- Can you offer three versions of the same activity—as a large group program, small group program, and individualized or mentored program? Could you reach more young people by offering the same activity in three formats?

- How can you use the new digital technologies (the Internet, social networking, online learning activities and video podcasts, etc.) in conjunction with each of the three types of programming?

Variety of Program Formats

There is so much competition for time that a youth ministry must be very creative in offering program formats that work for young people and their families today.

- How much variety in program formats does your congregation's youth ministry incorporate: weekly, bi-weekly, monthly, extended time, full day, overnight, weekend, weeklong, after-school, etc.?

- What are the most popular formats? Which formats are underutilized?

How can you use the variety of program formats to make it easier for youth to participate and/or to attract more youth participation? Can you offer the same program in multiple formats to increase participation?

CHAPTER FIVE

family and household faith

T he Continuing Influence of Parents and the Family on the Faith of Youth

One of the most significant, and to many startling, findings in the National Study on Youth and Religion (NSYR) is the impact of parental faith and religiosity on the beliefs and practices of teenagers. NSYR found: "of parents who report that their faith is *extremely* important in their daily lives, 67% of their teens report that faith is extremely or very important in their daily lives; only 8% of those parents' teens report that faith is not very or not important in their lives."[1] The opposite is also true: parents for whom faith is somewhat or not at all important have teens who believe the same thing. Smith concludes, "In sum, therefore, we think that the best general rule of thumb is this, 'We'll get what we are.' By normal processes of socialization, and unless other significant forces intervene, more than what parents might *say* they *want* as religious outcomes of their children, most parents most likely will end up getting religiously of their children what they themselves *are*."[2]

The importance of parental faith and practice on the lives of children and teens is clear.

> *Contrary to popular misguided cultural stereotypes and frequent parental misconceptions, we believe that the evidence clearly shows that the single most important social influence on the religious and spiritual lives of adolescents is their parents. Grandparents and other relatives, mentors, and youth workers can be very influential as well, but normally, parents are most important in forming their children's religious and spiritual lives. . .the best social predictor, although not a guarantee, of what the religious and spiritual lives of youth will look like is what the religious and spiritual lives of their parents do look like. Parents and other adults most likely "will get what they are." This recognition may be empowering to parents, or alarming, or both. But it is a fact worth taking seriously in any case.[3]*

Smith and Denton, authors of the National Study of Youth and Religion, conclude: "The best way to get most youth involved in and serious about their faith communities is to get their parents more involved in and serious about their faith communities."[4]

It is clear from the NSYR research that parents are the most influential factor in faith transmission, but how do parents influence their teen's religious loyalty. In her book *Choosing Church*, Carol Lytch found that it is very important for parents to link teens to their churches, the primary place were they develop religious commitment through socialization and religious experience.

- *First, the early religious nurture of parents in linking the child to the church and teaching the child the stories, symbols, and practices of their faith is the source for many of the enduring traits of identity, religious experience, and patterns of thought and action.*
- *Second, the parents' role of linking the child to the church continues to be important in the teen years. Parents influence teens in what they believe and how they practice their faith by maintaining a church attendance rule even into the teen years.*
- *Third, one of the most important things parents do is choose a church that is attractive to teens. If parents choose a church that attracts teens by*

the sense of belonging, meaning, and competencies that it offers, parents facilitate the link between the teen and the church that is crucial for developing religious loyalty.[5]

The Study of Exemplary Congregations in Youth Ministry confirms the continuing influence of parents and the family on young people. Young people are influenced by the faith of their parents and family in a number of significant, overlapping ways. (See Tables 10 and 11 for more details.)

CHART 6

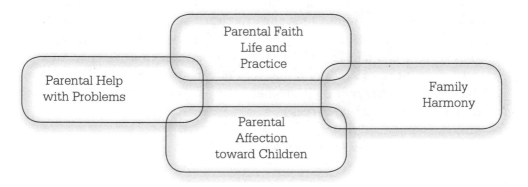

These four overlapping influences describe the role of family and household faith, adding another influence to the youth-friendly culture of the whole congregation and the effective age-level ministry with youth. Three Faith Assets focus on life within the family, parental faith influence, and faith practices at home.

Asset 25. Possess Strong Parental Faith: Parents possess and practice a vital and informed faith.

Asset 26. Promotes Family Faith Practices: Parents engage youth and the whole family in conversations, prayer, Bible reading, and service that nurture faith and life.

Asset 27. Reflects Family Harmony: Family members' expressions of respect and love create an atmosphere promoting faith.

Two Family and Household Faith Assets describe the role of the congregation in equipping and support parents and family life.

Asset 28. Equips Parents: The congregation offers instruction and guidance that nurture parental faith and equip parents for nurturing faith at home.

Asset 29. Fosters Parent-Youth Relationships: The congregation offers parent-youth activities that strengthen parent-youth relationships.

Parental Faith

Asset 25. Possess Strong Parental Faith: Parents possess and practice a vital and informed faith. A vital and informed parental faith includes understanding the Christian faith, participating in worship, praying, and engaging in service and mission. Young people are in households and relationships with parents where mature faith is cultivated and modeled.

The NSYR research tells us that parents will end up getting religiously of their children what they themselves are. The strong, vital, mature faith of parents in the EYM congregations is surely one of the most important contributors to nurturing sons and daughters of vital, committed Christian faith. These are parents who are committed to Jesus Christ and experience the presence of God in their daily lives and relationships with others. Their faith helps them decide what is right or wrong and take responsibility for serving those in need. Here are the most important characteristics of the faith of parents in the EYM Study. (See Table 11 for complete results. The highest rating is "9" indicating a response of "Always" or "Almost Always True.")

- *My faith helps me know right from wrong. (8.24)*
- *I have a sense of sharing in a great purpose. (8.20)*
- *I have had feelings of being in the presence of God. (8.12)*
- *I have a sense of being saved in Christ. (8.09)*
- *I am spiritually moved by the beauty of God's creation. (7.89)*
- *God helps me decide what is right or wrong behavior. (7.88)*
- *I have found a way of life that gives me direction. (7.72)*
- *Religious faith is important in my life. (7.37)*
- *My life is committed to Jesus Christ. (7.72)*
- *My life is filled with meaning and purpose. (7.33)*
- *I have a real sense that God is guiding me. (7.30)*
- *I feel God's presence in my relationships with other people. (6.87)*
- *I seek out opportunities to help me grow spiritually. (6.65)*
- *I try to apply my faith to political and social issues. (6.65)*
- *I talk with other people about my faith. (6.42)*
- *I give significant portions of time and money to help other people. (6.12)*
- *I care a great deal about reducing poverty in the U.S. and throughout the world. (5.96)*
- *I feel a deep sense of responsibility for reducing pain and suffering in the world. (5.90)*

Parents in the EYM congregations seek out opportunities to grow spiritually. The overwhelming majority of parents are involved in spiritual support groups in their churches. They reported that they belonged to at least one church group in which others will prayer with them and for them as needed (7.23); in at least one church group in which they can talk about spiritual issues (6.99); and in at least one church group in which it is possible to talk about personal problems (5.88).

Family Faith Practices

Asset 26. Promotes Family Faith Practices: Parents engage youth and the whole family in conversations, prayer, Bible reading, and service that nurture faith and life. Parents not only know and live Christianity themselves, they draw their teenagers into faith practices. Parents pray with their adolescents at table, at family celebrations, during times of crises and over individual and family decisions. Service is a way of life. Together parents and young people The Effective Christian Education Study (Search Institute. 1990) found that family religiousness was *the* most important factor in faith maturity.

> *Of the two strongest connections to faith maturity, family religiousness is slightly more important than lifetime exposure to Christian education. The particular family experiences that are most tied to greater faith maturity are the frequency with which an adolescent talked with mother and faith about faith, the frequency of family devotions, and the frequency with which parents and children together were involved in efforts, formal or informal, to help other people. Each of these family experiences is more powerful than frequency with which an adolescent sees his or her parents engage in religious behavior like church attendance.[6]*

The Effective Christian Education Study found that families that express faith do the following things: often talk about religious faith, often have family devotions, prayer, or Bible reading at home, and often have family projects to help other people.

The research also found that youth in families that often express faith do the following things *twice* as often as those families that do not express faith: read the Bible and prayer when alone, read and study about the Christian faith, are spiritually moved by the beauty of God's creation, and have often felt God's presence in their life.

Youth in families where faith is often expressed by a parent in word and deed are *three* times more likely to participate in family projects to help others and *twice* as likely to spend time helping other people than youth from families that did not express faith. Search Institute surveys of 217,000 sixth- to twelfth-grade youth in public schools (1999–2000) found that youth who say their parents "spent lots of time helping others" are almost twice as likely themselves to serve others. Among young people whose parents model helping, 61% volunteer at least one hour per week. Among those whose parents do not model helping, only 36% volunteer. People who live lives of service, justice, and advocacy often point to early experiences in their family as being normative.

Families that express faith also have an impact on participation in church life and service activities. Twice as many youth in families that express faith are involved in a church youth group, go to church programs or events that include children and adults, go to church camp or work camp, and regard a religious faith as a very or most important influence in life. Their attendance at worship services is almost 20% higher than youth from families that never express faith.

It is evident that youth who are most likely to mature in faith are those raised in homes where faith is part of the normal ebb and flow of family life. The Effective Christian Education Study provides convincing evidence of the power present in the religious practices of a home. Religious practices in the home virtually *double* the probability of a congregation's youth entering into the life and mission of Christ's church.

In the EYM Study young people were asked how their parents influenced their faith life, they people identified six ways that parental faith influences them. Confirming the findings from the Effective Christian Education Study, five of the six influences identified by the young people focus on family religiousness: talking about faith, serving others and God, and reading the Bible.

CHART 7

Parental Faith Influences	Mother	Father
1. Values are focused on serving others and God	7.41	6.88
2. Positive influence on my religious faith	7.23	6.21
3. Talked with me about my relationship with Jesus Christ	6.75	5.43
4. Attending Sunday worship	6.54	5.76
5. Talked with my parent about religious faith	4.89	3.95
6. Reading the Bible	4.10	3.48

When asked "How often does your family sit down together and talk about God, the Bible, or other religious things?" one in four young people said their family does this on a weekly or daily basis, and 40% once or twice a month. The combination of parental faith and parental faith influences promote a family which engages in faith practices at home. These are parents who read the Bible and pray with their teenagers, and include them in faith-informed discussions of family decision and budgets. Young people know about their parents' vital faith not only from observing them at church, but also from conversations about faith in the midst of everyday life. Young people in exemplary congregations explore understandings of God and matters of faith in their families. Faith instruction in these congregations does not all occur in their youth ministries; families reinforce what's learned at church through intentional faith practices and conversations at home.

The Practices of Faith

Reflecting on his research in faith practices, sociologist Robert Wuthnow writes,

> *Effective religious socialization comes about through embedded practices; that is, through specific, deliberate religious activities that are firmly intertwined with the daily habits of family routines, of eating and sleeping, of having conversations, of adorning spaces in which people live, of celebrating the holidays, and of being part of a community. Compared with these practices, the formal teachings of religious leaders often pale in significance. Yet when such practices are present, formal teachings also become more important.*[7]

This echoes the biblical directive to parents in Deuteronomy 6:7, "You shall teach them diligently to your sons and shall talk of them when you sit in your house and when you walk by the way and when you lie down and when you rise up." Parents have the assignment and joy of talking about the things of God in informal, repetitive ways in the normal routines of life. To talk about them "diligently" is similar to the language of sharpening a knife on a whetstone, repeatedly rubbing the edge to sharpen it for effective service. When "you sit in your house" speaks of the opportunities parents have to spend time in conversation with their sons and daughters about the activity of God in their lives. When "you walk by the way" hints at the aspect of modeling the characteristics and practices of a maturing Christian. Finally, "when you lie down and when you rise up" points toward the first and last things of the day, such as family prayers and devotional times.

Lawrence O. Richards makes the point clearly when he states, "The modeling of committed parents, the intimacy of family love, and the opportunity to see the implications of God's Laws as they were followed, together constituted the most powerful educational design ever devised."[8] Parents who sense their responsibility for the primary religious instruction of their children and modeling that lifestyle in everyday actions and conversations can make a significant difference in Christian maturity.

David Anderson and Paul Hill in *Frogs without Legs Can't Hear: Nurturing Disciples in Home and Congregation* describe four central family faith practices that when consistently acted upon at home and nurtured and supported by congregations contribute to developing families of faithful Christians who live their faith at home and in the world. The EYM Study, the Effective Christian Education Study, and the research of Robert Wuthnow affirm the significance of these four family faith practices.

1. **Caring Conversation.** Christian values and faith are passed on to the next generation through supportive conversation. Listening and responding to the daily concerns of young people makes it easier to have meaningful conversations regarding the love of God, and are ways to express God's love to others. Hearing their parents "faith stories" is one of the most important influences on the faith of children and teenagers.

2. **Family Devotions and Prayer.** The Christian faith shapes the whole of our lives and involves a lifetime of study, reflection, and prayer. Family devotions provide a way to learn more about the Bible and Christian tradition as a family, and apply the teachings to daily life as a follower of Jesus Christ. This understanding of a devotional life includes, but is not limited to, public worship, bedtime prayers, Bible reading and study, table grace, evening and morning prayers, and praying alone at any time of the day or night.

3. **Family Rituals and Traditions.** Families identify themselves and tell their family stories through daily routines, celebrations, and rituals. Family rituals can take many forms from daily rituals such as mealtime, bedtime, leaving and returning; celebrations such as birthdays, anniversaries, and special achievements; church year rituals at home such as Advent and Lent; milestones such as births and deaths, first day of school and graduations, and so on. Family rituals and traditions speak volumes about what the family values, believes and promotes, and how much the family values its faith.

4. **Family Service.** Engaging in service with one's family is a powerful opportunity for growing in faith. Both youth and adults are more likely to have a growing, strong faith when their family serves others together: in the home, in the congregation, in the community and world.

Family Harmony

Asset 27. Reflects Family Harmony: Family members' expressions of respect and love create an atmosphere promoting faith. Families and households find ways to navigate the challenges and stresses of daily life with approaches marked by respect, equal regard, open communication, and cooperation. Parents, grandparents and others practice individual accountability, forgiveness and reconciliation modeling faith in action and generating an atmosphere where faith can be referenced and discussed.

Young people in the EYM Study live in families where there is a high degree of family harmony as expressed in the interest that parents show their teens, close family relationships, and doing things as a family. In addition, young people experience parental affection from their parents and parental assistance with problems, They also experience a *lack* of parental verbal abuse. Each of these four features of family life influence the faith of young people and contribute to the development of a vital Christian faith in their lives. The findings from the youth survey demonstrate the significance of these features. (The highest rating is "9" indicating a response of "Always" or "Almost Always True.")

Family Harmony (7.19)
- *My mother is interested in me. (7.85)*
- *My father is interested in me. (7.35)*
- *We do things as a family. (7.31)*
- *My father and mother get along. (7.24)*
- *We are close as members of a family. (7.04)*
- *We are considerate of each other. (6.82)*
- *We have a feeling of love in our family. (6.74)*

Parents Are Affectionate toward Children (6.83)
- *Mother says things like I love you or I'm proud of youth. (7.42)*
- *Mother hugs, kisses, puts arms around me. (7.26)*
- *Father says things like I love you or I'm proud of youth. (6.60)*
- *Father hugs, kisses, puts arms around me. (6.04)*

Parents Help with Problems (6.02)
- *My mother helps me when I have a problem. (6.93)*
- *My family and I often talk about things that are important to me. (6.49)*
- *When I do something wrong, my mother takes the time to help me see why it was wrong. (6.25)*
- *My father helps me when I have a problem. (6.01)*
- *My mother gives me a chance to talk over rules I don't understand or like. (5.68)*
- *When I do something wrong, my father takes the time to help me see why it was wrong. (5.52)*
- *My father gives me a chance to talk over rules I don't understand or like. (5.23)*

Congregations Equip Parents to Pass on Faith and Strengthen Family Relationships

Asset 28. Equips Parents: The congregation offers instruction and guidance that nurture parental faith and equip parents for nurturing faith at home. Congregations provide strong adult faith formation, emphasizing adult discipleship and offering strong preaching, Bible studies, small groups and many forms of adult Christian education. Programs develop parental faith and prepare parents for nurturing the faith of their children and adolescents.

Asset 29. Fosters Parent-Youth Relationships: The congregation offers parent-youth activities that strengthen parent-youth relationships. Parent-youth programs focus on adolescent-specific issues such as family communication, adolescent independence, decision-making, choosing friends, sexual expression, and conflict resolution; as well as faith themes such as studying the Bible together, discussing case studies from youth culture, and exploring popular media. Parent-youth programs enhance the capacity of parents and teenagers to communicate and work together on matters of faith and life.

How are EYM congregations equipping parents to pass on faith to their young people? Parents, adult leaders in youth ministry, pastors, and youth ministers in the EYM Study agree that parents are equipped to pass on faith and family relationships are strengthened when congregations make intentional efforts to:

1. Provide education and resources parents need to teach their youth Christian concepts of right and wrong.
2. Show parents how to foster the development of moral values in their teens.
3. Encourage families to teach service as a way of life through their involvement in helping activities.
4. Encourage parent-youth communication through classes on how to discuss adolescent issues with youth.
5. Help youth and their parents deal with conflict.
6. Help provide opportunities for teens and parents to interact.
7. Help parents learn how to promote the faith of their children.
8. Help parents share their faith with their youth at home by such things as rituals, faith conversations, etc.
9. Establish a network of care and support for youth and their families
      (See Table 12 for complete results.)

In EYM congregations equipping parents to pass on faith to their young people involves a number of intentional practices and programs that deepen the faith of parents, teach about the unique developmental and socio-cultural characteristics of youth today, provide resources and skills training for teaching moral values and sharing faith at home, engage parents and their young people in service activities, develop communication skills and conflict resolution skills, and establish support groups for parents and for families. Congregations in the EYM Study created networks of support to provide a framework in which parents can deepen their faith, grow in their ability to raise teenagers, and expand their capacities to nurture faith in their young people.

EYM congregations strengthen family relationships by providing programs, activities, resources, and experiences that help parents become more involved in the lives of their youth, teens and parents to interact, parents recognize and adopt wise methods of discipline, and parents teach Christian concepts of right and wrong.

The Family–Congregation Partnership

EYM congregations invite parents into partnership with the church in nurturing the faith of their sons and daughters. The partnerships between the congregation and the families of their youth create a working synergy that enables the congregation, its youth ministry, and the families to nurture and support the lives and faith of their young people.

In many EYM congregations parents were directly involved in the congregation's youth ministry relationships and activities, serving as leaders/facilitators for Bible study groups, mission trips, retreats, worship, and small groups. Many adult leaders in youth ministry are parents and grandparents of youth. In some cases, they began serving while their teenager was in the congregation's youth ministry and continued after their sons and daughters had grown. Parental participation is not feared in these youth ministries, it is encouraged and the complexities generated are navigated.

Congregations involve parents in planning processes to shape the direction of youth ministry. Parents exercise their partnership by participating in assessment and planning. They become the eyes and ears for the youth minister as they listen to what other parents are saying and experiencing. These parents provide realistic perspectives on what is going well in the congregation's ministry with youth as well as identify challenges that need attention in their own families and the families of the community.

Conclusion

Family matters! Parent faith and influence matters! Family faith practices matter! The Study of Exemplary Congregations in Youth Ministry clearly shows the continuing influence of parents and the family on the development of a vital Christian faith in young people. The parents in the EYM Study possess a mature, committed Christian faith and this has a profound influence on the lives of young people. Family faith practices—caring conversations, family devotions and prayer, family rituals and traditions, family service—influence the faith lives of young people. EYM congregations have a role to play by equipping parents to pass on faith and strengthening family relationships, contributing to the influence of parents and the whole family on the development of youth of vital Christian faith. Given parents profound influence in the lives of their teens, youth ministries involved them directly in youth programs and activities, becoming a potential source of growth in faith for both teenagers and their parents.

Resources for Further Study: Family

Anderson, David W. *From the Great Omission to Vibrant Faith: Renewing the Role of the Home in Renewing the Church.* Bloomington: Vibrant Faith, 2009.

Anderson, David W. and Paul Hill. *Frogs without Legs Can't Hear: Nurturing Disciples in Home and Congregation.* Minneapolis: Augsburg Fortress, 2003.

DeVries, Mark. *Family-Based Youth Ministry.* Downers Grove: InterVarsity, 2004.

Garland, Diana. *Family Ministry—A Comprehensive Guide.* Downers Grove: InterVarsity, 1999.

Haynes, Brian. *Shift: What It Takes to Finally Reach Families Today.* Loveland: Group, 2009.

Holmen, Mark. *Faith Begins at Home.* Ventura: Regal, 2005.

Holmen, Mark. *Building Faith at Home.* Ventura: Regal, 2007.

Joiner, Reggie. *Think Orange: Imagine the Impact When Church and Family Collide.* Colorado Springs: David C. Cook, 2009.

Joiner, Reggie. *The Orange Leader Handbook: A Think Orange Companion.* Colorado Springs: David C. Cook, 2010.

Jones, Timothy Paul, editor. *Perspectives on Family Ministry: Three Views.* Nashville: B&H Academic, 2009.

Kehrwald, Leif, editor. *Families and Faith: A Vision & Practice for Parish Leaders.* New London: Twenty-Third, 2006.

Kehrwald, Leif. *Youth Ministry and Parents.* Winona: Saint Mary's, 2004.

Roehlkepartain, Jolene and Eugene. *Embracing Parents: How Your Congregation Can Strengthen Families.* Nashville: Abingdon, 2004.

Wigger, Bradley. *The Power of God at Home.* San Francisco: Jossey-Bass, 2003.

Resources for Further Study: Parents

Benson, Peter. *Sparks: How Parents Can Help Ignite the Hidden Strengths of Teenagers*. Minneapolis: Search Institute, 2008.

Burns, Jim. *Confident Parenting*. Grand Rapids: Bethany, 2008.

Clark, Chap and Dee Clark. *Disconnected: Parenting Teens in a MySpace World*. Grand Rapids: Baker, 2007.

Doe, Mimi. *Nurturing Your Teenager's Soul*. New York: Perigee, 2004.

Hoolihan, Patricia. *Launching Your Teen into Adulthood: Parenting through the Transition*. Minneapolis: Search Institute, 2008.

Housman, Brian. *Engaging Your Teen's World: Becoming a Culturally Savvy Parent*. Grand Rapids: Brazos, 2009.

Mueller, Walt. *The Space Between: A Parent's Guide to Teenage Development*. Grand Rapids: Youth Specialties/Zondervan, 2009.

Parrott, Les and Leslie. *The Parent You Want to Be: What You Are Matters More Than What You Do*. Grand Rapids: Zondervan, 2007.

Thompson, Kate. *Parenting Preteens with a Purpose: Navigating the Middle Years*. Minneapolis: Search Institute, 2008.

Websites: Parents and Families

- *Center for Parent-Youth Understanding: www.cpyu.org*
- *Faith Inkubators: www.faithink.com*
- *Fuller Youth Institute: www.fulleryouthinstitute.org*
- *Home Word (Jim Burns): www.homeword.com*
- *LifelongFaith Associates: www.lifelongfaith.com*
- *Parent Further (Search Institute): www.mvparents.com*
- *Parent Link (Group Publishing): www.theparentlink.com*
- *PARENTEEN (Chap Clark): www.parenteen.com*
- *Search Institute: www.search-institute.org*
- *Vibrant Faith Ministries: www.tyfi.org*

TABLE 10

Six Dimensions of Family Influence: Youth Responses

Overview

Six Dimensions of Family Influence	Rating[*]
1. Family Harmony (Lack of Family Disharmony)	7.19
2. Parents Are Affectionate toward Children	6.83
3. Lack of Parental Verbal Abuse	6.41
4. Parents Help with Problems	6.02
5. Mother Influences My Faith	6.15
6. Father Influences My Faith	5.41

The Six Dimensions with Items

1. Family Harmony (Lack of Family Disharmony)   7.19

- My mother is interested in me. (7.85)
- My father is interested in me. (7.35)
- We do things as a family. (7.31)
- My father and mother get along. (7.24)
- We are close as members of a family. (7.04)
- We are considerate of each other. (6.82)
- We have a feeling of love in our family. (6.74)

Mean scores: highest rating is "9," indicating a response of "Always" or "Almost Always True."

2. Parents Are Affectionate toward Children   6.83

- Mother says things like I love you or I'm proud of youth. (7.42)
- Mother hugs, kisses, puts arms around me. (7.26)
- Father says things like I love you or I'm proud of youth. (6.60)
- Father hugs, kisses, puts arms around me. (6.04)

3. Lack of Parental Verbal Abuse   6.41

4. Parents Help with Problems   6.02

- My mother helps me when I have a problem. (6.93)
- My family and I often talk about things that are important to me. (6.49)
- When I do something wrong, my mother takes the time to help me see why it was wrong. (6.25)
- My father helps me when I have a problem. (6.01)
- My mother gives me a chance to talk over rules I don't understand or like. (5.68)
- When I do something wrong, my father takes the time to help me see why it was wrong. (5.52)
- My father gives me a chance to talk over rules I don't understand or like. (5.23)

5. Mother Influences My Faith   6.15

- Values are focused on serving others and God (7.41)
- Positive influence on my religious faith (7.23)
- Talked with me about my relationship with Jesus Christ (6.75)
- Mother attending Sunday worship (6.54)
- Talked with my mother about religious faith (4.89)
- Mother reading the Bible (4.10)

6. Father Influences My Faith   5.41

- Values are focused on serving others and God (6.68)
- Importance of religion in my father's life (6.40)
- Positive influence on my religious faith (6.21)
- Father attending Sunday worship (5.76)
- Talked with me about my relationship with Jesus Christ (5.43)
- Talked with my father about religious faith (3.95)
- Father reading the Bible (3.48)

TABLE 11

Seven Dimensions of Parental and Family Faith Qualities: Parent Responses

Overview

Seven Dimensions of Parental and Family Faith Qualities	Rating*
1. God Consciousness	8.23
2. Moral Responsibility	7.97
3. Family Orientation	7.02
4. Centrality of Faith	6.99
5. Use of Faith Support Group	6.70
6. Desire for Participating in Leadership, Community, and Spirituality	6.49
7. Social Responsibility	6.16

The Seven Dimensions with Items

1. God Consciousness   **8.23**

- I have a sense that my prayers have been answered by God. (8.53)
- I have a sense of sharing in a great purpose. (8.20)
- I have had feelings of being in the presence of God. (8.12)
- I have a sense of being saved in Christ. (8.09)

Mean scores: highest rating is "9," indicating a response of "Always" or "Almost Always True."

2. Moral Responsibility   7.97

- The kind of moral decisions I make now will affect my future happiness. (8.31)
- God helps me decide what is right or wrong behavior. (7.88)
- When people wrong other people, they sin against God. (7.71)

3. Faith Orientation   7.02

- My faith helps me know right from wrong. (8.24)
- I have found a way of life that gives me direction. (7.72)
- Religious faith is important in my life. (7.37)
- Our family talks about God, the Bible, and other religious things. (4.76)

4. Centrality of Faith   6.99

- I am spiritually moved by the beauty of God's creation. (7.89)
- My life is committed to Jesus Christ. (7.72)
- My life is filled with meaning and purpose. (7.33)
- I have a real sense that God is guiding me. (7.30)
- I feel God's presence in my relationships with other people. (6.87)
- I seek out opportunities to help me grow spiritually. (6.65)
- I talk with other people about my faith. (6.42)
- I help others with their religious questions and struggles. (5.76)

5. Use of Faith Support Group   6.70

- I belong to at least one church group in which others will prayer with me and for me as needed. (7.23)
- I belong to at least one church group in which we talk about spiritual issues. (6.99)
- I belong to at least one church group in which it is possible to talk about personal problems. (5.88)

6. Desire for Participating in Leadership, Community, and Spirituality   6.49

- I am interested in experiencing a great sense of community or family in my church. (6.91)

- I am interested in making more friends at church. (6.58)

- I am interested in getting more help with my spiritual journey. (6.49)

- I am interested in having my talents and abilities better used by my church. (5.96)

7. Social Responsibility   6.16

- I try to apply my faith to political and social issues. (6.65)

- I give significant portions of time and money to help other people. (6.12)

- I care a great deal about reducing poverty in the U.S. and throughout the world. (5.96)

- I feel a deep sense of responsibility for reducing pain and suffering in the world. (5.90)

TABLE 12

Ways that Congregations Equip Parents

Theme: Congregational Faith	Parents	Adult Leaders	Pastors and Youth Ministers*
• Parents are shown how they can foster the development of moral values in their children.	5.70	-	5.27
• Youth ministry provides education and resources parents needs to teach their youth Christian concepts of right and wrong,	5.20	4.40	4.12
• Youth ministry provides help for teaching Christian concepts of right and wrong.	5.08	6.25	-
• Youth ministry encourages families to teach service as a way of life through involved in helping activities.	5.27	5.52	4.81
• Youth ministry encourages parent-youth communication through classes on how to discuss adolescent issues with youth.	4.89	3.67	3.58
• Youth ministry helps youth and their parents deal with conflict.	4.71	5.21	4.13
• Youth ministry provides opportunities for teens and parents to interact.	4.60	4.95	-
• Youth ministry provides classes to help parents learn how to promote the faith of their children.	4.37	3.84	-
• Youth ministry gives special assistance to parents coping with non-traditional family issues.	4.20	4.74	3.67

*Mean scores: highest rating is "9," indicating a response of "Always" or "Almost Always True."

• Youth ministry helps parents recognize and adopt wise methods of discipline.	3.66	4.30	-
• Youth ministry helps parents share their faith with their youth at home by such things as rituals, faith conversations, etc.	-	-	3.98
• We have established a network of care and support for youth and their families.	-	5.46	6.36

APPLICATION
TOOL 9

Evaluating Faith Assets: Family and Household Faith

Use this worksheet as a guide to reflect on the practice of the Family and Household Faith Assets in your congregation. First, rate your congregation on each of the items in the second column. Then, list in the third column things you already do to strengthen each quality. Finally, identify other things you could do to strengthen the Family and Household Faith Assets.

Assets	Rating Your Congregation *
25. Possess Strong Parental Faith	_____ Our congregation offers faith formation programs and resources for adults, and in particular parents, to deepen their understanding and practice of the Christian faith.
	_____ Our youth ministry offers faith formation programs and resources to deep parents' understanding and practice of the Christian faith.

What We Do Now:

What We Could Do Better:

* ★ = *Needs Work*   ★★ = *Okay*   ★★★ = *Great*

26. Promotes Family Faith Practices

Our congregation and youth ministry helps parents develop family faith practices by providing church programs/activities and household resources so that families can engage in:

_____ Caring Conversations

_____ Family Devotions and Prayer

_____ Family Rituals and Traditions

_____ Family Service

What We Do Now:

What We Could Do Better:

28. Equips Parents

Our congregation and youth ministry equips parents to pass on faith to their young people by offering programs and activities that:

_____ teach about the unique developmental and socio-cultural characteristics of youth today

_____ provide resources and skills training for teaching moral values and sharing faith at home

_____ engage parents and their young people in service activities

_____ develop communication skills and conflict resolution skills

_____ establish support groups for parents

What We Do Now:

What We Could Do Better:

29. Fosters Parent-Youth Relationships

Our congregation and youth ministry strengthens family relationships by providing programs, activities, resources, and experiences so that:

_____ parents become more involved in the lives of their youth

_____ teens and parents interact together

_____ parents recognize and adopt wise methods of discipline

What We Do Now:

What We Could Do Better:

APPLICATION
TOOL 10

Principles for Family-Friendly Congregations and Youth Ministries

- **Focus on the family as a system**. Recognize the power of the family system on the faith and values of adolescents. When we minister with adolescents it is important to recognize the entire family context from which they come and will return.

- **Build on family strengths**. All too often our ministry efforts focus on what is wrong with families or on correcting family problems. Focus on promoting family strengths, healthy values, and effective family life skills. Help families discover their mission, unique gifts, and strengths. Teach skills for family living and growing in faith; support and encourage families.

- **Respect the individual and cultural differences among families**. Families come in all different sizes, shapes, and colors. Recognize this diversity and incorporate distinct features in our ministry and programming to respond effectively to the diversity.

- **Respond flexibly to family needs; offer a variety of programs, activities, and strategies.** Family life is dramatically different today than it was only two or three decades ago. The diversity in family structure and family ethnic heritages, the pressures of family time and commitments, and the changing work patterns require flexible rather than rigid policies, programming, and scheduling. Gone are the days when a one-program-fits-all approach will work.

- **Reach out to families, rather than demand participation in programs**. Offer programs, services, and resources for families at home or in home-like settings. The basis for our ministry with families should not be participation in church programs. The issue is not how many people come to a program, but how many families you are reaching through a variety of programs, activities, and strategies. Decrease reliance on gathered programming as the primary way to minister with families, and increase the emphasis on reaching out to families at-home or in small groups of families. A contemporary approach to families strikes a balance between gathered programs and a variety of activities and strategies designed for home use by one family or a cluster of families.

- **Treat families as partners in ministry.** Instead of working in isolation, develop a partnership approach which includes assessing the needs of families with adolescents, consulting with parents on the direction of youth ministry, inviting parents to participate in the planning of programs and to take leadership roles at church programs or in home groupings. We treat parents as partners when . . .

  - We support families with diverse programs, resources and strategies.
  - We incorporate a family perspective into the life and programs of the congregation.
  - We build a bridge between youth programming and the home.
  - We consider carefully the impact on families when developing programs, policies and ministry strategies.

Criteria for Family-Friendly Programming

When designing programs and activities be sure to keep in mind several important criteria for family-friendly programming.

- The program accounts for the different family forms represented by the families of adolescents (for example, single-parent, blended, and dual career families).
- The program accounts for the variety of ethnic groups in the church and their particular needs.
- The scheduling of the program reflects the busy and, often, complex calendar of families with adolescents.
- The program addresses the needs of the adolescent in relation to his or her family or the overall needs of the entire family.
- The program improves the capacity for families to master the family life cycle developmental issues appropriate to families with adolescents.
- The program has a process that helps the participating adolescents and their families deal with the change and growth the program encourages.
- Parents are involved in planning, implementing, and evaluating the program.
- The program improves the relationship between youth ministry and the family.
- The program empowers the family to share and live the Christian faith at home, and helps them grow together as a family.
- The program provides families with resources and activities for in-home use.
- The program helps families connect with other families in family groupings or intergenerational groupings to share their faith, celebrate their faith, and/or serve others.

APPLICATION
TOOL 11

Strategies for Family Faith Formation

For the good of families and the whole Christian community, congregations can provide opportunities to equip homes as centers of faith formation at every stage of life. Congregations and youth ministries can make family faith formation a focus of everything they do as a church community, using an array of approaches and strategies to nurture faith at every stage of the family life cycle and in all the diverse forms and structures of the contemporary family. They can educate and enrich parents and the whole family to embed foundational religious practices—faith conversations, family devotions and prayer, Bible reading, service, and rituals and traditions—into the daily experience of family life. Congregations and youth ministries can strengthen the partnership between home and congregation by focusing on empowering, resourcing, and supporting the development of the family as the center of faith formation.

To help your congregation and youth ministry strengthen its approach to families, here are a variety of strategies to engage parents and the whole family.

Strategy 1. Utilize church ministries and programming to teach, model, and demonstrate family faith practices, and then provide the resources for families to live the practice at home.

Churches can utilize Sunday worship and church programs and activities to teach, model, and demonstrate faith practices that families can incorporate into home life, and provide them with specific resources to live their faith at home. Weekly worship and church events are significant opportunities for families to experience faith practices—conversations, devotions and prayer, Bible reading and reflection, service, and rituals and traditions—which can be extended into the home.

Strategy 2. Involve the whole family in congregational life, programs, and leadership roles.

Most ministry activities of congregations have involved persons as individuals, not as families. What is missing in current practice are more ways families can participate *together* in the mission, ministries, and programs of the church. Start with ministries and programs where at least one family member is already active and incorporate family or parent-teen participation. Assess all of the possibilities in your congregation to promote whole-family experiences. Without adding more programming, congregations can involve the whole family. For example:

- Redesign adolescent Christian education programming or adult Bible study programs to incorporate family learning programs or parent-teen learning programs as an integral part of the program year.
- Involve the whole family in worship roles, such as reading the Scripture on Sunday, leading prayer, decorating the environment for worship, singing in the choir as a family, greeting people as they arrive for worship, collecting the offering, and so on.
- Redesign existing service projects for teens and adults into whole-family service projects.
- Involve the whole family in congregational leadership, such as taking leadership roles in summer vacation Bible school or organizing the annual church festival.

Strategy 3. Offer family and intergenerational learning programs, as well as parent-teen programs.

Congregations can design programming that involves and engages the whole family in faith formation. In his report of the NSYR research (*Soul Searching*), Christian Smith observes, "Faith formation of children and teens would probably best be pursued in the larger context of family ministry, that parents should be viewed as indispensable partners in the religious formation of children and youth." Most congregations would do well to transform their over-emphasis on age-group learning and incorporate family-centered learning programs or intergenerational learning programs, which involve the whole community: singles, couples, families with children/teens, empty nest families, and older adult families.

There are a number of possibilities for learning programs that involve the whole family and/or the whole community:

- monthly large group family or intergenerational learning programs (that can replace or be integrated with age-group programming)
- family workshops through the year focused on family faith practices, church year seasons, and/or family-focused topics
- family cluster or small group learning programs (at the church or in homes)
- family-centered (small group or large group) lectionary-based Scripture reflection
- family-centered or intergenerational vacation Bible school
- family retreats and camps
- family Bible study

Congregations can also plan programs for parents and teens on common areas of interest and need, such as parent-teen community, making vocational decisions, cultural/media influences, social issues, and so on.

One model for family/intergenerational learning that is being used in thousands of churches incorporates the following elements:

1. Welcome, community building and opening prayer

2. Part 1: An All-Ages Learning Experience for the whole assembly that introduces the theme or topic for the program.

3. Part 2: In-Depth Learning Experiences that probe the theme or topic, organized for all ages (intergenerational) *or* for specific age-groups (families with children or children-only, adolescents, young adults, and adults), and conducted in one of three formats:

   - *Whole Group Format*: learning in small groups with the whole group assembled in one room (age-specific or all ages small groups);

   - *Age Group Format*: learning in separate, parallel groups organized by ages;

   - *Learning Activity Center Format*: learning at self-directed or facilitated activity centers (age-specific and/or all ages learning centers).

4. Part 3. An All-Ages Contributive Learning experience in which each generation teaches the other generations.

5. Part 4. Reflection on the learning experience and interactive group sharing.

6. Closing Prayer

Source: Intergenerational Faith Formation, Mariette Martineau, Joan Weber, and Leif Kehrwald (New London: Twenty-Third, 2008).

Strategy 4. Develop family faith formation around life-cycle milestones.

Milestones are significant moments in life's journey that provide the opportunity for individuals and their families to experience God's love, and grow in faith through sacred and ordinary events both in the life of the congregation and in daily life. Milestones faith formation provides a natural opportunity to create a partnership between the congregation and the home. Milestones faith formation uses four elements to shape this vital partnership:

- *Naming* the sacred and ordinary events that are recognized in the life of a congregation and those that take place in our daily lives—our beginnings, endings, transitions, achievements, failures, and rites of passage—creates rituals and traditions that shape our identities and give us a sense of belonging to the family of Jesus Christ.

- *Equipping* brings the generations together, builds community, invites conversation, encourages storytelling, and provides information. Opportunities are provided here to model faith practices for the home.

- *Blessing* the individual, and marking the occasion in a worship service and in the home, says that it is *all* about faith. God is present in all of daily life, making the ordinary sacred.

- *Gifting* offers a tangible, visible item that serves as a reminder or symbol of the occasion being marked, as well as a resource for the ongoing nurture of faith in daily life.

During the adolescent years milestones such as confirmation, receiving a driver's license, and graduations (middle school, high school) provide an opportunity for family faith formation. For each milestone, a congregation can provide faith formation that includes: (1) rituals and traditions; (2) intergenerational learning programs (building community, inviting conversation, encouraging storytelling, providing information, and modeling faith practices for individual and families); (3) a blessing of the individual and marking the occasion in a worship service and in the home; and (4) a tangible, visible item that serves as a reminder or symbol of the occasion being marked, as well as a resource for the ongoing nurture of faith in daily life at home.

For resources see:

- *Faith Stepping Stones*. Faith Inkubators.

- *Milestones Ministry Manual for Home and Congregation*. Vibrant Faith Ministries. Bloomington: Vibrant Faith Ministries, 2007.

- *Shift—What It Takes to Finally Reach Families Today.* Haynes, Brian. Loveland: Group, 2009.

- *Take It Home: Inspiration and Events to Help Parents Spiritually Transform Their Children.* Mark Holmen. Ventura: Gospel Light, 2008.

Strategy 5. Offer a variety of developmentally-appropriate family or parent-teen service projects.

Congregations can offer a variety of developmentally-appropriate family or parent-teen service projects where families can choose from different levels of commitment from beginner experiences to advanced projects that are local, regional, national, and international. Each mission/service project includes a learning component that focuses on understanding the issue being addressed, exploring the teachings of Scripture and tradition, developing the skills for mission and service, and then, upon completion of the project, reflecting upon the involvement. Mission projects are "developmental" with projects geared to different levels of involvement and challenge including:

- local mission projects lasting anywhere from a few hours to one day in length

- short-term mission trips lasting anywhere from two to five days and requiring an overnight stay on location

- weeklong mission trips within the United States as well as to foreign countries, designed for those who are ready to take the next big step in service.

- global expedition trips of 10 to 14 days that provide the opportunity to be immersed for a longer period in the targeted community and culture

Strategy 6. Provide at-home resources for the core family faith practices.

Congregations can provide families with a variety of resources—print, audio, video, and online—to help families embed faith practices in family life at each stage of life, including resources for parents at each stage of life, for in-home celebration of church year feasts and seasons, for extending Sunday worship into the home, for celebrating milestones, for engaging in service, and so many more. Churches can use their websites and digital communication to resource and connect families, delivering timely faith formation resources to the home, providing social networking among families to share faith stories and practices, and providing support, for parents.

Strategy 7. Use the Internet to resource and connect families.

Congregations can create their own online presence (website) as the centerpiece of their online faith formation. They can deliver faith formation experiences and resources anytime and anywhere, reaching people wherever they go online (home, work, school, vacation, coffee house). They can also promote continuing faith growth and practice by using their online presence and digital communication tools to extend relationships and faith formation initiated in a face-to-face learning settings. Churches can use a variety of online digital media strategies for faith formation including:

- A resource center with daily, weekly and seasonal resources for the family, including faith conversation activities, family devotions and prayer, Bible reading activities, service projects, and rituals and traditions

- A parenting center with "how to" parenting articles and videos, faith enrichment resources, a "gathering space" for parents to interact, a blog staffed by parent mentors, parent-generated ideas and activities, links to highly rated parent and family websites

- A milestones and life transitions center with sections for each milestone/transition that include rituals, blessings, commentaries, personal stories, a "gathering space" for sharing stories and ideas

- A virtual chapel sharing not only audio and video clips of some of the sermons and other worship experiences but also extending it through the daily posting of images, songs, meditations, inspirational stories, prayers of the people, and online worship exercises.

- A calendar of events with locations, times, and descriptions, with Web-streamed audio and video recordings of select offerings.

- Themed "gathering spaces" for synchronous and asynchronous interaction, including live text-based chat and live audio/video conferences, threaded discussions, collected blog links, self-paced tutorials on a range of topics, and so on.

- A community directory that includes "home pages" with pictures, contact information, and other self-determined personal information. Each individual can include more of his or her personal dreams, goals, and activities through statements or interactive blogs.

- A library pod with access to e-journals, e-books, archived streaming video of speakers and events, a clearinghouse-type collection of links to resources, and other Internet-mediated resources.

- A mission/service opportunity clearinghouse for local, national, and international internships, volunteer opportunities, and jobs.

- A learning center with courses and webinars on topics such as faith themes, Bible studies, life issues, and Christian practices, self-paced and facilitated by church staff and church members at scheduled times.

- Small group gatherings online for faith sharing, Bible study, and book discussions

Strategy 8. Focus on parents—parent faith formation and parental training.

Congregations can equip parents of teenagers for their parenting roles and sharing faith with teens through classes, workshops, retreats, and/or support groups. These could include such things as parenting classes, parent-youth discussion times, parent support groups, seminars for parents of younger youth as they enter adolescence, seminars for parents of older youth as they provide for college, and so forth. Churches can provide stand-alone parent programs, as well as incorporating parent faith formation and parent education into existing faith formation programs and support groups for parents. Parent workshops and educational programs need to have content that is relevant to parents and processes that help parents learn and want to participate in new learning. Here are several tips for designing and leading effective educational experiences for parents.

- Create a supportive, caring environment for learning. Greet parents, provide time for them to get acquainted with one another, and encourage mutual support during and after the experience.

- Actively engage parents in the learning. The amount they learn will be in direct proportion to how much they put into the experience.

- Let parents be the experts. Show that you value their knowledge and experience by giving them opportunities to contribute to the learning experience.

- Tie the learning activities around the parents' experiences and values so they know "this is for me and about my family."

- Focus the content on real needs, issues, and concerns, not just on content that parents ought to know. If, for example, you want to help parents teach their teens about healthy concepts of right and wrong, first identify the ways this connects with parents' needs or concerns regarding moral values, then develop the experience to reflect those concerns.

- Include information and skills parents can put into action immediately. Such application reinforces and helps parents internalize what they learn.

- Demonstrate how to use skills and practices during the program so that parents have a direct experience of how to use the skills or practice at home.

- Provide resources that parents can use for their own personal growth and with their family. Consider developing a parent website with resources and links to websites to enhance and expand the learning experience.

APPLICATION TOOL 12

Sample Survey: Parents of Teenagers

Please indicate your *interest* in the following topics.

		Rating *		
1.	How to communicate better with my teenager.	N	S	M
2.	How to help my teen develop healthy concepts of right and wrong.	N	S	M
3.	How to help my teen learn and practice the Christian faith.	N	S	M
4.	More about how to talk with my teen about sexuality.	N	S	M
5.	How to effectively discipline my teen.	N	S	M
6.	More about the development and life issues of my teenager.	N	S	M
7.	Participating in a support group where parents talk with other parents about common issues and concerns of being a parent.	N	S	M
8.	Participating in service projects with my teens or with other adults.	N	S	M
9.	How to deal with conflict in family relationships.	N	S	M
10.	How to promote the faith of my teenager.	N	S	M
11.	How to share faith at home through rituals and traditions, faith conversations, prayer, and devotions.	N	S	M

*Rating: None, Some, Much

12. Which of the following would improve your home life?
    (Rank them from 1 - most important to 5 - least important.)

    _____ to talk more openly with my teenager

    _____ to spend more time together as a family

    _____ to get along better with my teenager

    _____ to share more responsibilities at home

    _____ to learn how to set boundaries and rules with my teenager

    _____ other:

13. Which of the following do you believe your family really needs to work on?
    (Check all that apply.)

    _____ communication   _____ privacy

    _____ fun times   _____ trust

    _____ religious life   _____ expectations of family members

    _____ discipline   _____ getting along together

    _____ other:

14. To the best of your knowledge, how well does the church's current programming meet
    your family's needs?

    _____ very well   _____ good

    _____ okay   _____ poorly

    _____ don't know

15. When is the best time for you to attend activities and workshops?

    _____ weekdays during the day (which days: _____)

    _____ weekday evening (which days: _____)

    _____ Saturday

    _____ Sunday morning   _____ Sunday afternoon   _____ Sunday evening

If you could ask for one thing from the church to help your family, what would it be?

CHAPTER SIX

congregational leadership

C ommitted and competent leadership is at the heart of the exemplary congregations' faithful and effective ministries with youth. These ministries combine knowledgeable pastors, valued youth ministers, committed adult leaders in youth ministry, with gifted young people and dedicated parents in "cultures of shared leadership." Pastors in EYM congregations, whether directly involved in the youth ministry or not, either lead or provide critical support to this culture and the youth ministry leadership team. The prime youth minister in the congregation (most often unpaid but publicly "called"), the adult leaders, parents and youth themselves each make their unique contributions to the teams' effectiveness. This chapter will explore the leadership of the pastor, the youth minister, adult leaders in youth ministry, and youth leader.

Leadership of the Pastor

Pastors matter immensely in effective youth ministry! And they matter in very specific ways! Pastors lead through their spiritual influence, their pastoral effectiveness; their love for and support of young people; and their support of youth ministry leaders. In the EYM congregations, pastors are the most influential persons among the many adults and youth sharing leadership in these effective ministries with youth.

How is the pastor significant? Each of the following *dimensions* (a grouping of questions) developed from the results of the surveys, reflect high mean scores (9 being the highest), indicating the importance of the pastor in the life of the congregation and youth ministry, and more importantly, in nurturing young people of vital, committed Christian faith. (See Table 13 for complete results.)

1. Pastor Supports Christian Education and Youth Ministry (8.05, adult leaders)
2. Effectiveness of Pastor's Leadership (7.90, adult leaders) (7.88, parents)
3. Pastor's Communication Skills (7.84, adult leaders) (7.38, parents)
4. Interpersonal Characteristics (7.80, parents)
5. Pastoral Support for Youth Staff (7.76, pastors and youth ministers)
6. Pastor Creates a Healthy Culture (7.39, pastor and youth ministers)
7. Pastor's Spiritual Influence (7.37, youth)
8. Pastor's Personal Characteristics (7.13, youth)
9. Pastor is a Good Counselor (7.02, adult leaders) (6.82, parents)
10. Mission is to Make Disciples (6.94, pastors and youth ministers)
11. Pastor Preaches to Make Disciples (6.80, adult leaders) (6.71, parents)

Each of these dimensions can be seen in the four Faith Assets which describe the traits and leadership of the pastor regarding youth and youth ministry within the congregation. Taken together these four Faith Assets describe how influential a pastor's role is in the overall faithfulness and effectiveness of a congregation's ministries with youth.

Asset 30. Spiritual Influence: The pastor knows and models the transforming presence of God in life and ministry.
Asset 31. Interpersonal Competence: The pastor builds a sense of community and relates well with adults and youth.
Asset 32. Supports Youth Ministry: The pastor understands, guides, and advocates for youth ministry.
Asset 33. Supports Leaders: The pastor affirms and mentors youth and adults leading youth ministry.

The Pastor's Spiritual Influence

Asset 30. Spiritual Influence: The pastor knows and models the transforming presence of God in life and ministry.

Pastors' witness to their own faith in speech and action does not go unnoticed in their churches. Youth ministers, adult leaders in youth ministry, parents, and young people name four ingredients of the pastor's spiritual influence: their pastor's expression of what they personally believe, their pastor's faith practices, the way their pastor's public ministry was an expression of an authentic faith, and the way their pastor's faith was integrated in their pastor's lifestyle. Furthermore, the pastor's personal faith and its undergirding theology seemed to be one of the critical elements in the faith maturity of the congregation.

Pastors influence young people, and the congregation, in the ways they talk about God, pray, and ask for forgiveness when they hurt someone. Young people report that their pastors have a direct and profound impact on them spiritually and relationally. They say that the "pastor's personal characteristics" model Christian life in a manner that gives faith integrity and inspires them to be faithful.

All four survey groups concur on the important characteristics of the pastor's spiritual influence: a devout faith and an exemplary life, the mission of Christ is first in his or her own life, a passion that people come to know Jesus Christ, a Christ-centered preaching, an active concern for the oppressed, shared shares leaders in the congregation, and an ability to relate well to youth. (See Table 13 for complete results.)

The Pastor's Interpersonal Competence

Asset 31. Interpersonal Competence: The pastor builds a sense of community and relates well with adults and youth.

The pastor's interpersonal competence as a leader has a significant influence on the congregation and youth ministry. Survey findings from all four groups provide a profile of the pastor's interpersonal competence: a good speaker and easy to understand, a good listener and easy to talk to, supportive and inspiring, an ability to relate well to members, skill in building a sense of congregational family. (See Table 13 for complete results.)

Pastors build relationships with youth, and they encourage and equip their congregations to do the same. They have a genuine interest in people, especially young people, and possess the capacity to make "heart to heart' connections with people of all ages. The relational ability of the pastor has a direct relationship to the capacity of the congregation to nurture mature levels of faith in youth and adults. Pastors have great influence in generating a culture in which effective ministry with youth can occur through their authenticity, directness, and compassion in relationships. This in turn cultivates authenticity, directness and compassion throughout the congregation, especially in the congregation's relationships with young people.

The Pastor's Support

Asset 32. Supports Youth Ministry: The pastor understands, guides, and advocates for youth ministry.

Asset 33. Supports Leaders: The pastor affirms and mentors youth and adults leading youth ministry.

Pastors have strong working relationships with their youth ministry leadership team. Pastors support the congregation's youth minister, value the work of adult leaders in youth ministry, and are involved in the strategic planning of ministries with youth. Pastors also have high levels of support for and commitment to Christian education and youth ministry.

Survey findings from adult leaders in youth ministry, pastors, and youth ministers identify several key characteristics of the pastor's support for youth ministry and for leaders: an enthusiasm for and involvement in Christian education, a deep commitment to youth ministry, and appreciation, interest, and trust in leaders. (See Table 13 for complete results.)

The EYM congregations reported strong working relationships between their pastor and their youth ministry leadership team. These pastors support the congregation's youth minister, value the work of adult leaders in youth ministry, and are involved in the strategic planning of ministries with youth.

The data from the surveys and the voices of youth ministers, adult leaders, parents and young people on the site visits converge to send a strong and detailed message from the EYM congregations: Pastors matter immensely in effective youth ministry! And they matter in very specific ways! Pastors lead through their spiritual influence, their pastoral effectiveness, their love for and support of young people, and their support of youth ministry leaders. In EYM congregations, pastors are the most influential persons among the many adults and youth sharing leadership in these effective ministries with youth.

When combined these four sets of strengths—spiritual influence, leadership, relationships, and support—a composite of powerful influence emerges. The effectiveness of the leadership of the pastor and the attitudes of the pastor regarding young people combine with the pastor's relational wisdom and skill to position pastors among the most influential factors in a congregation's youth ministries.

Leadership of the Youth Minister

When the pastors in all 131 EYM congregations were asked to respond to the open-ended question regarding the reasons for the effectiveness of their congregation's youth ministry, "we credit the outstanding leadership provided by the youth minister" was second only to a "great variety of high quality relationships and practices." It may be that the high quality relationships and practices might even be a result of these effective youth ministers' leadership.

The pastors who cited the importance of outstanding leadership of youth ministers were specific about the contributions these youth ministers were making. They reported that the youth minister is committed to establishing a close relationship with the youth of the congregation, and that he or she has established a high level of trust with both congregational adults and the youth. In their congregation the youth minister is experienced, well trained, and extremely competent; and has been serving for a number of years (a long tenure).

Most of these youth ministers in the EYM congregations were not salaried. About a third of them, those in the larger congregations, were paid and paid well. The other two thirds, those in the smaller congregations, while not "salaried fulltime or not at all," were "compensated" through strong support from adult leaders in youth ministry, parents, and youth and given ample resources for their work as well as regular continuing education.

Six Faith Assets describe the strengths of the primary youth minister in the congregation. The youth minister is both a competent leader with theological and ministry knowledge and skill, and a faith-filled role model for youth and adults.

Asset 34. Provides Competent Leadership: The youth minister reflects superior theological, theoretical, and practical knowledge and skill in leadership.

Asset 35. Models Faith: The youth minister is a role model reflecting a living faith for youth and adults.

Asset 36. Mentors Faith Life: The youth minister assists adult leaders and youth in their faith life both one-on-one and in groups.

Asset 37. Develops Teams: The youth minister reflects a clear vision and attracts gifted youth and adults into leadership.

Asset 38. Knows Youth: The youth minister knows youth and the changes in youth culture, and utilizes these understandings in ministry.

Asset 39. Establishes Effective Relationships: The youth minister enjoys effective relationships with youth, parents, volunteers, and staff.

Survey findings from youth, parents, and adult leaders in youth ministry describe the most important characteristics of the youth minister's personal qualities, ministry competence, and leadership. Youth ministers in the EYM study possess: a vitality of faith and an exemplary life, a commitment to youth, ability to help youth on their spiritual journey, the capacity to relate well with youth and adults, knowledge of Scripture and the Christian faith, good organizational and delegation skills, the ability to discover people's gifts and strengths, effectiveness in recruiting, training and supporting adult and youth leadership, the ability to assist a congregation in supporting youth ministry, the capacity to handle conflict, and a commitment to caring for their own spiritual, social and physical health. (See Table 14 for complete results.)

One of the key elements for effective youth ministry is the relational ability of the youth minister: establishing close relationships with young people, and modeling and fostering significant relationships among young people and adults in the congregation. Like a bridge that has anchors in two land masses, the youth minister has influence in both the adult and youth worlds. Adults may not grasp their crucial role in influencing youth without someone guiding them in the process. By teaching and modeling for the congregation the importance of building closer bonds with young people, youth ministers can not only set the pace for volunteers and lay a solid foundation for team work with other staff, they can also foster a congregational community that nurtures teenage faith maturity.

One unique feature of the youth ministers in the study is that they all had served in the same congregation for many years, developing connections and networks of influence and leadership. It appears that several factors contribute to the effectiveness and longevity of youth ministers in the EYM Study.

1. A congregation with high expectations "calls" a person of strong faith and passion for ministry with youth.
2. Once that person has been called, the congregation supports them with prayer, resources, ongoing education and networks of support.
3. The person who has been called thrives in this culture of high expectations, ample resources, ongoing learning and strong support. The youth minister deepens his or her commitment, expands personal investment, and fires the imagination. Full of spirit and hope, the youth minister stays for years, even decades.
4. The youth minister's faithfulness and effectiveness inspires the congregation to higher expectations, imagination and support. And forward it goes over long periods of expanding impact in the lives of young people.

Youth and Adult Leadership in Youth Ministry

A cluster of five Faith Assets describe youth and adult leadership—people of a vibrant and informed Christian faith who are "called" to youth ministry leadership. They are in significant relationships with each other and with the young people of the congregation. They prepare for their ministry through training and apprenticeships in their leadership roles.

Asset 40. Equipped for Peer Ministry: Youth practice friendship, care-giving, and outreach and are supported by ministry training and caring adults.

Asset 41. Establish Adult-Youth Mentoring: Adults engage youth in the Christian faith and life supported by informed leadership.

Asset 42. Participate in Training: Youth and adults are equipped for ministry in an atmosphere of high expectations.

Asset 43. Possesses Vibrant Faith: Youth and adult leaders possess and practice a vital and informed Christian faith.

Asset 44. Provides Competent Adult Leaders: Adults foster authentic relationships and utilize effective practices in youth ministry with a clear vision strengthened by training and support.

Adult Leadership in Youth Ministry

The adult leaders in youth ministry are women and men of mature faith. They are aware of the presence and activity of a living God in their lives and are committed to reflecting on their relationships with God and practicing faith in their daily lives. Adult leaders have a real sense that God is guiding them in daily life. Their thinking is informed by substantive understandings of God as reflected in Scripture and their faith traditions.

Moreover, this awareness and understanding of God has a central place in their life's direction, their speaking and their decision-making, leading them to be more morally responsible and socially conscious. Their faith forms the substance and sets the tone of youth ministry practices. They live their faith both at church and in the community, carrying in their lives manifold indications that God is present in their lives and influential in their decisions.

When pastors and youth ministers were asked in an open-ended question, "Why do you think your congregation's youth ministry is able to accomplish this while so many other congregations struggle at it?", one of the top five answers was that their congregation's effectiveness is due to the dedicated participation of volunteer adults and parents. Comments about adult leaders in youth ministry included their love and passionate commitment for youth, their willingness to be trained and attend monthly or weekly orientation sessions, and their longevity resulting in little turnover in leadership. On the open-ended question, "The youth ministry of our congregation would die if. . .," the most common response of pastors and youth ministers was: "if we lose our committed, loving, and dedicated adult leaders in youth ministry." Some of these pastors and youth ministers referred to specific to adult leaders, identifying their passion for youth ministry and commitment to Christ, their care for young people, and their interest in serving.

The Faith of Adult Leaders in Youth Ministry

The strong, vital, mature faith of adult leaders in youth ministry is one of the most important contributors to youth ministries that nurture young people of vital, committed Christian faith. Adult leaders are committed to Jesus Christ and experience the presence of God in their daily lives and relationships with others. Their faith helps them decide what is right or wrong, and take responsibility for serving those in need. They feel competent when teaching the Bible and faith traditions of the church (history, beliefs, practices), and talking with other people about their faith. They seek out opportunities to help me grow spiritually. (See Table 15 for complete results.)

Relational Characteristics

Adult leaders form trusted relationships with young people and their parents as evidenced in the high scores from the survey findings. Adult leaders enjoy spending time with youth, and youth enjoy spending time with them. They feel that they are effective working with youth, and make good decisions in their work with youth. They know how to nurture youth's spiritual walk. (See Table 15 for complete results.)

Training

A systematic plan for training adult leaders in youth ministry is a vitally important part of youth ministry, no matter the size of congregation or the number of leaders. Effective adult youth leaders are the result of intentional efforts at recruiting, training, and encouraging adults with the requisite gifts willing to give of themselves to ministry. There is a strong relationship between effective adult leaders and the training provided in youth ministry as identified in the survey findings from adult leaders, pastors, and youth ministers. (See Table 15 for complete results.)

Adult leaders in EYM congregations express satisfaction with their ministry. They are satisfied with the opportunities given to them to use their abilities in youth ministry and feel appropriately appreciated and affirmed as an adult leader.

The Leadership of Adults

The adult leaders in youth ministry sense a call to work with youth and follow this call with passion and dedication. One can see this passion in the observations of the study's site researchers: "There is a team of dedicated volunteer youth leaders who are spiritual role models, deeply invested in the lives of the youth they teach." "The youth leaders do a great job of greeting and talking with the students and making them feel welcome." "A cadre of strong passionate leaders, paid staff and hundreds of committed lay people working in teams, generate the spirit and culture that are at the heart of this ministry." A youth in one of the congregations remarked: "They (adult leaders) will go to the ends of the earth for us."

The "twenty-something" pre-med student in one EYM congregation serves as one of the co-leaders of the team that guides youth and family ministry. She's joined on this leadership team by a mother of three young men in the congregation. These two adult leaders dedicate many long hours, go off to get training, and are designated as the unpaid, yet called youth ministers in their church.

Adult leaders at another EYM congregation go beyond Sunday morning in their involvement with young people. They attend the Wednesday evening youth Bible study and build relationships with their class members and friends who come with them. One student said of an adult youth leader: "He brings me to concerts and spends time with me." A young woman said of her faith mentor: "She gets on my level." Another youth said, "The adults get behind what you are doing. They help you with your school work and they repeat stuff so you can remember."

Dedicated adult leaders were particularly present in the congregations with confirmation ministries. As a dimension of confirmation at one EYM congregation adult leaders are "Shepherds" maintaining weekly contact with a young person for five months. During these weekly contacts they journal, talk about faith issues, discuss concerns of the young person, and play together.

A final distinctive characteristic of the adult leaders in the study is their dedication and long-tenured service. Adult leaders who serve for longer periods of time seem to be an important positive factor in the faith maturity of youth. Longevity among leaders is a vision to be stated and nurtured. Congregations build an environment in which youth ministry is valued and long-term youth ministry leadership a calling. They discuss with current adult leaders the expectations of those who serve in youth ministry. Churches provide resources to sustain adult youth leadership long term.

Youth Leadership

One of the significant discoveries in the study was the large number of young people in leadership. Congregations, large and small, intentionally involve youth in leadership. They develop youth leaders, share real responsibilities, and delegate tasks. They encourage young people in leadership by providing resources and training throughout the life and ministries of their congregations.

Young people lead congregational activities: teaching classes, guiding worship, serving on committees, and helping with programs and events. As a result, these young people mature in their faith, develop important leadership skills, and are drawn more deeply into the life of the congregation. Young people who are apprenticed into leadership are more likely to develop more mature levels of faith. Congregations develop strategies for discovering and utilizing young people's strengths and spiritual gifts.

Youth lead through expressions of faith and servant witness. They speak privately and publically about their faith with others in the congregation. They bring their friends to worship, Bible studies, youth activities, mission trips, retreats, and youth events. Younger youth watch their older peers and learn from their example. Congregations benefit from this witness of young people—young people lead others in the church to greater engagement in ministry.

Young people in EYM congregations are given opportunities to exercise their gifts and talents in worship, education, music, and service. They are considered as able and gifted as the adults in the congregation. Many congregations utilize Bible studies around spiritual giftedness and gift inventories as a framework for identifying young peoples' gifts and strengths. Identifying these young peoples' gifts and apprenticing them into leadership begins in the early grades and continues through high school.

Youth also lead through relationships with their peers. Many of the churches in the study have embedded a sense of responsibility for mentoring the young into the culture of the congregation. High school youth are apprenticed into leadership by serving as mentors, small group co-leaders, and big brothers and sisters to their younger counterparts. They often serve as team leaders in their youth ministries. As young people lead youth ministry activities adults are guiding, mentoring and coaching.

Youth, parents, adult leaders, pastors, and youth ministers all affirm the importance peer ministry in their congregations. Survey findings identified five strong characteristics of the practice of peer ministry in EYM congregations.

1. Our peer ministry youth have intentionally established friendships with other youth who need help.
2. Our peer ministers are likely to stick-up for someone who is laughed at or mocked.
3. Adult mentors guide peer ministers' efforts to do ministry work.
4. Our youth have had peer ministry training in how to reach others needing help or friendship.
5. Troubled youth at school have sought help from our peer ministers.

EYM youth ministries take an "empowerment approach" to leadership. They develop youth leaders, share real responsibilities with them, and delegate them tasks. They encourage young people in leadership by providing resources and training throughout the life and ministries of their congregations.

Conclusion

At its best youth ministry is a team effort. Congregations may imagine that one person can be hired or enlisted to lead or manage or do their youth ministry, thus relieving the church or further responsibilities for work with young people. However, the EYM Study emphasizes the power of involving the entire congregation with its variety of people, relationships, and practices in ministry with youth.

When the pastors and youth ministers in all 131 EYM congregations were asked to respond to the open-end question regarding the key structural/organizational components to your youth ministry, they emphasized a team approach to youth ministry. They identified a leadership group that works with the youth minister to provide oversight and direction. This group was named in a variety of ways: a youth executive board, a youth ministry committee or team, a youth council, and so on. They also described a team approach involving youth and adults. This often took the form of an adult leader working with a number of youth in planning and carrying out one or more youth events.

Leadership teams, made up of youth, adult youth leaders, parents, and other church members work together to envision and oversee youth ministry and the variety of its programs and activities. Leadership teams are responsible for planning and tending the varied practices and relationships of the youth ministry. The teams do not have to be large to be effective—smaller churches in the EYM Study have teams of three to four people.

Jeffrey Jones reminds us about the importance of a team approach in congregations.

> *The leader of the future isn't a person. It is a team. It is a group of people gifted and called by God to lead. It is a community drawn together by a sense of the possible within a congregation and committed to making God's kingdom just a bit more real in their time and place. This fact alone changes the notions of leadership that pastors and congregations have operated under for years. It breaks down barriers between professional and lay leaders. It refocuses our attention on gifts and call as being the basis for ministry.*

The focus on gifts and call leads us to a new humility about leadership. It reminds us that no one has all the gifts, but all the gifts are present within the Body. This is why a leadership team is essential for the future. When the challenges before us are great we need to take advantage of every gift God has given. That is only possible if we approach the task of leadership as a team.

Someone will need to see his or her primary call as bringing together the group . . . That responsibility requires the eyes of Jesus to see the gifts in others and call them into ministry . . . The team leader's responsibility will be to gather those who are needed, guide the development of a common vision for their work, and support and encourage their efforts.

No matter what size the congregation, pastors and youth ministers in EYM congregations do not do youth ministry alone. The congregation—leadership teams, adult leaders, parents, and youth leaders—work together to make youth ministry vibrant and effective. Committed and competent leadership is at the heart of the EYM congregations' faithful and effective ministries with youth. These ministries combine knowledgeable pastors, valued youth ministers, committed adult and youth leaders, with dedicated parents and supportive church leadership councils and teams in "cultures of shared leadership."

For Further Study: Leadership

Barton, Ruth Haley. *Strengthening the Soul of Your Leadership*. Downers Grove: InterVarsity, 2008.

Blanchard, Ken, et al. *Leading at a Higher Level*. Upper Saddle River: Prentice Hall, 2007.

Blanchard , Ken and Phil Hodges. *Lead Like Jesus*. Nashville: W, 2005.

Doohan, Leonard. *Spiritual Leadership: The Quest for Integrity*. New York: Paulist, 2007.

Geoffrion, Timothy. *The Spirit-Led Leader*. Herdon: Alban, 2005.

Harney, Kevin. *Leadership from the Inside Out: Examining the Inner Life of a Healthy Church Leader*. Grand Rapids: Zondervan, 2007.

Jones, Jeffrey D. *Heart, Mind, and Strength: Theory and Practice for Congregational Leadership*. Herdon: Alban, 2008.

McCormick, Blaine and David Davenport. *Shepherd Leadership*. San Francisco: Jossey Bass, 2003.

Maxwell, John C. and Tim Elmore, executive editors. *The Maxwell Leadership Bible*. Nashville: Thomas Nelson, 2007.

Robinson, Anthony B. *Leadership for Vital Congregations*. Cleveland: Pilgrim, 2006.

Sofield, Loughlan, and Carroll Juliano, SHCJ. *Collaboration: Uniting Our Gifts in Ministry*. Notre Dame: Ave Maria, 2000

Sofield, ST,. Loughlan and Donald Kuhn. *The Collaborative Leader*. Notre Dame: Ave Maria, 1995.

For Further Study: Developing Leaders

DeVries, Mark. *Sustainable Youth Ministry.* Downers Grove: InterVarsity, 2008.

Eckert, Ann Marie. "Youth Ministry Leadership." *Leadership for Catholic Youth Ministry: A Comprehensive Resource.* New London: Twenty-Third, 2009.

Eckert, Ann Marie with Maria Sanchez-Keane. *Total Youth Ministry: Youth Leadership Development.* Winona: Saint Mary's, 2004.

McKee Jonathan and Thomas W. McKee. *The New Breed: Understanding and Equipping the Twenty-First Century Volunteer.* Loveland: Group, 2008.

Malloy, Sue. *The Equipping Church: Serving Together to Transform Lives.* Grand Rapids: Zondervan, 2001.

Morgan, Tony and Tim Stevens. *Simply Strategic Volunteers: Empowering People for Ministry.* Loveland: Group, 2005.

Powell, Kara and the Fuller Youth Institute. *Essential Leadership: Ministry Team Meetings that Work.* Grand Rapids: Zondervan, 2009.

Trumbaurer, Jean Morris. *Created and Called: Discovering Our Gifts for Abundant Living.* Minneapolis: Augsburg Fortress, 1998.

Trumbaurer, Jean Morris. *Sharing the Ministry: A Practical Guide for Transforming Volunteers into Ministers.* Minneapolis: Augsburg Fortress, 1998

Wilson, Marlene, general editor and author. *Group's Volunteer Leadership Series.* Loveland: Group, 2004.

TABLE 13

Leadership of the Pastor

Overview

Responses from Youth: 2 Dimensions	Youth[*]
Pastor's Spiritual Influence	7.37
Pastor's Personal Characteristics	7.13

Responses from Parents: 5 Dimensions	Parents
Effectiveness of Pastor's Leadership	7.88
Interpersonal Characteristics	7.80
Pastor's Communication Skills	7.38
Pastor is a Good Counselor	6.82
Pastor Preaches to Make Disciples	6.71

Responses from Adult Leaders in Youth Ministry: 5 Dimensions	Adult Leaders
Pastor Supports Christian Education and Youth Ministry	8.05
Effectiveness of Pastor's Leadership	7.90
Pastor's Communication Skills	7.84
Pastor is a Good Counselor	7.02
Pastor Preaches to Make Disciples	6.80

*Mean scores: highest rating is "9," indicating a response of "Always" or "Almost Always True."

Leadership of the Lead Pastor: 3 Dimensions	Pastor and Youth Minister
Pastoral Support for Youth Staff	7.76
Pastor Creates a Healthy Culture	7.39
Mission is to Make Disciples	6.94

Pastor's Spiritual Influence: Comparison of Responses

* Youth Survey Dimension: "Pastor's Spiritual Influence"
* Parent and Adult Leader Survey Dimension: "Effectiveness of Pastor's Leadership" and "Pastor Preaches to Make Disciples"
* Pastor and Youth Minister Survey Dimension: "Pastor's Mission is to Make Disciples" and "Pastor Creates a Healthy Culture"

Characteristics of Pastor's Spiritual Influence	Youth	Parents	Adult Leaders	Pastor and Youth Minister
Is a person of devout faith.	8.21	-	-	-
Leads an exemplary life.	7.93	8.38	8.40	-
Shares leadership with members chosen for leadership by the congregation.	7.91	8.23	8.16	7.63
Shows the mission of Christ to be first in his or her own life.	7.86	8.37	8.26	7.87
His or her passion is that people come to know Jesus Christ.	7.62	-	-	7.70
Helps people use the resources of faith in coping with personal problems.	7.52	7.92	7.84	7.77
Treats the Bible as the final authority in all matters of faith.	7.40	-	-	-
Relates well to youth.	7.23	7.58	7.51	-

Creates an atmosphere in the congregation that is enlivened by the Gospel spirit of freedom and love.	7.08	7.20	7.28	7.01
When he or she is through preaching, you are conscious of Jesus Christ.	6.93	7.47	7.48	7.36
Helps members feel confident in sharing their faith with non-members.	6.81	6.55	6.62	5.94
Preaches sermons that awaken listeners to their sinfulness and need for a Savior.	6.49	6.46	6.60	6.19
People are converted as a result of his or her ministry.	6.46	6.25	6.44	5.96
Shows an active concern for the oppressed.	-	7.83	7.91	7.16
People are changed as a result of his or her ministry.	-	7.46	7.67	7.28

Pastor's Interpersonal Competence: Comparison of Responses

- Youth Survey Dimension: "Pastor's Personal Characteristics"
- Parent Survey Dimension: "Pastor's Communication Skills," "Pastor's Interpersonal Characteristics" and "Pastor is a Good Counselor"
- Adult Leader Survey Dimension: "Pastor's Communication Skills"
- Pastor and Youth Minister Survey Dimension: "Pastor Creates a Healthy Culture"

Characteristics of Pastor's Spiritual Influence	Youth	Parents	Adult Leaders	Pastor and Youth Minister
The pastor is a good speaker.	7.39	7.53	7.60	-
The pastor is good listener.	7.24	6.78	7.04	-
The pastor is supportive.	7.22	7.07	7.28	-
The pastor is a easy to understand.	7.20	7.55	7.64	-
The pastor is easy to talk to.	6.92	6.78	6.95	-
The pastor is inspiring.	6.83	6.99	-	-

The pastor is around when needed.	-	6.65	6.80	-
The pastor promotes activities which build a sense of congregational family.	-	7.73	-	7.43
The pastor gives pastoral service to all people with needs.	-	7.63	-	7.61
The pastor has trouble relating to members. (Reverse-scored)	-	8.11	-	-
The pastor is insensitive to the congregation. (Reverse-scored)	-	8.49	-	-
The pastor creates opportunities for people to air their differences.	-	-	-	6.89

Pastor's Support: Comparison of Responses

- Adult Leader Survey Dimension: "Pastor Supports Christian Education and Youth Ministry"
- Pastor and Youth Minister Survey Dimension: "Pastor Support for Youth Staff"

Characteristics of Pastor's Support	Adult Leaders	Pastor and Youth Minister
The pastor is enthusiastic about Christian education	8.33	-
The pastor shows a deep commitment to youth ministry.	8.07	-
The pastor is involved in doing Christian education.	7.71	-
I feel trusted by my pastor.	-	8.23
The pastor or supervisor shows an interest in what I am doing.	-	7.90
Doing things in new and creative ways is appreciated by my pastor or supervisor.	-	7.89
The pastor relates well to youth.	-	7.02

TABLE 14

Leadership of the Youth Minister

Overview of Four Dimensions of the Leadership of the Youth Minister

Dimensions	Youth	Parents	Adult Leaders*
1. Youth Minister's Positive Characteristics	7.87	-	-
2. Youth Minister's Competence	-	8.00	7.95
3. Youth Minister's Leadership	-	8.14	-
4. Youth Minister's Effectiveness	-	-	7.83

Youth Minister's Positive Characteristics and Competence: Comparison of Responses

Characteristics of Youth Minister's Positive Characteristics and Competence	Parents	Adult Leaders	Pastors and Youth Ministers
• Our youth minister is a person of devout faith.	8.23	-	-
• Our youth minister is a good counselor of youth.	8.06	-	-
• Our youth minister tries to do things in new and creative ways.	7.98	-	-
• I enjoy spending time with our youth minister.	7.91	-	-

*Mean scores: highest rating is "9," indicating a response of "Always" or "Almost Always True."

Our youth minister is an effective model for adult youth workers of how to do youth ministry	7.93	8.06	8.04
Our youth minister keeps up with changes in the youth culture.	7.87	-	
Our youth minister leads an exemplary life.	7.87	8.25	8.26
Our youth minister's leadership style produces other leaders.	7.79	-	
Our youth minister does a good job of helping me on my spiritual journey.	7.73	-	-
The youth ministry regularly accomplishes goals under our youth minister's leadership.	7.80	7.96	7.95
Our youth minister is a good delegator.	7.79	7.68	7.53
Our youth minister easily recruits adult youth workers.	7.65	-	7.35
Our youth minister is a good organizer.	7.69	7.84	7.66
Our youth minister makes good decisions about youth ministry.	-	8.23	8.28
Our youth minister is competent.		8.50	8.51
Our youth minister makes working with parents an important part of his or her work.	-	7.40	7.16
I relate well to our youth minister.	-	8.06	8.23

Youth Minister's Leadership and Effectiveness: Comparison of Responses

Characteristics of Youth Minister's Leadership and Effectiveness	Parents	Adult Leaders
I trust our youth minister.	8.56	-
I respect our youth minister.	8.54	-
Our youth minister is well equipped to train adult youth workers.	7.87	-
Our youth minister's leadership style produces other leaders.	7.59	-

- Our youth minister is effective.   -   8.28
- Doing things in new and creative ways is appreciated
  by my youth minister.   -   8.20
- Our youth minister shows an interest in what I am doing.   -   7.94
- Our youth minister is well equipped to prepare parents
  for youth ministry leadership.   -   7.37

TABLE 15

Adult Leaders in Youth Ministry

1. Faith Characteristics: Results from Adult Leaders in Youth Ministry Survey

Dimension: God Consciousness   8.57*

- I have a sense that my prayers have been answered by God. (8.72)
- I have a sense of sharing in a great purpose. (8.59)
- I have a sense of being saved in Christ. (8.51)
- I have had feelings of being in the presence of God. (8.45)

Dimension: Moral Responsibility   8.06

- The kind of moral decisions I make now will affect my future happiness. (8.27)
- God helps me decide what is right or wrong behavior. (8.09)
- When people wrong other people, they sin against God. (7.82)

Dimension: Centrality of Faith   7.47

- My life is committed to Jesus Christ. (8.17)
- I am spiritually moved by the beauty of God's creations. (8.09)
- My life is filled with meaning and purpose. (7.67)
- I have a real sense that God is guiding me. (7.64)
- I feel God's presence in my relationships with others. (7.40)
- I seek out opportunities to help me grow spiritually. (7.35)
- I talk with other people about my faith. (7.07)
- I help others with their religious questions and struggles. (6.33)

*Mean scores: highest rating is "9," indicating a response of "Always" or "Almost Always True."

Dimension: Theological Competence   **6.70**

- I feel incompetent when teaching the Bible and faith traditions of the church (history, beliefs, practices). (Reverse scored) (7.20)
- I feel inadequate in discussing theological issues. (Reverse scored) (6.97)
- My youth ministry is theologically based. (6.82)
- I have a good grasp of theological concepts. (6.49)
- I am confident in my knowledge of Scripture. (6.04)

Dimension: Social Responsibility   **6.56**

- I try to apply my faith to political and social issues. (6.92)
- I give significant portions of time and money to help other people. (6.69)
- I feel a deep sense of responsibility for reducing pain and suffering in the world. (6.44)
- I care a great deal about reducing poverty in the U.S. and throughout the world. (6.21)

2. Relational Characteristics: Results from Adult Leaders in Youth Ministry Survey

Dimension: Positive Relationship with Youth   **7.07**

- I enjoy spending time with youth. (7.92)
- I feel I make good decisions in my work with youth. (7.36)
- I feel competent working with youth. (7.27)
- My youth enjoy spending time with me. (7.25)
- I am effective working with youth. (7.13)
- Young people open up to me easily. (6.94)
- Youth affirm me often. (6.82)
- I have a philosophy of youth ministry. (6.51)
- I know how to nurture youth's spiritual walk. (6.46)

Dimension: Youth Workers' Relationship with Parents   **6.93**

- I feel respected by the members of my congregation. (7.50)
- I relate well to parents of youth. (7.05)
- I feel valued and loved by the parents of youth. (6.99)
- Working parents is an important part of my work. (6.19)

3. Satisfaction: Results from Adult Leaders in Youth Ministry Survey

Adult Worker Satisfaction   **6.82**

- I am satisfied with the opportunities given to me to use my abilities in youth ministry. (7.42)
- I am seeing results from our youth ministry. (7.08)
- Youth ministry is leading the congregation to place a high priority on youth ministry. (6.66)
- Youth ministry has an agreed-upon philosophy of youth ministry. (6.63)
- I feel appropriately appreciated as an adult youth worker. (6.61)
- I receive the affirmation I would like. (6.57)

4. Training for Adult Leaders in Youth Ministry

- Adult Leader Survey Dimension: "Training of Adult Youth Workers" (5.52) and "Training Emphasis" (5.12)
- Pastor and Youth Minister Survey Dimension: "Training Leaders" (5.83)

	Adult Leaders	Pastors and Youth Ministers
• Adult youth workers gather to coordinate and plan Christian education.	7.46	-
• Adult youth workers and teachers are carefully screened.	-	7.24
• Adult youth workers gather to discuss the goals and objectives of Christian education	6.30	-
• Adult youth workers meet to help each other deal with specific problems and challenges.	6.14	-
• Adult youth workers gather for their own spiritual formation.	5.61	-
• Adult youth workers are given instruction in effective teaching methods	5.57	-
• Adult youth workers and teachers are carefully trained before teaching or leading a program.	5.50	6.33

• People in our congregation willing participate in training programs that equip them for service.	5.39	5.47
• In-service training events are provided for adult youth workers.	5.20	-
• Our congregation's youth minister has a systematic plan for training adult youth workers.	-	4.63
• Evaluation is a regular part of training leaders in our church.	4.50	5.40
• Adult youth workers are evaluated.	2.65	-

APPLICATION TOOL 13

Pastor Reflection Tool

Use this reflection tool to view your ministry through the eyes of the EYM findings on the pastor's influence in the congregation and youth ministry. Identify your strengths and areas for growth.

The Pastor's Spiritual Influence

		Rating*			
1.	The pastor is a person of devout faith.	1	2	3	4
2.	The pastor leads an exemplary life.	1	2	3	4
3.	The pastor shows the mission of Christ to be first in his or her own life.	1	2	3	4
4.	The pastor's passion is that people come to know Jesus Christ.	1	2	3	4
5.	The pastor treats the Bible as the final authority in all matters of faith.	1	2	3	4
6.	The pastor shows an active concern for the oppressed.	1	2	3	4
7.	The pastor creates an atmosphere in the congregation that is enlivened by the Gospel spirit of freedom and love.	1	2	3	4
8.	When the pastor is through preaching, you are conscious of Jesus Christ.	1	2	3	4
9.	The pastor preaches sermons that awaken listeners to their sinfulness and need for a Savior.	1	2	3	4

*Rating: 1= needs growth/improvement, 2=satisfactory, 3=good, 4=a real strength

	Rating

10. People are converted as a result of the pastor's ministry.　　　1　2　3　4

11. People are changed as a result of the pastor's ministry.　　　1　2　3　4

12. The pastor helps members feel confident in sharing their faith with non-members.　　　1　2　3　4

13. The pastor shares leadership with members chosen for leadership by the congregation.　　　1　2　3　4

14. The pastor helps people use the resources of faith in coping with personal problems.　　　1　2　3　4

15. The pastor relates well to youth.　　　1　2　3　4

The Pastor's Interpersonal Competence

16. The pastor is a good speaker and easy to understand.　　　1　2　3　4

17. The pastor is good listener and easy to talk to.　　　1　2　3　4

18. The pastor is supportive.　　　1　2　3　4

19. The pastor is inspiring.　　　1　2　3　4

20. The pastor gives pastoral service to all people with needs.　　　1　2　3　4

21. The pastor relates well to members.　　　1　2　3　4

22. The pastor is sensitive to the congregation.　　　1　2　3　4

23. The pastor promotes activities which build a sense of congregational family.　　　1　2　3　4

24. The pastor creates opportunities for people to air their differences.　　　1　2　3　4

The Pastor's Support

25. The pastor is enthusiastic about Christian education. 1 2 3 4

26. The pastor shows a deep commitment to youth ministry. 1 2 3 4

27. The pastor is involved in doing Christian education. 1 2 3 4

28. The pastor trusts the leaders in youth ministry. 1 2 3 4

29. The pastor shows an interest in what I am doing. 1 2 3 4

30. The pastor appreciates leaders doing things in new and creative ways. 1 2 3 4

31. The pastor relates well to youth. 1 2 3 4

Planning for Growth

Use these questions for each learning need you have selected.

- What is the learning need or area for growth?
- *How can you go about learning or improving in this area?* Consider independent learning, mentoring/coaching, small group learning, and organized educational programs such as courses, workshops, conferences. Consider online learning resources, courses, and programs as well.
- *How will you go about learning/improving?* Develop a learning plan which addresses the following elements:
  - What do you want to learn?
  - How will you go about learning it?
  - What material resources will you need?
  - What people resources will you need?
  - How long will it take you?
  - How will you know you demonstrate your proficiency in this area?
  - How will you evaluate your learning experience?

APPLICATION TOOL 14

Youth Minister Reflection Tool

Use this reflection tool to view your ministry through the eyes of the EYM findings on the youth minister. Identify your strengths and areas for growth.

		Rating*
1.	The youth minister is a person of devout faith.	1 2 3 4
2.	The youth minister leads an exemplary life.	1 2 3 4
3.	The youth minister cares for his or her own spiritual, social, and physical well-being.	1 2 3 4
4.	The youth minister has a good working knowledge of the Bible.	1 2 3 4
5.	The youth minister has a good working knowledge of the Christian faith.	1 2 3 4
6.	The youth minister relates well to a diversity of young people.	1 2 3 4
7.	The youth minister is a good counselor of youth.	1 2 3 4
8.	The youth minister keeps up with changes in the youth culture.	1 2 3 4
9.	The youth minister does a good job of helping youth on their spiritual journey.	1 2 3 4
10.	The youth minister assists the congregation in understanding the goals and activities of youth ministry, and in supporting youth ministry.	1 2 3 4

*Rating: 1= needs growth/improvement, 2=satisfactory, 3=good, 4=a real strength

11. The youth minister regularly accomplishes the youth ministry's goals.

1 2 3 4

12. The youth minister is a good organizer.

1 2 3 4

13. The youth minister works well with teams of adults and youth in leading the youth ministry and providing programs and activities.

1 2 3 4

14. The youth minister makes good decisions about youth ministry.

1 2 3 4

15. The youth minister tries to do things in new and creative ways.

1 2 3 4

16. The youth minister is a good delegator.

1 2 3 4

17. The youth minister's leadership style produces other leaders.

1 2 3 4

18. The youth minister discovers the gifts and talents of adults and youth for ministry.

1 2 3 4

19. The youth minister is an effective model for adult youth workers of how to do youth ministry.

1 2 3 4

20. The youth minister recruits adult and youth leaders in youth ministry.

1 2 3 4

21. The youth minister trains adult and youth leaders in youth ministry.

1 2 3 4

22. The youth ministry shows appreciation for adult and youth leaders doing things in new and creative ways.

1 2 3 4

23. The youth minister relates well to parents and adult leaders in youth ministry.

1 2 3 4

24. The youth minister makes working with parents an important part of his or her work.

1 2 3 4

25. The youth minister is well equipped to prepare parents for youth ministry leadership.

1 2 3 4

Planning for Growth

Use these questions for each learning need you have selected.

- What is the learning need or area for growth?

- *How can you go about learning or improving in this area?* Consider independent learning, mentoring/coaching, small group learning, and organized educational programs such as courses, workshops, conferences. Consider online learning resources, courses, and programs as well.

- *How will you go about learning/improving?* Develop a learning plan which addresses the following elements:

  - What do you want to learn?

  - How will you go about learning it?

  - What material resources will you need?

  - What people resources will you need?

  - How long will it take you?

  - How will you know you demonstrate your proficiency in this area?

  - How will you evaluate your learning experience?

APPLICATION TOOL 15

Servant Leadership Reflection

The *Heart* of the Servant Leader—Motivation

Rating*

1. I depend on the work of the Holy Spirit in my life and relationships. R O F C

2. I actively seek and encourage feedback on my leadership. R O F C

3. I take personal risk to support and protect others. R O F C

4. I share credit for the result of my group's efforts. R O F C

5. I avoid letting my own self-interests and needs negatively impact my leadership. R O F C

The *Head* of the Servant Leader—Leadership Point of View

6. I align my leadership point of view to that of the Scriptures. R O F C

7. I treat growth and development of people as being equally important as producing results. R O F C

8. I develop, communicate, and reinforce a clear vision and set of rank-ordered operating values for my group. R O F C

9. I communicate my leadership point of view to members of my organization. R O F C

*Rating Scale: R = rarely, O = once in a while, F = frequently, C = consistently

The *Hands* of the Servant Leader—Leadership Behavior

10. I practice the role of a performance coach, empowering others for their work.   R O F C

11. I test for understanding and establish clear performance goals when assigning tasks within my group.   R O F C

12. I apply different leadership styles depending on the development level of the individuals assigned to perform specific tasks.   R O F C

13. I praise progress and am actively engaged in day-to-day coaching.   R O F C

14. I take positive action to resist the temptations to manipulate the fears and pride of others to get things done.   R O F C

The *Habits* of the Servant Leader—Daily Recalibration

15. I call upon the Holy Spirit to guide my words, thoughts, actions, and behaviors.   R O F C

16. I practice the discipline of solitude.   R O F C

17. I employ prayer as my first response instead of my last resort in meeting the challenges, temptations, and opportunities of my work.   R O F C

18. I seek God's wisdom in the study of Scripture to stay focused on being a servant leader.   R O F C

19. I maintain active accountability relationships to keep making progress on my good intentions as a servant leader.   R O F C

My Most Important Learning Needs

- The leadership motivation-related actions (Heart) I need to focus on for improvement are:

- The leadership point of view-related actions (Head) I want to focus on for improvement are:

- The leadership behavior-related actions (Hands) I want to focus on for improvement are:

- The leadership habits I want to focus on for improvement are:

Servant Leadership Bible Study

To explore more deeply the biblical teaching on Servant Leadership read and reflect upon each of the ten passages below. Focus on one per day as part of your daily prayer time. Reflect on Bible's understanding and how you can grow as a servant leader who walks in the footsteps of *the* servant leader, Jesus Christ.

1. John 13:1-17 (Jesus, Servant Leader)
2. Mark 10:35-45 (To Serve, Not Be Served)
3. Isaiah 52:13—53:12 (Jesus, The Suffering Servant)
4. Mark 9:33-37 (The First Must Be Last)
5. Luke 22:24-30 (The Greatest Is the One Who Serves)
6. Revelation 5:1-14 (Jesus, the Ultimate Servant Leader)
7. 1 Timothy 5:1-25 (Servant Leadership and Power)
8. Hebrews 4:14-16 (Leading by Serving)
9. Acts 4:36-37, 9:26-30, 13—14 (Barnabas, Servant Leader)
10. Philippians 2:19-24 (Timothy, Servant Leader)

Learn More about Servant Leadership

Blanchard, Ken and Phil Hodges. *Lead Like Jesus.* Nashville: W, 2005.

Doohan, Leonard. *Spiritual Leadership—The Quest for Integrity.* New York: Paulist, 2007.

Geoffrion, Timothy. *The Spirit-Led Leader.* Herdon: Alban, 2005.

Harney, Kevin. *Leadership from the Inside Out—Examining the Inner Life of a Healthy Church Leader.* Grand Rapids: Zondervan, 2007.

Jones, Jeffrey D. *Heart, Mind, and Strength: Theory and Practice for Congregational Leadership.* Herdon: Alban, 2008.

McCormick, Blaine and David Davenport. *Shepherd Leadership.* San Francisco: Jossey Bass, 2003.

A P P L I C A T I O N
T O O L   1 6

Spiritual Leadership: Deepening Your Spiritual Life

Use as many of the following questions as you wish to help you reflect on your spiritual life today and, perhaps, ways that you would like to grow in your spiritual life as a leader.

1. Which spiritual practices do you engage in?

	Daily	Weekly	Monthly	Yearly
• Solitude and silence				
• Reflecting on Scripture (Lectio Divina)				
• Daily Examen: God in Daily Life				
• Keeping Sabbath				
• Weekend worship at your church				
• Daily devotional and Bible reading				
• Keeping a journal				
• Praying in nature				
• Contemplative prayer				
• Scriptural prayer				
• Intercessory prayer				
• Praise prayer				
• Thanksgiving prayer				
• Jesus prayer				
• Other:				
• Other:				

2. How is your prayer life today? Consider the following questions:

    *   When do you pray?
    *   Where do you pray?
    *   What do you do during your prayer time—e.g., read the Bible, contemplate, listen to music, be silent, or recite traditional prayers?

    *   What do you pray *for* or pray *about*?

3. How has your prayer life changed or grown or evolved over the course of your life? What was your prayer life like when you were a child? a teenager? a young adult? a midlife adult? an older adult? (Answer as many as apply to you.)

4. Which prayer traditions have been helpful to you? How? When? Why, or why not?

5. What new ways of praying have you tried? Have they been helpful? How? Why, or why not?

6. Has there ever been a time when you made no effort to pray and "gave things a rest," either inadvertently or on purpose, in your prayer life? Why? What was this like? Looking back, can you see any benefits from this experience?

7. Have you ever felt "stuck" in your prayer? When? How? What do you do about it?

8. Has they ever been a time when you couldn't pray, but felt sustained by the prayers offered on your behalf?

9. Have you experienced any change in God's faithfulness to you?

10. Have you experienced any change in your faithfulness to God?

11. When were the prayer times when you felt closest to God? Why?

12. Would you say that prayer is an integral part of your everyday life today? Why or why not? If not, how could it be?

Resources for Developing Your Spiritual Life

Barton, Ruth Haley. *Strengthening the Soul of Your Leadership.* Downers Grove: InterVarsity, 2008.

Barton, Ruth Haley Barton. *Sacred Rhythms: Arranging Our Lives for Spiritual Transformation.* Downers Grove: InterVarsity, 2006.

Benson, Robert. *In Constant Prayer.* Nashville: Thomas Nelson, 2008.

Calhoun, Adele Ahlberg. *Spiritual Disciplines Handbook—Practices That Transform Us.* Downers Grove: InterVarsity, 2005.

McLaren, Brian. *Finding Our Way Again—The Return of the Ancient Christian Practices.* Nashville: Thomas Nelson, 2008.

Redmont, Jane. *When in Doubt, Sing: Prayer in Daily Life.* Notre Dame: Sorin, 2008.

Rhoades, Tricia McCary. *Sacred Chaos: Spiritual Disciplines for the Life You Have.* Downers Grove: InterVarsity, 2008.

Rupp, Joyce. *Prayer.* Maryknoll: Orbis, 2007.

Thompson, Marjorie. *Soul Feast: An Invitation to the Christian Spiritual Life.* Louisville: Westminster/John Knox, 2005.

Wicks, Robert J. *Prayerfulness—Awakening the Fullness of Life.* Notre Dame: Sorin, 2009.

Wolpert, Daniel. *Creating a Life with God: The Call of Ancient Prayer Practices.* Nashville: Upper Room, 2003.

Wolpert, Daniel. *Leading a Life with God: The Practice of Spiritual Leadership.* Nashville: Upper Room, 2003.

APPLICATION
TOOL 17

A Checklist for Developing Leadership

The checklist includes the major tasks of developing leaders (adult and youth). Rate your effectiveness in each area. Then identify the areas you need to improve and develop a plan for improvement.

Inviting People into Leadership
<u>Rating*</u>

1. We list all the tasks and positions for which leaders are needed.   1 2 3 4 5

2. We write a job description for each leadership position.   1 2 3 4 5

3. We use a variety of personal strategies for inviting leaders.   1 2 3 4 5

4. We use a variety of church-wide strategies for inviting leaders.   1 2 3 4 5

5. We survey the congregation to discover ministry gifts, abilities, and interests (e.g., a time and talent survey).   1 2 3 4 5

6. We search throughout the year for persons with leadership potential.   1 2 3 4 5

7. We maintain an up-to-date database of potential leaders.   1 2 3 4 5

8. We select each prospective leader based on a thorough knowledge of both the job and the person.   1 2 3 4 5

9. We interview each person and explain the responsibilities involved.   1 2 3 4 5

10. We carefully screen prospective leaders through background checks.   1 2 3 4 5

11. With each leader, we establish a clear agreement regarding the responsibilities and terms of his or her service.   1 2 3 4 5

*1 = do not do this   2 = poor   3 = satisfactory   4 = good   5 = a real strength

Preparing and Training Leaders

12. We customize the training to each leader and leadership position.　　1 2 3 4 5

13. We use a variety of learning approaches including independent learning, mentoring, small group learning, and training programs (workshops, courses, conferences, etc.)　　1 2 3 4 5

14. We provide an orientation program for all leaders.　　1 2 3 4 5

15. We develop a training plan to prepare for leaders/facilitators/teachers for their responsibilities.　　1 2 3 4 5

16. All leaders participate in the training they need.　　1 2 3 4 5

17. We evaluate the effectiveness of the training with leaders.　　1 2 3 4 5

Supporting Leaders

18. We authorize/commission/bless leaders to begin their service.　　1 2 3 4 5

19. We provide leaders with the resources and information they need.　　1 2 3 4 5

20. We gather information and evaluate the work of leaders.　　1 2 3 4 5

21. We express and celebrate the congregation's appreciation for leaders.　　1 2 3 4 5

We need to strengthen or improve the following areas of our approach to developing leaders . . .

APPLICATION
TOOL 18

Sample Adult and Youth Leader Interest Finder

Name _____

Address _____

Day phone: _____ Evening: _____

E-mail _____

Which age group are you a member of? ☐ 14–18 ☐ 18–30 ☐ 31–55 ☐ 56–70 ☐ 71+

Occupation_____

Marital Status: ☐ Single   ☐ Married   ☐ Separated   ☐ Divorced   ☐ Widowed

Ages of children (if applicable): _____

Availability
☐ Weekday evenings: _____
☐ Friday evening
☐ Saturday
☐ Sunday morning
☐ Sunday afternoon
☐ Sunday evening

Leader Involvement Interests (indicate all that interest you)

☐ I would like to be part of the leadership team responsible for overall <u>coordination</u> of youth ministry.

☐ I would like to help with <u>planning</u> specific programs or activities. (Please check Area of Interest below.)

☐ I would like to <u>conduct</u> or <u>lead</u> specific programs or activities. (Please check area of interest below.)

☐ I would like to help with <u>support</u> tasks (communication, logistics, facility set-up, etc.). (Please check area of interest below.)

Age Groups

I prefer to work with youth in: (check as many as apply)

☐ grades 6-8

☐ grades 9-10

☐ grades 11-12

Youth Ministry Interest and Involvement

Our youth ministry needs your gifts and talents. You can select from a wide variety of leadership positions based on your interests and availability. Please review the list and indicate as many of the leadership positions that interest to you. We will contact you very soon about your choices.

- ☐ **Community Life**
    - ☐ plan and lead social activities
    - ☐ plan and lead sports activities
    - ☐ plan and lead outdoor activities
    - ☐ plan and lead trips
    - ☐ hospitality at youth programs—greeting people, making people feel welcome

- ☐ **Christian Education**
    - ☐ teach a class
    - ☐ assist a teacher
    - ☐ lead a small group

- ☐ **Bible Study Small Group Leader**

- ☐ **Youth Gatherings**
    - ☐ plan and organize programs
    - ☐ serve as a presenter at youth gatherings
    - ☐ serve as a small group leader
    - ☐ manage facilities and logistics

- ☐ **Service Projects**
    - ☐ plan and organize service projects
    - ☐ lead service projects
    - ☐ be a group leader on a mission trip

- ☐ **Prayer and Worship**
    - ☐ prepare prayer services and special worship services
    - ☐ lead a prayer or worship service
    - ☐ lead a prayer group
    - ☐ teach a course on prayer
    - ☐ be a spiritual guide for a young person

- ☐ **Music and Drama**
    - ☐ Lead music at programs
    - ☐ Play a musical instrument: _____
    - ☐ Sing as part of a choir or group
    - ☐ Work on drama presentations
    - ☐ Mentoring Program: work with one-on-one with a young person

- ☐ **Family Programs and Activities**
    - ☐ plan and organize family or parent-teen programs and activities
    - ☐ take a leadership role in presenting a family or parent-teen program
    - ☐ plan and organize parent workshops
    - ☐ take a leadership role in presenting a family or parent-teen program

- ☐ **Retreats**
    - ☐ plan and organize a retreat program
    - ☐ work as a group leader on the retreat
    - ☐ provide support (cooking, set-up, materials)

- ☐ **Media, Arts, and Internet**
    - ☐ Prepare media presentations for youth programs
    - ☐ Manage the website
    - ☐ Create content for the website
    - ☐ Create artwork for youth programming and promotional information
    - ☐ Design promotional materials—print or digital (advertisements, brochures)
    - ☐ Work on a newsletter (print or digital)
    - ☐ Provide decorations for events
    - ☐ Take photos of events

- ☐ Administration
    - ☐ plan and implement fund raising projects
    - ☐ Write articles about the youth ministry
    - ☐ Manage database and keep records
    - ☐ Manage communication
    - ☐ Manage registrations and finances
    - ☐ Manage program logistics (facility, materials, transportation, etc.)

Personal Skills I Bring to Youth Ministry

Skills, interest and hobbies I'm willing to teach interested youth (fishing, outdoor activities, woodworking, cooking, car repair, computers, sewing, craft making, knitting, chess, radio controlled models, art, etc.)

Resources I Can Offer Youth Ministry

For example: use of recreation equipment, vacation cabin, boat, discounts for purchases, novelty items for prizes, use of season tickets for events, business connections, access to facilities, etc.

APPLICATION
TOOL 19

Sample Evaluation of a Ministry Position

Name: _____ **Telephone:** _____

Name of ministry position: _____

Term of the position: from _____ to _____

1. This ministry position has been satisfying for me because:

2. The major frustrations in this ministry position have been:

3. I used the following skills in this ministry position:

4. The training I received for this position included:

5. I felt supported in this position in the following ways:

6. I received the following resources which assisted me in this position:

7. I would have been able to do this ministry better if:

8. The highlights of this ministry for me have been:

9. The major accomplishments which have been achieved through this ministry include:

10. A person following me in this ministry position needs to know:

Please rate each of the following as they enabled you to do this ministry effectively and faithfully by circling the appropriate response:

Rating*

1. The way in which the position was explained before you began.	1 2 3
2. Opportunity to contribute to program planning.	1 2 3
3. Satisfaction with the program plan we are following.	1 2 3
4. Accuracy of your job description.	1 2 3
5. Quality of the orientation to the youth ministry and its goals.	1 2 3
6. Quality and extent of training before you began.	1 2 3
7. Quality and extent of in-service training.	1 2 3
8. Quality and extent of the support you receive.	1 2 3
9. Quality of the supervision and feedback you receive on your job.	1 2 3
10. Opportunity to express your opinions on how our program is going.	1 2 3
11. Degree to which your work is recognized and properly appreciated.	1 2 3
12. The challenge and responsibility you feel in doing your job.	1 2 3

13. Specific ministry opportunities you would like to explore in the future:

14. Factors in your situation that would influence your next ministry position:

Additional comments:

*1 = inadequate   2 = average   3 = outstanding

embracing the spirit and culture of youth ministry in your congregation

The Study of Exemplary Congregations in Youth Ministry is rich in implications for developing and enhancing a congregation's ministry with young people. We have described a new framework for youth ministry, the forty-four Faith Assets, as a way to embrace a more holistic and comprehensive approach to developing a vital, Christian faith in young people. Throughout the book, we have identified the most important findings and provided strategies and tools that congregations can use to implement the research. In this concluding chapter we want to highlight some of these significant findings and suggest several necessary cultural shifts that congregations need to make to truly embrace the "spirit and culture of youth ministry."

Developing Youth of Vital, Committed Christian Faith

Pay Attention to the Culture of the Whole Church

While confirming the power of several well known youth ministry practices, the EYM Study pointed to a congregational culture of the Spirit—something more basic and central in establishing vital faith in youth. The research points to the value of a congregation's culture endowed with a palpable sense of the living, active presence of God at work among the people of the whole congregation, its ministries with youth, its parents, the ministries of the congregation, and its congregational leaders (pastor, youth minister, youth and adult leaders) as providing the most powerful, pervasive influence these congregations have on young people long-term. It is the communal awareness of participation in God's presence and action that permeates the values, relationships, and activities of these congregations, giving rise to an atmosphere, a culture of the Spirit focused on mission and the transformation of life that seems to make them so influential in the lives and faith of young people.

The congregational culture of the Spirit generates four spheres of relationships and practices that intersect and powerfully impact the lives of young people in the EYM congregations.

- *First, these congregations' basic ministries are thoroughly intergenerational. Young people are welcomed and expected to participate and lead in church-wide ministries, including worship, education, fellowship, outreach, and decision-making.*
- *Second, these congregations have developed age-level youth ministries marked by trusted relationships and custom-designed ministry practices and activities within a caring atmosphere of high expectation. There are multiple nurturing relationships and activities intentionally planned to create an atmosphere of respect, growth and belonging.*
- *Third, these congregations educate parents in the faith and equip them for at-home caring conversations, prayer, ritual, Bible reading, and service; and parents and many families are engaged in faith practices at home.*
- *Fourth, these congregations are blessed with competent, faith-filled, leadership from the pastor to the youth minister to the youth and adult leaders who are committed to young people and developing their faith lives.*

Aligning and integrating the intergenerational ministries of the congregation with adolescent age-level ministries and the families/households of the young people, supported by competent, faith-filled leaders (pastors, youth ministers, and youth and adult leaders), generates intersecting arenas of influence that seem to make the work of these congregations so significant in the lives of their committed Christian youth.

Recognize the Power of the Congregation's Theological Commitments

The research shows that the theological commitments of the congregation as a whole become the theological commitments of the congregation's youth ministry. For example, because of the centrality of the Gospel and discipleship in congregational life, knowing Jesus Christ and following him in discipleship are at the core of these congregations' youth ministries. A second example of this dynamic at work is the alignment of the mission/vision statements of the congregation and its youth ministry, reflecting striking similarities of both identity and mission. In part, the power of these congregations and their youth ministries lies in the integration of vision and mission.

When one sets the findings of the EYM Study alongside Scripture and Christianity's long standing understandings of God, humans and ministry one finds significant parallels and alignments. These EYM congregations see God as personal, living presence at work in the community of faith. They understand the community of believers as the ongoing concrete, historical presence of the body of Christ able to bear God's presence and life-giving work in the lives of young people. The entire congregation, not just an individual pastor or youth minister, is understood to be the prime location where the "sociality" of ministry is most faithfully and effectively accomplished. These relationships are accompanied with Bible study, mutual care giving, prayer, and sacrificial commitments in service of God, each other and the world. It seems that their commitments and practices point to and reflect the best of Christianity's understandings of God and the Church. We believe this faithfulness to the Christian tradition to be one of the factors in the depth and breadth of the EYM congregations' effectiveness.

Nurture the Power of Faithful, Multi-Generational Christian Relationships

The hospitality afforded young people was palpable in the EYM congregations. At Sunday worship adults and youth greet each other and groups of adults gather for informal conversation with young people before and after the services. Young people bring their friends to worship because they are valued and the worship services engage them. Young people feel at home in these safe and nurturing communities where their participation, energy, concerns, questions, and faith life are valued. They turn to adults in the congregation for guidance and care. Young people come to know a living and active God through relationships in the community. They get to know Jesus Christ through the witness of believers and ongoing relationships with persons and communities who know Him. The

EYM study presents a picture of welcoming congregations who respect and value young people and their youth ministries. These youth are surrounded by multiple, reinforcing spheres of relational Christian influence, and immersed in a larger, multi-generational community of quality relationships informed by faith in Jesus Christ.

The findings of the EYM study, undergirded by the relational character of God, encourage congregations to use their gifts of community-building as central, shaping elements of their youth ministries. This ministry of community-building has several focal points: relationships between "youth and adults" and between "youth and youth" need to be a priority in congregations; these relationships need to take on a quality and character informed by faith and discipleship; relationships within families need to be nurtured; young people's need for significant relationships both inside and outside the church need attention; and in Christian communities, the focus might well be on the sociality of God and Jesus Christ as the center of all relationships.

The goal of youth ministry is not just to build better relationships, to get along, or to celebrate each other. The goal is for young people to get to know God and serve each other and the world. The Greek word *koinonia* is most often translated as community and used to refer to the communion of saints with each other and with God. If young people experience wholesome friendships in the presence of God and God's people, they can grow in life and faith through these relationships. If these young people are also drawn into relationship with God, the resulting communion bonds them closer together as brothers and sisters in Christ. Other young people can be drawn to God through the witness of God's presence expressed in the love present in their community of faith.

Focus on Discipleship

The purpose of youth ministry in EYM congregations can be summarized in a single goal: *making disciples of Jesus Christ.* These congregations focus their youth ministries on Jesus Christ and engage young people in discipleship, witness, and service that transforms their lives. Effective youth ministries make a significant impact on the personal of faith of young people by deepening their relationship with Jesus, helping them understand the Christian faith better, applying their faith to daily life and serious life choices, and sharing their faith with others.

For EYM congregations youth ministry is first and foremost God conversation and God thinking (theology); then it is working out God's claim on their lives (discipleship and vocation); and, finally, it is God's call into the world (vocation and missiology). At its core, ministry with youth (and adults) is making disciples and apostles. Based on EYM Study we recommend consider the following strategies for strengthening your congregations focus on youth discipleship.

- *Engage adults and youth in thinking about and talking about God's active presence in their lives, relationships, congregation, and world. These conversations can take place in a variety of settings, such as small groups talking about Bible passages, creedal beliefs, faith questions, movie clips, or case studies. It is important that these settings be interactive so every participant can speak, listen and respond.*
- *Pursue ever fuller understandings of Jesus Christ—past, present, and future—through activities such as experiential study of the Gospels, sharing stories of the presence of Christ in each others lives, discipleship groups, and action-reflection service projects and mission trips.*
- *"Bear God to each other" in trusted relationships. Begin by modeling these trusting relationships within the youth ministry leadership team of adults and youth. Develop multiple mentoring relationships with adolescents by engaging adults within the congregation in the lives of young people.*
- *Develop sacred spaces, sacred times and sacred practices for nurturing the spiritual lives of young people and their adult leaders as integral to youth ministry programming.*
- *Incorporate prayer—regular disciplines of personal, small group and congregational prayer—in the flow of everything that happens in youth ministry. Reflect on "Where is God in this experience/activity/relationship?" "How would we know God's guidance in what we are doing or going to do?" "Have we talked with God about this?" "Are we listening or watching for God to lead us?"*
- *Engage in experiential Bible study using a variety of formats for interactive study that combines prayer, reading and discussion of Scripture texts with personal and corporate application and action in response to the group's "conversation" with the Bible and each other.*

Engage Parents and Families in Faith Practice at Home and Church

The Study of Exemplary Congregations in Youth Ministry affirmed what so many other studies have shown: the family matters! parental faith and influence matters! family faith practices matter! The parents in the EYM Study possess a mature, committed Christian faith and this has a profound influence on the lives of young people. Family faith practices—caring conversations, family devotions and prayer, family rituals and traditions, family service—influence the faith lives of young people. Congregations have a important role to play by equipping parents to pass on faith and strengthening family relationships, contributing to the influence of parents and the whole family on the development of youth of vital Christian faith. Congregations can equip parents and the whole family through intentional practices and programs that:

- *deepen the faith of parents*
- *teach about the unique developmental and socio-cultural characteristics of youth today*
- *provide resources and skills training for teaching moral values and sharing faith at home*
- *engage parents and their young people in service activities*
- *develop family and parent-teen communication skills and conflict resolution skills*
- *establish support groups for parents and for families*
- *provide family-centered or parent-teen educational programs*

Apply Common Youth Ministry Practices and Approaches Contextually

The EYM Study identified nine youth ministry practices that were incorporated in each congregation's youth ministry: (1) peer ministry and youth leadership, (2) retreats, (3) service and mission trips, (4) Bible study and religious education, (5) prayer and spiritual formation, (6) spiritual support groups, (7) youth-oriented worship, (8) special events, and (9) family and intergenerational activities. EYM congregations take these common practices and approaches of youth ministry and develop custom-designed, innovative ways to address the particular needs of youth, their families, and the congregation.

The exploration into custom-designed youth ministry practices and approaches reveals that developing a contextually unique expression of a long-standing, common practice can bring fresh meaning and impact to youth ministry. By considering the unique needs and context of youth, leaders can contextualize common practices, making them distinctive and fresh. Second, it also reveals that the variety and scope of youth ministry practices is important. No one strategy will fit everyone. To reach and minister to a larger audience of youth means that the type of events, functions, and opportunities must be varied. Third, it is important to balance congregational integration of young people with age-level ministry practices and support for their families. Effective youth ministry addresses young people's developmental, social, and spiritual needs through "age-level oriented" practices, as well as intergenerational experiences and activities within the larger body of believers and their families.

Cultivate Faith-Filled, Competent, and Committed Leadership

In youth ministry faithful, competent leadership makes the critical difference. In the EYM congregations the excellence in leadership began with the pastor and permeated the entire congregation's life and ministry especially as it focused on young people. No matter what size the congregation, pastors and youth ministers do not do youth ministry alone—it is a team approach. The youth ministry team, adult leaders, parents, and youth leaders work together with the pastor and youth minister.

Pastors matter immensely in effective youth ministry! And they matter in very specific ways! Pastors lead through their spiritual influence, their pastoral effectiveness, their love for and support of young people, and their support of youth ministry leaders. In the EYM congregations, pastors are the most influential persons among the many adults and youth sharing leadership in these effective ministries with youth. The pastor doesn't have to be directly involved in all the relationships and practices of youth ministry, but the direction of the congregation's youth ministry requires the pastor's advocacy, guidance and support.

Effective youth ministers—full time or part time, paid or volunteer—possesses an essential set of qualities and skills: a vitality of faith, a commitment to youth, the capacity to relate well with youth and adults, knowledge of Scripture and the Christian faith, the ability to discover other's gifts and strengths, effectiveness in recruiting, training and supporting adult and youth leadership, the ability to assist a congregation in supporting youth ministry, the capacity to handle conflict, and a commitment to caring for his or her own spiritual, social and physical health.

Youth ministers work in a team approach with a leadership group that provide oversight and direction. Leadership teams, made up of youth, adult youth leaders, parents, and other church members work together to envision and oversee youth ministry and the variety of its programs and activities. Leadership teams are responsible for planning and tending the varied practices and relationships of the youth ministry.

Embracing the "Spirit and Culture of Youth Ministry"

One of the most important contributions of the Exemplary Youth Ministry Study is the identification of forty-four Faith Assets that contribute to the development of a vital Christian faith in young people. The Faith Assets are a roadmap for developing congregations and youth ministries that promote youth of vital, committed Christian faith. Adopting the Faith Assets mindset and framework can be transformational in both thinking and practice. The Faith Assets suggest a shift in the congregation's priorities, energy, and resources. Consider the following transformations in the journey toward a Faith Assets approach to youth ministry.

A Faith Assets mindset and framework counteracts so many stereotypes about youth ministry. For example, it confronts the "deficit mentality"—the popular misconception that we need to "solve the youth problem" or that we need to intervene to help youth through their many crises. It also counteracts the continual search for the one magic formula, activity, or program that will turn a

CHART 8

From . . .	To . . .
• Youth ministry is made up of many seemingly unrelated activities without a clear mission or purpose.	• The Faith Assets framework helps to integrate diverse activities into a larger framework that promotes a vital Christian faith in young people—a living discipleship in Jesus Christ.
• It often is unclear what to do in the youth ministry that will make a difference in youth's lives.	• The Faith Assets framework provides specific practices that the congregation and youth ministry can implement to make a lasting difference in the faith lives of young people.
• The focus is primarily on youth-focused programming and adult leader-to-youth relationships.	• The Faith Assets framework broadens the focus to the culture of the congregation—the intergenerational community, the family and household, the youth ministry, and congregational leadership.
• Youth in the congregation are the responsibility of the youth minister and adult leaders.	• Everyone in the congregation recognizes his or her responsibility for youth—and his or her power to influence the faith growth of young people. Young people are welcomed into the total life of the congregation, and invited into leadership roles.
• Parents are only superficially involved in the youth ministry (providing services and being informed about youth programs).	• Parents and the family are essential for developing the faith life of youth at home and active partners in the youth ministry through family and parent-teen activities and parent education.
• The youth minister is primarily a program leader, planner, and mentor for youth in the congregation.	• The youth minister empowers and equips teams of adults and youth to plan and conduct programs, and serves as the congregation's advocate and voice for youth and youth ministry.
• The pastor delegates youth ministry to others and is only minimally involved with young people.	• The pastor recognizes his or her influence and impact on youth and the youth ministry, and exercises a variety of roles, especially advocacy, guidance, and support for youth ministry.

youth ministry into superstar status. It also counteracts the myth that only large congregations with lots of resources and staff can do effective youth ministry. In an asset-building approach, every congregation has Faith Assets. It is only a question of how many. Congregations need to discover those that are already at work and then chart a plan for developing more assets. An asset-building approach offers very tangible qualities and practices that every congregation can adopt that contribute to an effective youth ministry and nurturing youth of maturing Christian faith.

The Faith Assets are a framework for strengthening the congregation *and* the youth ministry. The challenge for congregational and youth ministry leadership is to identify which assets are at work and which are not, and then chart a direction for the future using the Faith Assets framework. There are many pathways to action using the Faith Assets. Congregations need to begin with their strengths and resources, and leverage them!

The Faith Assets are cumulative. They build on each other. The more the better for everyone involved: the congregation, leaders, families, and young people. The key is working toward the "tipping point" in your congregation when the cumulative effect of the forty-four Faith Assets creates a congregational spirit and culture that maximizes efforts to nurture youth of vital, committed Christian faith.

APPLICATION
TOOL 20

The Faith Assets Framework

The Faith Assets are elements or building blocks that describe congregational culture and constitute a framework for congregations to use in developing the faith of young people. The study points to these forty-four elements as ways and means through which congregations have over time, with great effort and struggle, built their capacities to influence the faith and lives of young people. It is important to remember that the forty-four Faith Assets are descriptive, not prescriptive. They are not *the* definitive list. They are part of a growing body of knowledge about faith maturing in youth and the role of the congregation-as-a-whole, the family, and the youth ministry. The Faith Assets are a roadmap for developing congregations and youth ministries that promote youth of vital Christian faith. They are cumulative. They build on each other. The more the better for everyone involved: the congregation, leaders, families, and young people. The key is working toward the "tipping point" when the cumulative effect of the forty-four Faith Assets creates a congregational spirit and culture that maximizes efforts to nurture youth of maturing Christian faith.

1. Congregational Faith and Qualities

Congregational Faith

Asset 1. Experiences God's Living Presence: The congregation possesses a sense of God's living presence in community, at worship, through study, and in service.

Asset 2. Makes Faith Central: The congregation recognizes and participates in God's sustaining and transforming life and work.

Asset 3. Emphasizes Prayer: The congregation practices the presence of God as individuals and community through prayer and worship.

Asset 4. Focuses on Discipleship: The congregation is committed to knowing and following Jesus Christ.

Asset 5. Emphasizes Scripture: The congregation values the authority of Scripture in its life and mission.

Asset 6. Makes Mission Central: The congregation consistently witnesses, serves and promotes moral responsibility, and seeks justice.

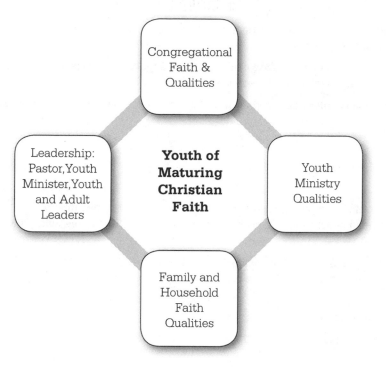

Four Clusters of Faith Assets

Congregational Faith & Qualities

Leadership: Pastor, Youth Minister, Youth and Adult Leaders

Youth of Maturing Christian Faith

Youth Ministry Qualities

Family and Household Faith Qualities

Congregational Qualities

Asset 7. Supports Youth Ministry: Youth and ministry with young people are high priorities for the congregation.

Asset 8. Demonstrates Hospitality: The congregation values and welcomes all people, especially youth.

Asset 9. Strives for Excellence: The congregation sets high standards, evaluates, and engages in continuous improvement.

Asset 10. Encourages Thinking: The congregation welcomes questions and reflection on faith and life.

Asset 11. Creates Community: Congregational life reflects high quality personal and group relationships.

Asset 12. Encourages Small Groups: The congregation engages members in study, conversation, and prayer about faith in daily life.

Asset 13. Promotes Worship: The congregation expands and renews spirit-filled, uplifting worship.

Asset 14. Fosters Ethical Responsibility: The congregation encourages individual and social moral responsibility.

Asset 15. Promotes Service: The congregation sponsors outreach, service projects, and cultural immersions both locally and globally.

Asset 16. Demonstrates Effective Practices: The congregation engages in a wide variety of ministry practices and activities.

Asset 17. Participate in the Congregation: Youth are engaged in a wide spectrum of congregational relationships and practices.

Asset 18. Assume Ministry Leadership: Youth are invited, equipped and affirmed for leadership in congregational activities.

2. Youth Ministry Qualities

Asset 19. Establishes a Caring Environment: Youth ministry provides multiple nurturing relationships and activities resulting in a welcoming atmosphere of respect, growth, and belonging.

Asset 20. Develops Quality Relationship: Youth ministry develops authentic relationships among youth and adults establishing an environment of presence and life engagement.

Asset 21. Focuses on Jesus Christ: Youth ministry's mission, practices, and relationships are inspired by the life and ministry of Jesus Christ.

Asset 22. Considers Life Issues: Youth ministry values and addresses the full range of young people's lives.

Asset 23. Uses Many Approaches: Youth ministry intentionally and creatively employs multiple activities appropriate to the ministry's mission and context.

Asset 24. Is Well Organized and Planned: Youth ministry engages participants and leaders in long range planning, implementation, evaluation, and innovation in an atmosphere of high expectations.

3. Family and Household Faith Assets

Asset 25. Possesses Strong Parental Faith: Parents possess and practice a vital and informed faith.

Asset 26. Promotes Family Faith Practices: Parents engage youth and the whole family in conversations, prayer, bible reading, and service that nurture faith and life.

Asset 27. Reflects Family Harmony: Family members' expressions of respect and love create an atmosphere promoting faith.

Asset 28. Equips Parents: The congregation offers instruction and guidance that nurture parental faith and equips parents for nurturing faith at home.

Asset 29. Fosters Parent-Youth Relationships: The congregation offers parent-youth activities that strengthen parent-youth relationships.

4. Leadership

Pastor

Asset 30. Exercises Spiritual Influence: The pastor knows and models the transforming presence of God in life and ministry.

Asset 31. Demonstrates Interpersonal Competence: The pastor builds a sense of community and relates well with adults and youth.

Asset 32. Supports Youth Ministry: The pastor understands, guides, and advocates for youth ministry.

Asset 33. Supports Leaders: The pastor affirms and mentors youth and adults leading youth ministry.

Youth Minister

Asset 34. Provides Competent Leadership: The youth minister reflects superior theological, theoretical, and practical knowledge and skill in leadership.

Asset 35. Models Faith: The youth minister is a role model reflecting a living faith for youth and adults.

Asset 36. Mentors Faith Life: The youth minister assists adult leaders and youth in their faith life both one-on-one and in groups.

Asset 37. Develops Teams: The youth minister reflects a clear vision and attracts gifted youth and adults into leadership.

Asset 38. Knows Youth: The youth minister knows youth and the changes in youth culture, and utilizes these understandings in ministry.

Asset 39. Establishes Effective Relationships: The youth minister enjoys effective relationships with youth, parents, volunteers, and staff.

Youth and Adult Leaders

Asset 40. Are Equipped for Peer Ministry: Youth practice friendship, care-giving, and outreach and are supported by ministry training and caring adults.

Asset 41. Establish Adult-Youth Mentoring: Adults engage youth in the Christian faith and life supported by informed leadership.

Asset 42. Participate in Training: Youth and adults are equipped for ministry in an atmosphere of high expectations.

Asset 43. Possess Vibrant Faith: Youth and adult leaders possess and practice a vital and informed Christian faith.

Asset 44. Demonstrate Competent Adult Leadership: Adults foster authentic relationships and utilize effective practices in youth ministry with a clear vision strengthened by training and support.

congregations participating in the study of exemplary congregations in youth ministry

T wenty-One Congregations Featured
in the Qualitative Research

1. Calvary Christian Center Assemblies of God, Louisville, KY
2. Cottonwood Assembly of God, Cottonwood, AZ
3. Newport Mesa Christian Center, Assemblies of God, Costa Mesa, CA
4. Rochester Covenant Church, Rochester, MN
5. Rolling Hills Covenant Church, Rolling Hills, CA
6. Thornapple Evangelical Covenant Church, Grand Rapids, MI

7. Grace Lutheran Church, Des Moines, WA
8. Hope Lutheran Church, Fargo, ND
9. Shared Lutheran Ministry of Fayette County, Fayette County, TX
10. First Presbyterian Church, Billings, MT
11. First Presbyterian Church, Fort Dodge, IA
12. Memorial Presbyterian Church, Saint. Augustine, FL
13. Saint. Michael's Catholic Parish, Albion, NE
14. The Catholic Parishes of Sacred Heart, Saint Benedict, and Saint Ann, Terre Haute, IN
15. Saint Mary's Catholic Parish, Pompton Lakes, NJ
16. New Colony Baptist Church, Billerica, MA
17. Oaks Baptist Church, Grand Prairie, TX
18. Travis Avenue Baptist Church, Fort Worth, TX
19. Common Cup Cooperative Parish, United Methodist Church, Portland, OR
20. First United Methodist Church, Valparaiso, IN
21. Myers Park United Methodist Church, Charlotte, NC

131 Congregations Participating
in the Quantitative Research

Assembly of God

Calvary Christian Center Assembly of God, Louisville, KY
Cottonwood Assembly of God, Cottonwood, AZ
Crossroads Of Life Assemblies of God, Duncanville, TX
Emmanuel Christian Center, Minneapolis, MN
Newport Mesa Christian Center, Costa Mesa, CA
Rocky Branch Assembly of God, Farmerville, LA

Evangelical Covenant

New Gate Covenant Fellowship, Hickory, NC
Forest Park Covenant, Muskegon, MI
Hope Community Covenant, Strathmore, AB, Canada
Rochester Covenant, Rochester, MN
Covenant Congregational, North Easton, MA
First Evangelical, Rockford, IL
Faith Covenant, Saint Petersburg, FL

First Covenant, San Francisco, CA
Lund Mission Covenant, Stockholm, WI
Salem Evangelical Covenant, Oakland, NE
Crossroad, Cottage Grove, MN
Rolling Hills Covenant, Rolling Hills, CA
Evangelical Covenant, Kingsburg, CA
Community Covenant, San Andreas, CA
Evangelical Covenant, International Falls, MN
Evangelical Covenant, Bemidji, MN
Redeemer Covenant, Tulsa, OK
Grace Covenant, Olympia, WA
Evangelical Covenant, Springfield, MA
Evangelical Covenant, Anoka, MN
Thornapple Covenant, Grand Rapids, MI
Maple Grove Covenant, Maple Grove, MN
Roseville Covenant, Roseville, MN
Cornerstone Covenant, Turlock, CA
Evangelical Covenant, Fort Collins, CO
Evangelical Covenant, Roseau, MN
Hope Covenant, Saint Cloud, MN

Evangelical Lutheran Church in America

Augustana Lutheran, West Saint Paul, MN
Bethany Lutheran, Elkhorn, NE
Calvary Lutheran, Apollo Beach, FL
Calvary Lutheran Church, Grand Forks, ND
Christ Lutheran, Jeffersontown, KY
First Lutheran, Warren, PA
Lutheran Church of the Incarnation, Poway, CA
Our Saviors Lutheran, Arlington Heights, IL
Saint Stephen Lutheran, Stow, OH
Trinity Lutheran, Marshalltown, IA
Grace Lutheran, Des Moines, WA
Hope Lutheran, Fargo, ND
Messiah Lutheran, Auburn, WA
Olivet Lutheran, Fargo, ND
Tri-County Ministry, Binford, ND
Lutheran Church of the Ascension, Citrus Heights, CA
Bethel Lutheran, Willmar, MN
Christ Lutheran Church, Charlotte, NC
Saint Johns Lutheran, Grove City, OH

Shared Lutheran Ministry of Fayette County, TX
Trinity Lutheran, Owatonna, MN

Presbyterian Church (USA)

Northmont United Presbyterian, Pittsburgh, PA
Harvey Browne Memorial Presbyterian, Louisville, KY
Newlonsburg Presbyterian, Murrysville, PA
First Presbyterian, Marietta, GA
Riverside Presbyterian, Jacksonville, FL
Setauket Presbyterian, Setauket, NY
First Presbyterian, Waunakee, WI
Watauga Avenue Presbyterian, Johnson City, TN
Canyon Creek Presbyterian, Richardson, TX
Preston Hollow Presbyterian, Dallas, TX
First Presbyterian, Farmington, NM
First Presbyterian, Tallahassee, FL
First Presbyterian, Nashville, TN
Westminster Presbyterian, Eugene, OR
Mount Pleasant Presbyterian, Mount Pleasant, SC
First Presbyterian, Billings, MT
First Presbyterian, Dalton, GA
White Memorial Presbyterian, Raleigh, NC
Kirk of Kildaire Presbyterian, Cary, NC
First Presbyterian, Fort Dodge, IA
Memorial Presbyterian, Saint Augustine, FL

Roman Catholic

Saint Egbert, Morehead City, NC
Saint Robert Bellarmine, Blue Springs, MO
Resurrection Parish, Wilmington, DE
Church of the Holy Spirit, Carterville, IL
Holy Family Catholic, Abilene, TX
Saint Francis of Assisi, Centerville, OH
Saint Mary Uxbridge, Uxbridge, MA
Saint Michael the Archangel, Cary, NC
Christ the King, Rochester, NY
Sacred Heart, Saint Benedict, and Saint Ann, Terre Haute, IN
Saint Bernard, Appleton, WI
Saint Colette, Livonia, MI
Saint Elizabeth Ann Seton, New Berlin, WI

Saint John the Evangelist, Spencerport, NY
Saint Joseph Saint Thomas, Kalamazoo, MI
Saint Margaret Mary, Omaha, NE
Saint Mary, Pompton Lakes, NJ
Saint Michaels, Albion, NE
Saint Paul on the Lake, Grosse Pointe Farms, MI
Saints Peter and Paul, Danville, KY

Southern Baptist

Ballwin Baptist, Ballwin, MO
Rolling Hills Baptist, Buford, GA
First Baptist Spartanburg, Spartanburg, SC
First Baptist Simpsonville, Simpsonville, SC
Gateway Baptist, Irmo, SC
First Baptist Mulvane, Mulvane, KS
Pleasantview Baptist, Derby, KS
Dawson Memorial Baptist, Honewood, AL
First Baptist, Richardson, TX
Southwest Park Baptist, Abilene, TX
Clearpoint Baptist, Pasadena, TX
Springhill Baptist, Springfield, MO
First Baptist McKinney, McKinney, TX
First Baptist Arlington, Arlington, TX
First Baptist Lubbock, Lubbock, TX
The Oaks Baptist, Grand Prairie, TX
Travis Ave Baptist, Fort Worth, TX

United Methodist

Cheshire UMC, Cheshire, CT
Common Cup Cooperative Parish, Portland, OR
First United Methodist, Ann Arbor, MI
First UMC, Brevard, NC
First United Methodist, Valparaiso, IN
Halifax United Methodist, Halifax, PA
Los Altos United Methodist, Los Altos, CA
Malibu United Methodist, Malibu, CA
Memorial UMC, Thomasville, NC
Meridian Street United Methodist, Indianapolis, IN
Myers Park UMC, Charlotte, NC
Platt Springs United Methodist, West Columbia, SC

Saint Andrews UMC, Littleton, CO
Saint Johns UMC, Rock Hill, SC
Saint Stephen UMC, Charlotte, NC
Westwood United Methodist, Cincinnati, OH
White Plains UMC, Cary, NC
Concord UMC, Knoxville, TN
Aldersgate UMC, Olathe, KS

how the quantitative study was conducted

Mark J. Brekke

T he Study of Exemplary Congregations in Youth Ministry (EYM)[1] was designed to use both quantitative and qualitative methodologies. Broadly, the quantitative part of the study was designed to map the domain of exemplary youth ministry as experienced by members of congregations practicing it, including how that domain, in general, differs from that of the "average" congregations. The qualitative part was designed to learn in greater depth and detail how specific congregations are doing exemplary youth ministry, and, if possible, identify patterns of approaches that appear to be working. In brief form, the full design included the following steps:

General

- *Determine the study definition of exemplary youth ministry.*
- *Identify and secure the participation of a sample of congregations doing exemplary youth ministry.*

Quantitative

- *Develop quantitative instruments (surveys) to measure characteristics of exemplary congregations and their members.*
- *Survey youth, parents, adult youth workers, the senior/lead pastor, and youth minister(s) in exemplary congregations.*
- *Identify, from the survey data, reliable item clusters, representing meaningful constructs (behaviors, attitudes, beliefs, programs, processes, policies, etc.).*
- *Determine whether EYM congregations differ from "average" congregations regarding the constructs by comparing EYM results to data from previous studies.*
- *Identify patterns of characteristics from pastors' and youth ministers' responses to open-ended survey questions regarding the important elements of their youth ministry.*

Qualitative

- *Develop structured interviews to get in-depth information from EYM congregations.*
- *Collect interviews and first-hand observations through site visits to selected EYM congregations.*
- *Identify patterns of characteristics from the site visit data.*

The remainder of this document describes, in detail, each of the above general and quantitative steps. The qualitative steps are described in a companion document.

Definition of Exemplary Youth Ministry

The project team defined "exemplary youth ministry" in terms of an observable end product: exemplary youth ministry is youth ministry that consistently produces "mature Christian youth." That is, exemplary youth ministry is youth ministry that produces high school graduates who:

1. *Believe God is present and active in the world.*
2. *Seek spiritual growth, both alone and with others.*

3. *Act out of a commitment of faith.*
4. *Are active with God's people.*
5. *Possess a positive, hopeful spirit.*
6. *Live out a life of service.*
7. *Live a Christian moral life.*

The seven characteristics of mature Christian youth were identified from two studies: *Effective Christian Education*[2] (ECE), which assessed evidences of a mature faith in youth and adults; and *Five Cries of Youth*[3-5] (5Cries), which described the concerns, behaviors, and beliefs of high school youth. Through factor analysis of the 38-item "faith maturity" scale from ECE, the EYM team found that there were four primary, well-defined factors within the faith maturity scale, corresponding to characteristics 1, 2, 3, and 6 above. 5Cries identified a similar set of factors related to the faith maturity of youth, and also identified factors corresponding to characteristics 4, 5, and 7. All seven factors were considered by the study team to be necessary to fully describe mature Christian youth.

Congregation Sample Selection

A 7 x 3 sampling frame was defined: 7 church bodies crossed with 3 congregation sizes (small = weekly worship attendance of less than 250; medium = 250-750; large = 751 or more). It was recognized that the definition of congregation size did not fit all church bodies well (for example, a Roman Catholic parish that worships 751 persons a week is not considered a large parish in the Roman Catholic church, and a congregation worshipping 249 persons is not a small Assembly of God congregation). However, the definition represented, in the experience of the study team, size categories that typically yield functionally different youth ministries. The sampling target was 315 total congregations with exemplary youth ministries, fifteen congregations in each of the twenty-one cells. Though the sample was not additionally stratified by other variables, it was desired that the total sample contain congregations from all major regions of the country, and congregations with significant percentages of members from minority racial/ethnic groups. Table A-1 shows a summary of the sampling and subsequent recruitment and participation of congregations.

The intent of the project was to study the "best of the best," so a two-stage sampling process was used. First, each church body was asked to nominate thirty congregations in each of the three size categories (ninety total per denomination) that were doing exemplary youth ministry by the study's definition. Church bodies used whatever means they desired to obtain nominations, and submitted nominations using "Congregational Assessment Form A" (Appendix A, available at www.exemplarym.com).

TABLE A-1

Summary of Congregation Sampling, Recruitment, and Participation *

DENOMINATION Size	A**	B	C	D	E	F	G	H
Assemblies of God								
Unknown	2	1	50.0%	0	0.0%	0	NA	0.0%
Small	5	4	80.0%	2	50.0%	1	50.0%	20.0%
Medium	9	8	88.9%	3	37.5%	3	100.0%	33.3%
Large	16	14	87.5%	7	50.0%	2	28.6%	12.5%
Baptist								
Unknown	21	14	66.7%	9	64.3%	0	0.0%	0.0%
Small	6	4	66.7%	3	75.0%	1	33.3%	16.7%
Medium	25	15	60.0%	8	53.3%	6	75.0%	24.0%
Large	34	17	50.0%	8	47.1%	10	125.0%	29.4%
Covenant								
Unknown	0	0	NA	0	NA	0	NA	NA
Small	34	15	44.1%	10	66.7%	10	100.0%	29.4%
Medium	51	38	74.5%	22	57.9%	13	59.1%	25.5%
Large	7	7	100.0%	3	42.9%	4	133.3%	57.1%

Percentages may exceed 100% because unknown congregation sizes were resolved with the survey administration.
**** A = # of Candidates Nominated; B = # Invited; C = % Invited (of Candidates); D = # Accepting; E = % Accepting; F = # Completing Survey; G = % Completing Survey (of Accepting); H = % Completing Survey (of Candidates)*

DENOMINATION Size	A**	B	C	D	E	F	G	H
Lutheran								
Unknown	4	3	75.0%	3	100.0%	0	0.0%	0.0%
Small	7	4	57.1%	3	75.0%	3	100.0%	42.9%
Medium	24	22	91.7%	17	77.3%	9	52.9%	37.5%
Large	14	14	100.0%	14	100.0%	9	64.3%	64.3%
Methodist								
Unknown	2	2	100.0%	0	0.0%	0	NA	0.0%
Small	18	12	66.7%	5	41.7%	4	80.0%	22.2%
Medium	29	24	82.8%	13	54.2%	10	76.9%	34.5%
Large	20	17	85.0%	12	70.6%	5	41.7%	25.0%
Presbyterian								
Unknown	1	1	100.0%	0	NA	0	NA	NA
Small	17	14	82.4%	13	92.9%	3	23.1%	17.6%
Medium	21	21	100.0%	17	81.0%	13	76.5%	61.9%
Large	10	10	100.0%	6	54.5%	5	83.3%	45.5%
Roman Catholic								
Unknown	7	3	42.9%	1	33.3%	0	0.0%	0.0%
Small	1	1	100.0%	1	100.0%	1	100.0%	100.0%
Medium	28	21	75.0%	5	23.8%	1	20.0%	3.6%
Large	59	37	62.7%	14	37.8%	18	128.6%	30.5%
TOTAL								
Unknown	36	23	63.9%	13	56.5%	0	0.0%	0.0%
Small	88	54	61.4%	37	68.5%	23	62.2%	26.1%
Medium	187	149	79.7%	85	57.0%	55	64.7%	29.4%
Large	161	117	72.7%	64	54.7%	53	82.8%	32.9%
GRAND TOTAL	**472**	**343**	**72.7%**	**199**	**58.0%**	**131**	**65.8%**	**27.8%**

Second, each nominated congregation was then sent a "validation form," "Congregational Assessment Form B," for the youth minister or senior/lead pastor to complete (Appendix B, available at www.exemplarym.com). Congregations that were nominated and returned Form B were considered "candidate congregations." The purpose of Form B was that someone internal to the nominated congregation verify that the congregation actually met the study criteria for doing "exemplary youth ministry." Form B contained a survey of thirty-six items. Thirty-four of the items were statements of observable youth behaviors related to the seven characteristics of mature Christian youth defined above. Items from the ECE faith maturity scale were used where applicable with modifications as necessary to make each statement an observable youth behavior. Additional items were drafted by the research team to fill out each of the seven characteristics. The two remaining items asked how many of the congregation's high school youth came from outside the congregation and how many eighth graders of four years ago are still active now as twelfth graders. For each of the thirty-six items, the respondent was asked for what proportion of the congregation's high school youth the statement was true, using a five-point scale (1 = Very few, 2 = Some, 3 = Half, 4 = Most, 5 = Almost All).

Cluster analysis was done on the Form B data from the first 374 candidate congregations from five church bodies (not Lutheran or Presbyterian). A structure similar in many respects, but not identical, to the seven characteristics of mature Christian youth was identified. It was found that the average item score, computed for each congregation, was correlated at 0.97 to the average of cluster scores derived from the cluster analysis. Consequently, for simplicity, the average item score was used as the "validation score" for each congregation. Both the mean and the median of the validation score was 3.0, and the standard deviation was 0.59. The structure and other statistics were later tested including Lutheran and Presbyterian candidates, and results were nearly identical.

Congregations with a validation score of 2.60 or greater were selected to be invited into the study. The value 2.60 was selected because it yielded a reasonable number of congregations in each of the twenty-one sampling cells, and yet it was not so low on the absolute scale as to be inconsistent with the study definition of "exemplary youth ministry."

The church body representatives on the study team were each allowed to make three types of adjustments to the list of selected congregations. First, congregations in which the youth minister or pastor had left since their nomination could be dropped from the list. Second, candidate congregations that did not meet the 2.60 score criteria could be added to the selected list based on the church body representative's personal knowledge of the congregation. Third, after several months of recruitment, it was found that congregations were somewhat more reluctant to respond positively to invitation than was expected by the study team, especially in certain denominations. The church body representatives were allowed to nominate and invite a supplemental sample of congregations from their church body that the representative knew, from their personal experience, to be practicing exemplary youth ministry.

Congregations were invited by letter with follow-up phone calls. Upon acceptance, each congregation was mailed surveys and instructions for their administration. Administration was conducted by members of each congregation. Completed surveys were mailed from each congregation to one of the three coordinating sites.

Congregation size was unknown for thirty-seven of the 472 nominated congregations. Since the 2.60 cutoff yielded enough congregations of known size, this information was not pursued at the time of congregation selection. The congregation size variable used for analysis was finally determined by the senior/lead pastor's response to a question on the Minister survey (or youth minister's if there was no pastor survey response).

The study did not sample a control group of congregations for comparison to the exemplary congregations. Instead, the research team had available to them the study datasets from four previous studies that included many questions relevant to youth ministry: *Effective Christian Education*[2] from 1988 (permission to use granted by Search Institute and downloaded from the American Religion Data Archive[6]); *Youth Ministry That Transforms*[7] from 1998-1999 (permission to use granted by Link Institute and data supplied by Brekke Associates, Inc.); *Survey of Catholic Youth Program Participants*[8] from 1996 (permission to use granted and data supplied by Center for Ministry Development); and *Young Adolescents and Their Parents*[9] from 1983-1984 (permission to use granted by Search Institute and downloaded from the American Religion Data Archive[10]). Each of these studies drew a random sample of congregations or individuals across the nation. The design was that by using selected questions from the past studies in the new EYM surveys, the EYM results could be compared statistically with the random sample in each of the previous studies. That is, the previous studies provided a surrogate control sample.

Instrument Development

Definition of the domain of study. In order to determine the domain of the study, the project team developed a model of the environment of the maturing Christian youth, presented in Chart 9. From the perspective of youth ministry, the primary influences on the maturing Christian youth are the youth minister, the senior/lead pastor, and the adult youth workers in the congregation. Past research has shown that parents and other youth are also very influential to faith development of youth, and that these relationships are active both inside and outside the life of the congregation. Finally, other adults, the media, and other activities, again both inside and outside the congregation also have an influence, though possibly of lesser degree. This model defined boundaries of people, relationships, and activities to study. That is, the intent of the study was to measure characteristics of these particular people in congregations and their relationships and activities with one another, with emphasis placed on youth, their parents, the senior/lead pastor, the youth minister, and the adult youth workers.

The project team identified 373 potential theoretical concepts to be measured by reviewing the findings of several studies, including:

- *Effective Christian Education[2]*
- *Survey of Catholic Youth Program Participants[8]*
- *Youth Ministry That Transforms[7]*
- *Five Cries of Youth[3-5]*
- *Youth Ministry and Spirituality Project[11]*
- *Youth and Religion Project[12]*
- *National Study of Youth and Religion[13]*

CHART 9
THE ENVIRONMENT OF THE MATURING CHRISTIAN YOUTH

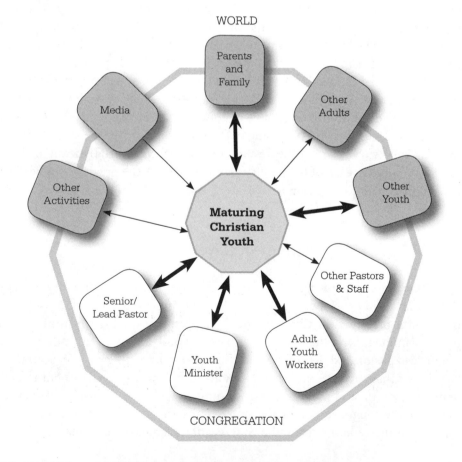

WORLD

Parents and Family

Media

Other Adults

Other Activities

Maturing Christian Youth

Other Youth

Senior/ Lead Pastor

Other Pastors & Staff

Youth Minister

Adult Youth Workers

CONGREGATION

A short rating form was developed with which each of the church body representatives rated the importance of each concept for the study (2 = Essential, 1 = Useful, 0 = Unimportant), and from whom or of whom each concept should be measured. Results were summarized, yielding a ranked list of concepts. The research team examined the 195 concepts that received an average rating of 1.8 or greater, combined close duplicates, and selected 127 concepts for study.

Selection and development of items. The next step was to find items to measure the concepts. First, items from the four "surrogate control" studies (discussed above) were identified that fit the concepts. Second, potential items from the following studies were identified:

- *Young Adolescents and Their Parents*[9]
- *Five Cries of Youth*[3-5]
- *A Study of Generations*[14]
- *Ministry in America*[15]
- *Study of Organizational Change*[16]
- *Congregational Tools for Effective Evangelism*[17]
- *Four Imperatives Study*[18]

Finally, additional items were written by the research team to fill out the desired concepts. The result was a collection of 1093 potential items.

The research team evaluated each potential item carefully. Minor modifications to items were made to use consistent language (e.g., "youth minister" throughout, replacing "youth leader" and "youth director"). Care was taken to leave items from the four "surrogate control" surveys unchanged. A few missing concepts were identified in the process of reviewing the items, so items were added accordingly. Four surveys were drafted: youth; their parents; adult youth workers; and pastor and youth minister. The selection of items for particular groups was informed by the second part of the concept ratings that the church body representatives completed, that of identification of from whom or of whom each concept should be measured. The draft surveys were reviewed by the church body representatives, and revised based on their feedback.

Pretest and analysis of items. The draft surveys were pretested with 262 individuals (12 pastors and youth ministers, 66 parents, 71 adult youth workers, and 113 youth) in seven congregations (3 Baptist, 1 Covenant, 1 Lutheran, and 2 Roman Catholic). In addition to answering each item, the respondents were asked to evaluate the quality of the item: item okay; item is hard to understand, unclear; item can have more than one meaning; item uses words that I do not understand; or, item is repetitious. Respondents were also asked to underline problem words or phrases.

Revision to final form. The responses to the pretest questionnaire, both item responses and item evaluations, were carefully analyzed by the research team. Items identified by the respondents as problematic were revised or thrown out. Items with poor distributions of response (i.e., that did not discriminate well) were discarded. Cluster analyses were performed to identify additional items that could be eliminated. Again, items from the four "surrogate control" surveys were used without change whenever possible. The result was four survey booklets (see Appendices C-F, available at www.exemplarym.com):

- *Pastor and Youth Minister Survey* containing 301 items (4 open-ended).
- *Parent Survey* containing 309 items.
- *Youth Worker Survey* containing 338 items.
- *Youth Survey* containing 354 items.

The final surveys contained a total of 760 items, of which thirty-one items were in all four surveys. 206 items were unique to the Youth Survey, forty-eight to the Parent Survey, sixty-nine to the Youth Worker Survey, and 124 to the Pastor and Youth Minister Survey.

Data Collection and Preparation for Analysis

Survey administration. Survey booklets were mailed to each participating congregation, together with instruction manuals and materials for administration (Appendices G-O, available at www.exemplarym.com). Congregations were asked to administer surveys to thirty of their 9th through 12th grade youth who were currently active in the congregation, thirty of their parents (one per household), thirty adult youth workers, the senior/lead pastor, and the youth minister (if different from the senior/lead pastor). If the congregation was small enough so that thirty in a particular group did not exist, the congregation was asked to survey as many as possible (i.e., the population within the congregation).

131 congregations completed a total of 5,793 surveys during the spring and fall of 2003, with congregations distributed across the twenty-one sampling cells as shown in Table A-1. The count of returned surveys of each of the four types is shown in Table A-2, again across the twenty-one sampling cells.

Table A-3 summarizes the number of respondents per congregation for each of the four surveys. The total population who might have been eligible for a survey in each congregation was not asked of the congregation; thus, the sampling fraction in each congregation is unknown.

TABLE A-2

Count of Returns for Each Survey Type

Congregation / Size	Pastors and Youth Ministers	Parents	Youth Workers	Youth
Assemblies of God				
Small	2	1	6	5
Medium	4	14	30	62
Large	3	14	46	51
TOTALS	9	29	82	118
Baptist				
Small	2	20	22	27
Medium	11	68	69	119
Large	3	14	46	51
TOTALS	29	228	299	512
Covenant				
Small	19	87	37	116
Medium	22	157	63	307
Large	37	107	52	196
TOTALS	116	199	86	401

Congregation / Size	Pastors and Youth Ministers	Parents	Youth Workers	Youth
Lutheran				
Small	5	25	16	30
Medium	16	133	117	162
Large	16	143	132	181
TOTALS	37	301	265	373
Methodist				
Small	6	14	19	43
Medium	18	120	118	181
Large	8	80	47	91
TOTALS	32	214	184	315
Presbyterian				
Small	6	38	16	34
Medium	22	225	154	245
Large	9	102	73	109
TOTALS	37	365	243	388
Roman Catholic				
Small	1	19	9	19
Medium	1	7	13	13
Large	30	218	161	291
TOTALS	32	244	183	323
Totals				
Small	41	204	125	274
Medium	94	724	608	981
Large	88	760	719	1175
TOTALS	223	1688	1452	2430

TABLE A-3

Summary of Congregation Sampling, Recruitment, and Participation

	Number of Respondents From Congregation				Number of Congregations Having 0 Respondents
	Mean	Standard Deviation	Min	Max	
Minister	1.70	0.54	0	3	4
Parent	12.89	7.78	0	30	4
Worker	11.08	8.10	0	54	1
Youth	18.55	18.86	0	212	2

Data capture. The questionnaire booklets were printed as a mark-sense, machine-scannable form. Each returned survey was examined before scanning, and light marks and marks in ink were corrected. Surveys that appeared to have been completed invalidly (such as making visual patterns using the marking ovals) were identified for exclusion in the analysis. A total of 5,793 survey booklets scanned. Scan counts were verified against the manual count of survey returns, and the electronic file from each scan batch was examined for scanner errors.

Data preparation. The electronic scan batch files were converted to a SAS® (version 7) dataset, with full variable and value labels. Multiple cross-checks of the data against the congregation nomination data and the scan logs were performed, and any inconsistencies were corrected. Missing and multiple marks were given missing data values which allowed the exclusion of the values, but not the respondents, from statistical procedures. Univariate statistics and frequency distributions were examined to confirm that all responses were within the correct range, the item distributions were reasonable, and that there were no items with extreme numbers of missing data. The data passed all such tests.

Records corresponding to surveys that had been identified as invalid were flagged for exclusion from further analyses (n = 12, 0.2% of total returns). On average, respondents answered 96.3% of the questions in their surveys. Records that contained less than 67% completed item responses were also flagged for exclusion (n = 209, 3.6% of total returns). After combining the exclusion criteria, the following were excluded: 1 Minister survey (0.45% of total Minister returns); 16 Parent surveys (0.95% of Parent returns); 22 Worker surveys (1.52% of Worker returns); and 178 Youth surveys (7.33% of Youth returns). A total of 5,576 surveys remained after these exclusions.

After data conversion, items were transformed in preparation for analysis. Items were recoded as necessary so that 1 was the lowest amount of "positive" response. Negatively worded items were reversed. Items with responses "Yes," "No," and "?" or "I don't know" were scored 3, 1, and 2, respectively. All items were then linearly translated to a 1 through 9 scale. For example: 3-response items initially scored 1, 2, 3 were linearly translated to scores of 1, 5, 9; 7-response items initially scored 1, 2, 3, 4, 5, 6, 7 were translated to 1, 2.33, 3.67, 5, 6.3, 7.67, 9.

Weighting the data. Since one particular congregation returned a disproportionately large number of surveys, a subsample of the returns from this congregation was randomly created for use in the cluster analyses. This process removed 24 Adult Youth Worker surveys and 182 Youth surveys from the cluster analysis. Otherwise, each (non-excluded) survey was given equal weight in the cluster analyses. The full total of 5,576 surveys were included for calculations of the final item means, standard deviations, and scale reliabilities. When scale means were compared with historical data, the data was specially weighted for each analysis (see "Comparisons of sub-cluster scores" below).

Identification of Reliable Item Clusters

Searching for structure. The author has previously published a discussion of the rationale behind doing cluster analysis.[19] That discussion is reproduced as background for the reader, edited to apply to the current study.

When the American public considers results of a survey, it most often thinks of "polls" which consist of just a few items, asked of a carefully selected sample of people. We are used to hearing the results of political polls, Gallup polls on a variety of issues, and exit polls during elections which report the percent answering a question a certain way (often "yes" or "no," or "which candidate"), with a "margin of error" of, usually, 3–4%.

While those types of surveys are very useful, they are also very limited. They answer single questions, but do not capture either the breadth of context and reasoning of the respondents, or the depth of meaning which underlies the respondents' answers. They are also unable to reveal anything about the way in which people "structure" their thinking on the issue. That is, typical polls do not capture the "cognitive constructs" ("dimensions," "compartments," "facets," "areas of concern," and so on) that often subconsciously underlie the answers.

This study of exemplary youth ministry was designed to do what the typical poll does not: to map and study the domain of exemplary youth ministry as it is lived, felt, perceived, and conceived by youth, parents, youth workers, pastors and youth ministers in congregations doing exemplary youth ministry today. There are several advantages to this kind of research. The primary one is that past research has shown that, once the domain is mapped, the boundaries and landmarks (the "conceptual structure") remain consistent both for a broad group of people (in this case congregations across many church bodies), and over a long period of time (often twenty years or more). For example, when Merton Strommen carried out trend analyses on the structure identified in his book, *Five Cries of Youth*, he found no change after fifteen years in four of the five constructs, and only slight change in the fifth. This kind of consistency and persistence of structure allows researchers to study trends over long periods of time, make decisions with lasting impact, and develop tools, materials, and curricula that have broad and continuing value.

One key feature of this more expansive and persistent research is the identification of what we call "item clusters." An item cluster is a set of interrelated items in which each item asks a slightly different question having to do with the same topic, issue, or cognitive construct, but asks it from a different angle or in a different way. A good item cluster is one that is "internally consistent" (a measure of "reliability"). That is, people who give a high rating to one item in a scattered set of perhaps five or six items tend to give a high rating to *all* of the items in the set. Simultaneously, those who give a low rating to one item also tend to give a low rating to the other items of the set.

A second feature of this research is that the item clusters are identified *by the respondents themselves* by the way they answer the full questionnaire, not by the researchers beforehand. Item clusters are developed using the data collected with the questionnaire. The researchers do not presuppose that certain items are related to certain others. True, they have developed the questionnaire with questions they think are probably related, but more so they developed the questionnaire hoping to include items that covered the entire domain of study. The respondents' answers to the items are then analyzed using techniques that identify which items are more tightly interrelated with each other than with the rest of the items in the questionnaire (more on the techniques below). The analysis is done blind to the content of the items: when interrelated sets of items are identified, they are formed without any attention to the content of the questions; only the consistency of the respondents' answers are taken into account. After each item set is found, the researchers then look at the content of the items in each set and identify and name the larger concept that each item set is describing. What results are item "clusters," each describing a discrete concept more accurately than any single item can, and together providing a map of the field of study.

An example might be helpful. Say that a researcher is interested in people's likes and dislikes regarding foods. So, the researcher develops a questionnaire that asks how much a person likes or dislikes different foods. The researcher puts items regarding virtually every type of food they can think of into the questionnaire. After surveying a few thousand people, the researcher applies the techniques to search for the structure of food likes and dislikes that underlie people's answers. Let's say that many interrelated item sets are identified, but let's examine one which contains: brownies, Hershey® bar, fudge sickle, cocoa puffs, and Nestlé's Quik®. The researcher examines this set and quickly realizes that the concept being described is "preference for chocolateness." That is, people who like one type of chocolate-flavored food tend to like others, and vice versa. By using this set of items to measure how much people like chocolate-flavored foods, the researcher gets a much more reliable answer than if only one of the items were used. By using item clusters such as this the researcher also gets the advantage of being able to study a smaller, but more thoroughly defined and manageable, set of concepts, as opposed to studying each individual item. Finally, since the researcher has identified a conceptual area with each item cluster, s/he is in a much better position to use the information to develop new materials which will be accepted or meet the needs of a group of people. Using our example, suppose the researcher found that people tended to like chocolate-flavored foods more than lime-flavored foods. The researcher could then reasonably predict that, all else being equal, a new chocolate desert would sell better than a new lime dessert.

Item clusters based on the original questionnaire items are often called "first-order" clusters. It is also possible to search for structure among the first-order clusters, using the same process as described above. This, then, yields a "second-order" structure, or "cluster families," that further defines the domain of study.

A way of thinking about all of this is to think of a map of the world. The whole map is the "domain of study." To know more about the domain, one might study individual people as "items." Those people group into cities, or "first-order clusters." Finally, the cities group into countries, or "second-order cluster families." Now one can begin to make sense of the domain, because the map now has delineated areas and landmarks.

When doing this type of research, it is important to understand that though the *structure* which one finds is generally stable and persistent over time, the *level* of each conceptual construct in the structure can vary dramatically between groups and over time. In our example above, the level or degree of liking chocolate-flavored foods might differ significantly between men and women, children and adults, different ethnic groups, or regions of the country. Or, it might change in one group over time (if, say, chocolate was found to be a carcinogen). The beauty of highly reliable item clusters is that one can be much more confident that observed differences or changes are real, because a cluster measures the construct more precisely and consistently than does a single item.

This study of exemplary youth ministry, then, used the process of searching for structure—i.e., building reliable item clusters—in order to: map and better describe the domain of youth ministry as experienced in congregations doing exemplary youth ministry; provide a framework for thinking about exemplary youth ministry; and, be able to compare groups on measures related to exemplary youth ministry.

Identification of item clusters. First-order item clusters were identified for each of the four surveys (Youth, Parent, Worker, and Ministers surveys). The same process, described following, was used for each survey.

Three mathematical methods—each blind to content, not informed by any preconceived categories, and designed to identify distinct, interrelated sets of items—were used to analyze the survey items:

- *Principal component (factor) analysis, with varimax rotation (using PROC FACTOR in SAS® version 8).*
- *Principal factor analysis, with varimax rotation (using PROC FACTOR in SAS® version 8).*

- *Homogeneous keying (using software developed by Brekke Associates, Inc., based upon the work of Loevinger, et al.20-22).*

All non-demographic items were entered simultaneously into analysis by each of the three methods. Each analysis was run without weighting.

For efficiency and since the Parent and Workers surveys shared a large number of items, they were analyzed together. That is, each set of three analyses were run on each of the two surveys, and the resulting six analyses were then used together to identify clusters.

In each analysis, the results of the three methods were compared using software written by Brekke Associates. The software identified item sets that met the following criteria:

- *At least three items.*
- *For each item, the factor load for each method is the highest factor load found for the item, or if not the highest load it is either 0.35 or greater or it is 0.30 or greater and within 0.1 of the highest load.*
- *For the Youth and Ministers surveys, one method's factor load could be less than the highest load for any given item. For the combined Parent/ Worker analysis, two methods' loads could be less than the highest load for an item.*
- *For at least one item in the set, the factor load for each of the three methods is the highest factor load found for the item.*

Item sets containing a large number of items (approximately fifteen or more) were analyzed again to see if item subsets existed within the set. Items that did not cluster in the first analysis were also analyzed separately and yielded a few additional item sets.

For each item set meeting these criteria, the software created a table that included the internal consistency reliability of the set (Chronbach's alpha), and, for each item, the exact text, the factor load by each method, item to total correlation, reliability with item removed, and a list of other identified item sets that include the item. Each set was then passed to one of the quantitative research co-directors who carefully examined the results and identified the item sets with the strongest combination of high factor loads, high reliability (0.55 or higher, with rare exceptions explained below), and meaningful, identifiable content. By examining the content of all of the items in the resulting "cluster," the researcher identified the concept that served to "skewer" the set, and gave the cluster a short description. That individual also evaluated the fit of "borderline items" (items with relatively low factor loads) to the rest of the cluster; generally, such items were discarded. Items that fell into multiple item sets were retained in a single cluster only if they contributed substantially to the cluster's reliability and if the item content was conceptually consistent with the overall cluster content. An item could finally be used in only one cluster, resulting in "discrete" clusters for each survey. All of the clusters identified through this multi-step process were given final review by the project director and the quantitative research co-directors.

The number of respondents to the Pastor and Youth Ministers Survey was 223. Consequently, the clustering process results were not as clean for ministers as for the other groups. In order to allow for comparisons between parents, workers, and ministers regarding their assessment of the maturity of their youths' faith, the seven first-order clusters having to do with that topic that were identified in the Parent/Worker analysis were used for the Ministers. The empirical analysis of the Ministers data showed indications that the seven clusters were likely present in the data, and it is possible that they would have been cleanly identified had the number of respondents been greater. The cluster reliabilities for ministers for the seven clusters ranged from 0.42 to 0.92 and averaged 0.71, which was considerably lower than for the parents and workers. The clusters were considered serviceable, however.

This process of analyzing the survey items yielded 194 discrete first-order item clusters, as summarized in Table A-4. The final discrete cluster tables are presented in Appendices P-W (available at www.exemplarym.com).

Computation of cluster scores. For each respondent, a score for each cluster was assigned by computing the mean of the respondent's answers to the cluster items. The respondent must have answered at least two-thirds of the cluster's items to be given a valid score. If not, the score was set to a missing value that excluded the score, but not the respondent, from statistical analyses.

A priori clusters and additional cluster scores. Items corresponding to the thirty-four items in the nomination validation form, Congregational Assessment Form B, were included in all surveys. The item sets defined in Form B were scored as clusters for purposes of comparisons across groups. Clusters that were identified by the *Youth Ministry That Transforms* study and used in EYM were also scored. A few meaningful clusters were identified that were subsets of larger clusters. For example, the Youth cluster "Parents Help With Problems" contains clusters "Mother Helps With Problems" and "Father Helps With Problems." These meaningful "sub-clusters" were also scored because they helped explicate the nuances of the overall structure.

Identification of second-order cluster families. The first-order discrete cluster scores (not including the a priori clusters and additional sub-clusters) were analyzed to determine whether a second-order structure existed. The same process was used as for the identification of first-order clusters, this time treating the first-order cluster scores as if they were items. For the second-order analyses, the

TABLE A-4

Summary of 1st and 2nd-order Cluster Analysis

	A	B	C	D	Number of Items in Discrete 1st-order Clusters				E	F
					Sum	Mean	Min	Max		
Minister	301	257	54	40	187	4.7	2	17	6	31
Parent	309	412*	59	48	245	5.1	2	17	6	46
Worker	338		62	51	257	5.0	2	17	5	48
Youth	354	343	69	55	313	5.7	2	13	5	45

A = Number of items in survey
B = Number of items used in 1st-order cluster analysis
C = Number of 1st-order clusters scored
D = Number of discrete 1st-order clusters used in 2nd-order cluster analysis
E = Number of 2nd-order clusters identified
F = Number of discrete 1st-order clusters grouped into 2nd-order clusters

*in combined analysis

TABLE A-5

Number and Percent of Items Used in Sub-clusters

	Number of Sub-clusters	Number (Percent) of Items in Sub-cluster		
		Mean	Min	Max
Minister	21	3.4 (76%)	1 (14%)	8 (100%)
Parent	12	2.8 (77%)	1 (33%)	7 (100%)
Worker	11	3.4 (82%)	1 (14%)	8 (100%)
Youth	44	2.8 (52%)	1 (14%)	13 (100%)

TABLE A-6

Summary of Comparison of Mean Sub-Cluster Scores between EYM and Prior Studies

A*	B	C	D	E	F	G

1. Youth: EYM versus "Effective Christian Education"

A*	B	C	D	E	F	G
1357	1069	2426	19	15 (79%)	13 (68%)	11 (58%)

Published in 1991. Subset used in analysis included Baptist / Lutheran / Methodist / Presbyterian. Covariaties include denomination, congregation size, race, political orientation, gender, live with, grade.

2. Youth: EYM versus "Young Adolescents and Their Parents"

A*	B	C	D	E	F	G
500	1241	1714	7	6 (86%)	6 (86%)	5 (71%)

Published in 1984. Subset used in analysis included 9th grade, ages 13-15, all denominations except EYM - Assemblies of God. Covariaties included race, live with, gender, age.

3. Youth: EYM versus CARA "Survey of Catholic Youth Program Participants"

A*	B	C	D	E	F	G
290	4394	4684	18	8 (44%)	6 (33%)	2 (11%)

Published in 1996. Subset used in analysis included Roman Catholic. Covariaties included race, grade point average, live with, grade, gender.

* A = N: EYM; B = N: Prior Study; C = N: Total; D = Number of Sub-Clusters Compared; E = Number (percent) of Comparisons Significant at $p < 0.05$; F = Number (percent) of Comparisons Significant at $p < 0.01$; G = Number (percent) of Comparisons Significant at $p < 0.001$

A	B	C	D	E	F	G

4. Parent: EYM versus "Effective Christian Education"

A	B	C	D	E	F	G
1027	1244	2271	12	11 (92%)	10 (83%)	9 (75%)

Published in 1991. Subset used in analysis included ages 30-59, Married / Remarried / Divorced / Separated, Baptist / Lutheran / Methodist / Presbyterian. Covariaties included denomination, congregation size, race, age, education, income, marital status, political orientation, gender.

5. Worker: EYM versus "Effective Christian Education"

A	B	C	D	E	F	G
942	2045	2987	11	10 (91%)	9 (82%)	7 (64%)

Published in 1991. Subset used in analysis included Baptist / Lutheran / Methodist / Presbyterian. Covariaties inlcuded denomination, congregation size, race, age, education, income, marital status, political orientation, gender.

6. Minister: EYM versus "Effective Christian Education"

A	B	C	D	E	F	G
50	221	271	1	1 (100%)	1 (100%)	1 (100%)

Published in 1991. Subset used in analysis included EYM Senior/Lead Pastors; Age 40+; White; Baptist / Lutheran / Methodist / Presbyterian. Covariaties included denomination, dongregation size, race, age, education, income, marital status, political orientation, gender.

7. Minister: EYM versus "Youth Ministry That Transforms"

A	B	C	D	E	F	G
102	1407	1509	20	17 (85%)	15 (75%)	14 (70%)

Published in 2001. Subset used in analysis included youth ministers; Assemblies of God / Baptist / Covenant / Lutheran / Methodist / Presbyterian. Covariaties included denomination, congregation size, race, age, education, marital status, political orientation, gender, region of the country, setting (rural/urban/suburban).

A	B	C	D	E	F	G
TOTALS			**88**	**68 (77%)**	**60 (68%)**	**49 (56%)**

Parents Survey and the Youth Workers Survey data were analyzed separately, since a number of the first-order clusters were unique to just one of the surveys. The resulting number of second-order cluster families and the number of first-order clusters that grouped into the second-order cluster families are presented in Table A-4.

Comparison of EYM to "Surrogate Control" Prior Studies

As discussed above, EYM did not include a control group. Rather, items from prior studies for which data was available were used in the EYM surveys so that the EYM data might be compared to the data from the prior studies. These studies, each of which used a random sample of congregations and/or individuals across the nation, were used as a "surrogate control" group. The prior studies used were:

- *Effective Christian Education[2]*
- *Survey of Catholic Youth Program Participants[8]*
- *Youth Ministry That Transforms[7]*
- *Young Adolescents and Their Parents[9]*

Sub-cluster development. The prior studies did not include all of the items used in EYM, so only some of the EYM first-order clusters contained items also in one or more of the prior studies. For each EYM cluster that contained prior study items, those items were used to compute a "sub-cluster" score. In the rare case that an EYM cluster contained items from multiple prior studies, multiple sub-cluster scores were computed, one for each of the prior studies. The number of items in an EYM cluster that came from a prior study ranged from one to all of the cluster items. Sub-cluster scores were computed regardless of the number of items, even though the reliability of the sub-cluster could have been significantly less than that of the EYM cluster. Table A-5 summarizes the number and percentage of items used in sub-clusters.

Comparisons of sub-cluster scores. Table A-6 summarizes the comparisons of sub-cluster scores between EYM and prior studies. Mean sub-cluster scores were compared using regression models with a dichotomous EYM variable (1 = EYM, 0 = prior study) as the primary independent variable. The data was stratified by study and, whenever possible, denomination. The data were to equalize the contribution of each study, denominations with studies, and congregations within denominations. When known, congregations were treated as primary sampling units (PSU), otherwise the individual survey was the PSU. For each analysis, the data were subset (both EYM and prior study) as necessary to most closely match denominations, age, and role (pastor, adult, youth, youth minister, etc.). All comparable demographic variables available in both EYM and the prior study were used as covariates in the analysis. These variables were collapsed into fewer categories as needed depending on the N-size available. Cross terms of the covariates with the dichotomous EYM variable were also included in the models. The analyses were performed using Proc Regress in SAS-callable SUDAAN.

Analysis of Open-Ended Survey Questions

The Pastor and Youth Minister Survey contained four open-ended questions:

- *Your congregation has been identified as one that is doing a good job of nurturing youth to mature Christian faith. Why do you think your congregation's youth ministry is able to accomplish this while so many other congregations struggle at it?*
- *Describe any key structural/organizational components to your youth ministry.*
- *Compared to other congregations in your area, what is distinctive about your youth ministry?*
- *Please complete this thought: The youth ministry at our congregation would die if . . .*

A qualitative content analysis was performed by one of the research co-directors on the written responses to the questions. The analysis yielded 20 content categories of responses (See Appendix 5).

Study Limitations

The EYM Study, like all studies, had limitations that were recognized by the researchers. Many such limitations have been pointed out in the discussion above. These and others are discussed in greater depth here.

Lack of true control group. As already discussed, the study lacked a true control group. Ideally, a randomly selected sample of congregations in each of the twenty-one sample cells would have been included in the study. This would have allowed for greater generalizability of the item cluster structure that was identified, comparisons could have been made between exemplary congregations and the population of congregations on all cluster scores. Unfortunately, resources were not sufficient to include another 130 congregations in the study. As it was, recruitment of even exemplary congregations proved to be much more difficult and costly than anticipated, and the study fell short of the targeted goal of fifteen congregations in each sample cell.

The use of prior study data as a surrogate for a control group was a cost-effective compromise. The studies provided data from randomly selected samples of congregations and/or individuals, similar to the ideal control group for EYM. Though not coincident in time with EYM, it is reasonable to hypothesize that scores on the dimensions measured by the surveys are unlikely to have risen since the time of the prior studies; if anything, they are more likely to have fallen, making the large number of significant differences found in the comparison analyses all the more striking.

It is unfortunate that only a limited number of comparisons could be made due to the limited number of questions from the prior studies that could be used in EYM. On the other hand, that is not a great surprise since there have been no prior studies of congregations doing exemplary youth ministry, and few, if any, previous studies regarding youth ministry have been so exhaustive. It is hoped that EYM has laid a foundation of constructs and their measurement that will serve future research in youth ministry well.

Sample. The sample of congregations was not random. The sampling process attempted to identify the "best of the best." Study of the best of the best was necessary to begin to understand youth ministry of the power and breadth that may be necessary for the future survival of the church. Similarly, sampling within congregations was not random. The study only wanted to know about the lives and activities of the truly active participants in the youth ministries of the congregations. Unfortunately, even in the best youth ministry programs, numbers are small. Consequently, random sampling did not make sense.

Because the sample was not a random sample of a defined population, the study makes no claim of generalizability of its findings. The study described the congregations that were in the study, but not necessarily any group of congregations outside the study.

Congregational Assessment Form B. The study team recognized that Form B had several weaknesses. As discussed, the questions asked for what proportion of the congregation's youth the statement is true. The primary problem was what defines "the congregation's youth"? What is the denominator? Is it those that are involved in the youth ministry regularly, those involved occasionally, confirmed youth, baptized youth, youth in the Catholic parish, or youth in the immediate community? Through long discussion, the study team concluded that church bodies looked at this issue in sometimes very different ways. At the root of the issue is the fact that the church bodies conceive of "membership" in the church differently. For many of the Protestant groups, membership is formal, requiring application and a reception ceremony. For other groups, membership is whoever shows up on a regular basis. For Roman Catholics, membership is whoever lives within the geographic territory of the parish. So, who are a congregation's youth? Ultimately, the decision was to let each respondent use their own definition of "the congregation's youth." The rationale was that if the congregation has the reputation for doing exemplary youth ministry (by the study's definition), and if the pastor or youth minister in the congregation indicated that a strong proportion of their youth (however they defined "their youth") was on their way to becoming mature Christian youth, then the study was interested in knowing what they were doing.

Form B, from a psychometric perspective, was also flawed by only requiring one respondent from each congregation. Statistically, the margin of error of a single measurement is infinite. However, used in conjunction with the fact that the congregation had been nominated for having a reputation for exemplary youth ministry, the study team felt that corroboration by a single, informed individual (i.e., the senior/lead pastor or youth minister) was sufficient to determine candidacy for the study.

Lower than desired participation. The study fell short of its participation goals both for congregations and individuals. Going into the study, the study team thought that congregations would be honored to be identified as doing outstanding work and would be inclined to participate. That was not the case. It appears that the growing disinterest in responding to surveys that has been observed throughout survey research in the past ten to fifteen years applies to churches as well as the general population. As mentioned above, the study members did everything they could to overcome this issue but finally were limited by resources and time.

The statistical analyses, of course, took the actual number of respondents and congregations into account. So, again, the fact that the study identified so many statistically significant differences is remarkable.

Sub-clusters. Cluster scores are created primarily for two reasons: higher precision and/or confidence in one's measurement of a construct (i.e., higher reliability); and greater efficiency in analysis. In the cases in which there were very few items used to compute a sub-cluster score, reliability was reduced to some extent. The analyses that were done, and their results, remain legitimate, however. The reader simply needs to take into account the fact that in some cases, constructs were not being measured with high reliability.

Mixed response sets for items in a single cluster. Ideally, all the items of a cluster would have the same response possibilities. Because the surveys included items from many prior studies, and because it was necessary to keep them unchanged in order to legitimately compare the EYM results to the prior study results, response sets varied across items, and, consequently, within some clusters. Whenever new items were created, the research team attempted to use the response set of an existing item that might cluster with the new item, but because the clusters were developed using blind, empirical methods, this did not entirely alleviate the problem.

For cluster analysis, if the items do not all have the same response set, it is preferable that all items in the analysis at least have the same range. For that reason, all items were translated to fit a 1-9 scale. This also made the interpretation of item means easier in some respects. Unfortunately, when a cluster has mixed response sets it is somewhat difficult sometimes to translate the 1-9 cluster score (mean item score) into the original responses, so interpretation of the "absolute meaning" of a cluster score can be troublesome. Even if the concept behind the response set is the same, the words don't necessarily line up. For example, one cluster combined 7- and 5-response scales in which the concept was "how often true." Here is how the response scales lined up on the 9-point scale:

7-response	5-response
1 = Never true	1 = Never or rarely true
2.33 = Rarely true	
	3 = Sometimes true
3.67 = True once in a while	
5 = Sometimes true	5 = True about half the time
6.33 = Often true	
	7 = Often true
7.67 = Almost always true	
9 = Always true	9 = Almost always or always true

As one can see, the words describing each response don't line up as well as one would like, particularly "Sometimes true." Fortunately, the experience of the study researchers is that many people tend to ignore the meaning of the words after a while when they answer the questions, especially when the responses are presented as letters to mark in long columns of responses (as most were in the EYM surveys). The middle response tends to become the midpoint for people, regardless of the words attached. Granted, this is not always true, but there is a tendency to move in that direction.

The study team considered using analytic procedures that attempt to rescale each item in a cluster so that the responses line up together from a statistical perspective (using nonmetric multidimensional scaling procedures such as reciprocal averaging[23]). It was decided not to do so for these reasons: (1) the study was designed to make group comparisons; (2) in the past, the research team's experience has been that there is not a dramatic difference to average group scores when such procedures are applied (though it does sometimes make a real difference if you are trying to build an instrument for assessing individuals); and (3) applying those procedures makes it even harder to figure out how to attach the words from the original responses to the cluster score, thus making explanation of the meaning of cluster scores more difficult.

Understanding the Nomenclature and Structure of the Quantitative Research

Items: individual questions or statements in the survey to which youth, parents, adult youth workers, youth ministers and pastors responded; over 750 appeared in the questionnaires. Some of these items were drawn from prior studies thereby providing possibilities of comparisons with historical populations.

> **Example—326: How true is each of these statements for you? I am keenly away of the presence of the presence of God.** It's one of a cluster of 8 items making up the dimension: A Personal Christianity.

Dimensions: clusters of items from the survey that have a strong coherent relationship to a common meaning or action; these clusters of items reveal the patterns of thought of the youth, parents, adult youth workers, youth ministers and pastors who filled out the surveys; over 90 emerged in the first round of analysis of the data.

> **Example—Y48: A Personal Christianity:** It consists of 8 items from the survey; it's one of the 12 dimensions making up the theme: Committed Christian Youth.

Themes: clusters of dimensions of the findings that have a strong coherent relationship to a common meaning or action; these clusters of dimensions reveal large patterns of thought of the youth, parents, adult youth workers, youth ministers and pastors who filled out the surveys; 14 emerged in the second round of analysis of items and dimensions.

> **Example—Committed Christian Youth:** It consists of 12 dimensions describing the faith of youth in the exemplary congregations.

summary of highest scoring themes in the quantitative study

T hemes are clusters of dimensions of the findings that have a strong coherent relationship to a common meaning or action. These clusters of dimensions reveal large patterns of thought of the youth, parents, adult youth workers, youth ministers, and pastors who filled out the surveys. A total of fourteen themes emerged in the second round of analysis of items and dimensions. All numbers reflect the mean with the highest score = 9.

The Strengths of Youth in Exemplary Congregations

As reported by Youth

1.	A Personal Christianity	7.74
2.	Moral Responsibility	7.37
3.	Defends and Supports Friends	6.86
4.	Faith Maturity	6.50
5.	A Personal Religiousness	6.36

As reported by Parents

1.	Positive Youth Response	7.98
2.	Youth Service Involvement	7.30
3.	Youth's Outreach	6.50
4.	Making Faith a Way of Life	6.44

As reported by Adult Youth Workers

1.	Positive Youth Response	7.98
2.	Youth's Service Involvement	7.26
3.	Youth's Outreach	6.50
4.	Making Faith a Way of Life	6.45

As reported by Pastors and Youth Ministers

1.	Positive Youth Response	8.12
2.	Youth Service Involvement	7.71
3.	Youth's Outreach	6.78
4.	Making Faith a Way of Life	6.48

The Strengths of Exemplary Congregations

As reported by Youth

1.	Pastor's Spiritual Influence	7.37
2.	Congregation's Biblical Emphasis	7.16
3.	Pastor's Personal Characteristics	7.13
4.	Warm, Challenging Climate	7.05

5.	Satisfied with Congregation	6.93
6.	Mission Effectiveness	6.71
7.	Congregation's Moral Guidance	6.60
8.	Congregation's Social Interaction	6.55
9.	Congregation Promotes Service	6.40
10.	Congregation's Openness	6.35
11.	Worship Services' Positive Characteristics	6.29

As reported by Parents

1.	Importance of the Church to Me	7.73
2.	Welcoming Atmosphere	6.96
3.	Teaches Core Christian Concepts	6.95
4.	Members Experience Love and Support	6.92
5.	Congregation Gives Moral Guidance	6.81
6.	Congregation Promotes Service	6.42
7.	Congregation Makes Me Think	6.36
8.	Satisfaction with Worship	6.27
9.	Congregation Open to Change	6.25

As reported by Adult Youth Workers

1.	Pastor Supports Christian Education and Youth Ministry	8.05
2.	Importance of this Church to Me	7.96
3.	Effectiveness of Pastoral Leadership	7.90
4.	Pastor's Communication Skills	7.48
5.	Welcoming Atmosphere	7.21
6.	Youth Worker's Satisfaction with Congregation	7.05
7.	Pastor is Good Counselor	7.02
8.	Congregation Gives Moral Guidance	6.96
9.	Pastor Preaches to Make Disciples	6.80
10.	Congregation Makes Me Think	6.68
11.	Congregation Promotes Service	6.43
12.	Satisfaction with Worship	6.40
13.	Congregation Open to Change	6.31

As reported by Pastors and Youth Ministers

1.	Awareness of Mission Statement	7.25
2.	Congregational Support for Youth Ministry	7.19
3.	Freedom to Disagree	6.75
4.	Climate of Warmth and Openness	6.63

The Strengths of Youth Ministries in Exemplary Congregations

As reported by the Youth

1.	Program Negatives (Reverse Score)	8.11
2.	Youth Minister's Positive Characteristics	7.87
3.	Emphasis on Prayer, Faith Study, Leadership; Safe and Caring Place	7.55
4.	Youth Gatherings have a Warm, Welcoming Climate	7.44
5.	Youth Ministry's Structural Core	7.36
6.	Impact on Personal Faith	7.28
7.	Emphasis on Participation in Congregation/Community	7.16
8.	Emphasis on Peer Ministry	7.14
9.	Youth Ministry's Desired Outcomes	6.75

As reported by Parents

1.	Adult Education Negatives (Reverse Scores)	8.15
2.	Youth Minister's Leadership	8.14
3.	Youth Minister's Competence	8.00
4.	Peer Ministry	6.64
5.	Teaching Moral Values	6.60
6.	Adult-Youth Mentoring	6.56
7.	Achievement of Desired Outcomes	6.52

As reported by Adult Youth Workers

1.	Youth Minster Competence	7.95
2.	Youth Minister's Effectiveness	7.83
3.	Youth Minister Characteristics	7.25
4.	Youth Ministry Roadblocks (Reverse Score)	7.17
5.	Adult Worker Satisfaction	6.82
6.	Achievement of Desired Outcomes	6.60
7.	Peer Ministry	6.55
8.	Adult-Youth Mentoring	6.31

As reported by Pastors and Youth Ministers

9.	Emphasizes Life as Calling	6.67
10.	Youth Ministry Effectiveness	6.08

The Strengths of Families in Exemplary Congregations

As reported by Youth

1.	Family Disharmony (Reverse Score)	7.19
2.	Parents are Affectionate	6.83
3.	Parental Verbal Abuse	6.41
4.	Mother Helps with Problems	6.29
5.	Mother Influences My Faith	6.15
6.	Father Helps with Problems	5.60
7.	Father Influences My Faith	5.41

As reported by Parents

1.	God Consciousness	8.23
2.	Moral Responsibility	7.97
3.	Family Disharmony	7.03
4.	Family Orientation	7.02
5.	Use of Faith Support Group	6.70

The Strengths of Pastors (Lead Pastors) in Exemplary Congregations

As reported by Youth

1.	Pastor's Spiritual Influence	7.37
2.	Pastor's Personal Characteristics	7.13

As reported by Parents

1.	Effectiveness of Pastor's Leadership	7.88
2.	Interpersonal Characteristics	7.80
3.	Pastor's Communication Skills	7.30
4.	Pastor is a Good Counselor	6.82
5.	Pastor Preaches to Make Disciples	6.71

As reported by Adult Youth Workers

1.	Pastor Supports Christian Education and Youth Ministry	8.05
2.	Effectiveness of Pastor's Leadership	7.90
3.	Pastor's Communication Skills	7.48
4.	Pastor is a Good Counselor	7.02
5.	Pastor Preaches to Make Disciples	6.80

As reported by Pastors and Youth Ministers

1.	Pastoral Support for Youth Staff	7.76
2.	Pastor Creates a Healthy Climate	7.39
3.	Mission is to Make Disciples	6.94
4.	Mentor	6.26

APPENDIX FOUR

themes from the quantitative study

Overview

Youth Survey Themes

1. Committed Christian Youth - 12
2. Congregational Characteristic and Influence - 12
3. Influence of Family - 5
4. Influential Factors of the Youth Ministry - 12
5. Involvement in Church Activities - 7

Parents' Themes

1. Committed Christian Youth - 7
2. Congregational Characteristics - 12
3. Effectiveness of Youth and Family Ministries - 12
4. Leadership of Lead Pastor - 5
5. Christian Spirituality - 6
6. Committed Christian Adults - 4

Adult Youth Workers' Themes

1. Committed Christian Youth - 7
2. Congregational Characteristics - 17
3. Effectiveness of Youth and Family Ministries - 14
4. Self-Perceived Competencies in Youth Ministries - 3
5. Personal Christianity of Youth workers - 7

Pastors' and Youth Ministers' Themes

1. Committed Christian Youth - 7
2. Congregational Characteristics - 4
3. Effectiveness of Congregation's Ministry to Parents and Youth - 8
4. Leadership of Lead Pastor - 4
5. Obstacles Within Youth Ministry - 3
6. Training for Youth Ministry – 5

Youth Survey Themes

1. Youth Survey Theme: Committed Christian Youth (Reliability: .94)

A	B	C	D	E	F *
.85	Y66	Y66: A Personal Religiousness	6.36	1.47	2231
.83	Y53	Y53: Seeks Spiritual Growth	5.76	2.02	2192
.82	Y50	Y50: Faith Maturity	6.50	1.50	2237
.80	Y52	Y52: Speaks Publicly About Own Faith	5.31	2.18	2176
.79	Y51	Y51: God Consciousness	5.38	2.32	2162
.74	Y48	Y48: A Personal Christianity	7.74	1.37	2247
.68	Y68	Y68: Moral Integrity	5.94	1.97	2124
.68	Y20	Y20: Defends and Supports Friends	6.86	1.47	2171
.67	Y19	Y19: Lives a Life of Service	5.35	1.81	2173
.64	Y49	Y49: Private Religious Study	4.34	2.09	2230
.63	Y7	Y7: Faith Impact of Church Involvement	6.83	1.75	2236
.58	Y18	Y18: Moral Responsibility	7.37	1.23	2244
.53	Y22	Y22: Considers a Religious Vocation	3.65	2.03	2200

*A = Dimension to Theme Correlation; B = Dimension Number; C = Dimension; D = Mean; E = Standard Deviation; F = Number of Respondents

2. Youth Survey Themes: Congregational Characteristics and Influence (Reliability: .94)

A	B	C	D	E	F *
.82	Y47	Y47: Congregation Promotes Service Activities	6.40	1.64	2214
.82	Y1	Y1: Warm, Challenging Climate	7.05	1.63	2237
.80	Y46	Y46: Congregation's Moral Guidance	6.60	1.68	2232
.79	Y64	Y64: Satisfaction With Congregation	6.93	1.63	2228
.79	Y5	Y5: Mission Effectiveness	6.71	1.66	2217
.78	Y3	Y3: Worship Services: Positive Characteristics	6.29	1.98	2191
.76	Y11	Y11: Pastor's Spiritual Influence	7.37	1.48	1937
.75	Y45	Y45: Congregation's Biblical Emphasis	7.16	1.66	2233
.69	Y12	Y12: Pastor's Personal Characteristics	7.13	1.82	2167
.67	Y4	Y4: Congregation's Social Interaction	6.55	1.59	2220
.65	Y6	Y6: Congregation's Openness	6.35	1.84	2196
.47	Y69	Y69: Congregation's Teaching Emphasis	5.89	2.05	1503

3. Youth Survey Themes: Influence of Family (Reliability: .82)

A	B	C	D	E	F *
.67	Y26	Y26: Parents Help With Problems	6.02	1.89	2234
.60	Y44	Y44: Mother Influences My Faith	6.15	1.90	2236
.59	Y24	Y24: Father Influences My Faith	5.41	2.22	2224
.59	Y67	Y67: Family Influences My Faith	4.73	1.77	2211
.56	Y28	Y28: Parents are Affectionate	6.83	2.05	2225
.49	Y23	Y23: Family Disharmony (Reverse-scored)	7.19	1.97	2201
.38	Y39	Y39: Parental Verbal Abuse (Reverse-scored)	6.41	1.85	2226

4. Youth Survey Themes: Influential Factors of the Youth Ministry (Reliability: .90)

A	B	C	D	E	F *
.78	Y65	Y65: Youth Ministry's Structural Core (Qualified youth workers, well run and organized, Christ-centered, safe and caring place)	7.36	1.50	2221
.74	Y13	Y13: Emphasis on Prayer, Faith, Study, Leadership, Safe and Caring Place	7.55	1.42	2223

*A = Dimension to Theme Correlation; B = Dimension Number; C = Dimension; D = Mean; E = Standard Deviation; F = Number of Respondents

.73	Y10	Y10: Youth Ministry's Desired Outcomes	6.75	1.73	2121
.71	Y8	Y8: Impact on Personal Faith	7.28	1.91	2224
.71	Y29	Y29: Youth Gatherings Have a Warm, Welcoming Climate	7.44	1.45	2225
.67	Y31	Y31: Help With Life Issues	5.82	1.78	2221
.66	Y2	Y2: Emphasis on Participation in Congregation and Community	7.16	1.58	2201
.57	Y9	Y9: Youth Minister's Positive Characteristics	7.87	1.31	2236
.41	Y40	Y40: Spiritual Support Group	8.39	1.58	2220

5. Youth Survey Themes: Involvement in Church Activities (Reliability: .72)

A	B	C	D	E	F *
.60	Y41	Y41: Leadership Development Activities	5.91	1.99	2226
.59	Y21	Y21: Church-Sponsored Trips	6.68	1.89	2233
.49	Y43	Y43: Church Friendships	6.71	1.88	2218
.38	Y42	Y42: Music Involvement	4.57	2.46	2243

6. Youth Survey Themes: Other Items

A	B	C	D	E	F *
NA	Y15	Y15: Faith-Influential Friends	6.40	1.79	2246
NA	Y32	Y32: Attractions of Youth Program	6.07	1.89	2235
NA	Y14	Y14: Emphasis on Peer Ministry	7.14	1.59	576
NA	Y37	Y37: Faith Influence of Relatives	4.97	2.18	2224
NA	Y36	Y36: Faith Influence of Other Adults	3.05	1.71	2240
NA	Y30	Y30: Program Negatives (Reverse-scored)	8.11	1.55	2201
NA	Y34	Y34: Faith Concerns (Reverse-scored)	6.18	1.93	2166
NA	Y33	Y33: Fine Arts Emphasis	3.67	2.07	2187
NA	Y35	Y35: Negative Pastoral Characteristics (Reverse-scored)	7.38	1.98	2130
NA	Y38	Y38: Salvation By Works (Reverse-scored)	4.81	2.51	2244

A = Dimension to Theme Correlation; B = Dimension Number; C = Dimension; D = Mean; E = Standard Deviation; F = Number of Respondents

Parent Survey Themes

1. Parent Survey Themes: Christian Spirituality (Reliability: .81)

A	B	C	D	E	F *
.73	R29	R29: Faith Orientation	7.02	1.21	1667
.67	R32	R32: Bible Reading	4.74	2.52	1654
.64	R39	R39: Salvation by Works (Reverse-scored)	5.74	2.23	1663
.48	R78	R78: Moral Responsibility	7.97	1.15	1657
.47	R31	R31: God Consciousness	8.23	1.50	1668
.43	R34	R34: Use of Faith Support Group	6.70	3.13	1658

2. Parent Survey Themes: Committed Christian Adults (Reliability: .72)

A	B	C	D	E	F *
.57	R30	R30: Centrality of Faith	6.99	1.34	1665
.53	R33	R33: Social Responsibility	6.16	1.41	1665
.49	R41	R41: Members' Expectations of the Congregation	6.60	1.51	1667
.45	R42	R42: Desire for Participating in Leadership, Community, and Spirituality	6.49	1.58	1665

3. Parent Survey Themes: Committed Christian Youth (Reliability: .90)

A	B	C	D	E	F *
.77	R74	R74: Evidence of Positive Spirit	5.35	1.77	1408
.77	R75	R75: Evidences Moral Responsibility	4.48	1.60	1203
.75	R73	R73: Seeks Spiritual Growth	4.72	1.70	1407
.72	R63	R63: Making Faith a Way of Life	6.44	1.23	1634
.67	R64	R64: Youth's Outreach	6.50	1.56	1619
.59	R65	R65: Youth's Service Involvement	7.30	1.41	1646
.59	R66	R66: Positive Youth Response	7.98	1.08	1613

*A = Dimension to Theme Correlation; B = Dimension Number; C = Dimension; D = Mean; E = Standard Deviation; F = Number of Respondents

4. Parent Survey Themes: Congregational Characteristics (Reliability: .92)

A	B	C	D	E	F*
.77	R18	R18: Congregation Open to Change	6.25	1.40	1583
.75	R48	R48: Congregation Makes Me Think	6.36	1.80	1658
.74	R15	R15: Teaches Core Christian Concepts	6.95	1.60	1667
.74	R22	R22: Members Experience Love and Support	6.92	1.44	1634
.72	R45	R45: Satisfaction With Worship	6.27	1.90	1652
.70	R16	R16: Congregation Gives Moral Guidance	6.81	1.67	1648
.69	R23	R23: Welcoming Atmosphere	6.96	1.62	1659
.67	R19	R19: Congregation Promotes Service Activities	6.42	1.65	1663
.64	R20	R20: Adult Education Effectiveness	5.96	1.64	1608
.62	R17	R17: Members Willing to Change	5.04	1.88	1643
.60	R77	R77: Importance of This Church to Me	7.73	1.44	1663
.47	R80	R80: Congregation's Social Interaction	5.18	1.72	1625

5. Parent Survey Themes: Effectiveness of Youth and Family Ministries (Reliability: .91)

A	B	C	D	E	F*
.83	R79	R79: Adult-Youth Involvement Together	5.28	1.77	1448
.81	R51	R51: Helps Parents With Parenting Issues	4.63	2.01	1283
.78	R50	R50: Achievement of Desired Outcomes	6.52	1.65	1591
.75	R21	R21: Teaching Moral Values	6.60	1.50	1549
.68	R26	R26: Peer Ministry	6.64	1.54	301
.65	R36	R36: Youth Minister Competence	8.00	1.09	1651
.64	R38	R38: Effectiveness of Parental Education	4.84	2.16	1408
.62	R25	R25: Adult-Youth Mentoring	6.56	1.47	603
.61	R35	R35: Youth Minister's Leadership	8.14	1.11	1651
.58	R49	R49: Congregation's Mission Outreach	5.82	1.70	1643
.56	R76	R76: Emphasis on Vocation	5.85	1.65	1500
.33	R24	R24: Adult Education Negatives (Reverse-scored)	8.15	1.28	1604

*A = Dimension to Theme Correlation; B = Dimension Number; C = Dimension; D = Mean; E = Standard Deviation; F = Number of Respondents

6. Parent Survey Themes: Leadership of Lead Pastor (Reliability: .92)

A	B	C	D	E	F *
.86	R43	R43: Effectiveness of Pastor's Leadership	7.88	1.19	1533
.84	R14	R14: Interpersonal Characteristics	7.80	1.33	1606
.77	R44	R44: Pastor Is a Good Counselor	6.82	1.84	1628
.75	R46	R46: Pastor's Communication Skills	7.38	1.66	1610
.72	R47	R47: Pastor Preaches to Make Disciples	6.71	1.71	1499

7. Parent Survey Themes: Other Items

A	B	C	D	E	F *
NA	R27	R27: Family Disharmony (Reverse-scored)	7.03	2.10	1652
NA	R28	R28: Faith Concerns (Reverse-scored)	6.19	1.98	1596

Adult Youth Worker Survey Themes

1. Adult Youth Worker Survey Themes: Committed Christian Youth (Reliability: .88)

A	B	C	D	E	F *
.77	W75	W75: Evidences Moral Responsibility	4.42	1.44	1119
.73	W73	W73: Seeks Spiritual Growth	4.70	1.48	1322
.73	W74	W74: Evidence of Positive Spirit	5.42	1.61	1273
.70	W63	W63: Making Faith a Way of Life	6.45	1.17	1394
.64	W64	W64: Youth's Outreach	6.50	1.48	1382
.56	W66	W66: Positive Youth Response	8.09	1.02	1397
.48	W65	W65: Youth's Service Involvement	7.26	1.46	1396

*A = Dimension to Theme Correlation; B = Dimension Number; C = Dimension; D = Mean; E = Standard Deviation; F = Number of Respondents

2. Adult Youth Worker Survey Themes: Congregational Characteristics (Reliability: .95)

A	B	C	D	E	F *
.89	W1	W1: Youth Workers' Satisfaction With Congregation	7.05	1.26	1411
.79	W43	W43: Effectiveness of Pastor's Leadership	7.90	1.29	1338
.78	W45	W45: Satisfaction With Worship	6.40	1.88	1419
.76	W48	W48: Congregation Makes Me Think	6.68	1.76	1416
.76	W47	W47: Pastor Preaches to Make Disciples	6.80	1.78	1305
.75	W18	W18: Congregation Open to Change	6.31	1.28	1382
.74	W46	W46: Pastor's Communication Skills	7.48	1.66	1385
.73	W49	W49: Congregation's Mission Outreach	6.04	1.71	1401
.73	W44	W44: Pastor Is a Good Counselor	7.02	1.98	1391
.72	W16	W16: Congregation Gives Moral Guidance	6.96	1.65	1417
.64	W23	W23: Welcoming Atmosphere	7.21	1.53	1419
.61	W76	W76: Emphasis on Vocation	6.19	1.59	1344
.61	W3	W3: Structural Openness to Change	6.25	1.55	1324
.60	W19	W19: Congregation Promotes Service Activities	6.43	1.63	1419
.58	W2	W2: Pastor Supports Christian Education and Youth Ministry	8.05	1.65	1304
.54	W77	W77: Importance of This Church to Me	7.96	1.29	1416
.52	W80	W80: Congregation's Social Interaction	5.22	1.75	1383

3. Adult Youth Worker Survey Themes: Effectiveness of Youth Ministry (Reliability: .94)

A	B	C	D	E	F *
.87	W50	W50: Achievement of Desired Outcomes	6.60	1.51	1402
.85	W52	W52: Effectiveness of Involving and Training	5.85	1.66	1350
.80	W51	W51: Helps Parents With Parenting Issues	5.23	1.88	1126
.80	W79	W79: Adult-Youth Involvement Together	5.02	1.64	1297
.75	W53	W53: Adult Worker Satisfaction	6.82	1.45	1403
.73	W5	W5: Youth Minister's Effectiveness	7.83	1.12	1422
.72	W36	W36: Youth Minister Competence	7.95	1.03	1423
.71	W54	W54: Youth Ministry Characteristics	7.25	1.41	1414

A = Dimension to Theme Correlation; B = Dimension Number; C = Dimension; D = Mean; E = Standard Deviation; F = Number of Respondents

.66	W4	W4: Training Emphasis	5.12	1.89	1345
.63	W26	W26: Peer Ministry	6.55	1.57	295
.63	W7	W7: Training of Adult Youth Workers	5.52	2.15	888
.62	W38	W38: Effectiveness of Parental Education	3.97	2.02	952
.58	W25	W25: Adult-Youth Mentoring	6.31	1.43	498
.40	W13	W13: Youth Ministry Roadblocks (Reverse-scored)	7.17	1.32	1400

4. Adult Youth Worker Survey Themes: Personal Christianity of Youth Workers (Reliability: .76)

A	B	C	D	E	F *
.65	W30	W30: Centrality of Faith	7.47	1.11	1425
.60	W32	W32: Bible Reading	5.58	2.28	1414
.56	W6	W6: Theological Competency	6.70	1.45	1411
.44	W31	W31: God Consciousness	8.57	1.04	1425
.39	W33	W33: Social Responsibility	6.56	1.40	1425
.38	W78	W78: Moral Responsibility	8.06	1.02	1422
.34	W40	W40: Salvation by Works (Reverse-scored)	6.15	2.74	1423

5. Adult Youth Worker Survey Themes: Self-Perceived Competence in Youth Ministry (Reliability: .75)

A	B	C	D	E	F *
.65	W8	W8: Positive Relationship With Youth	7.07	0.95	1420
.57	W11	W11: Adult Workers' Creativity	6.72	1.20	1394
.53	W10	W10: Youth Workers' Relationship with Parents	6.93	1.06	1419

6. Adult Youth Worker Survey Themes: Other Items

A	B	C	D	E	F *
NA	W9	W9: Personal Support Group	7.40	1.86	1419
NA	W34	W34: Use of Faith Support Group	7.95	2.21	1417
NA	W12	W12: Youth-Adult Disconnect (Reverse-scored)	7.53	1.39	1405

*A = Dimension to Theme Correlation; B = Dimension Number; C = Dimension; D = Mean; E = Standard Deviation; F = Number of Respondents

Pastor and Youth Ministry Survey Themes

1. Pastor and Youth Minister Survey Themes: Committed Christian Youth (Reliability: .83)

A	B	C	D	E	F *
.74	M54	M54: Evidences Moral Responsibility	4.52	1.21	202
.68	M53	M53: Evidence of Positive Spirit	5.61	1.45	216
.66	M48	M48: Making Faith a Way of Life	6.48	1.08	219
.64	M52	M52: Seeks Spiritual Growth	4.86	1.28	218
.53	M49	M49: Youth's Outreach	6.78	1.30	218
.48	M51	M51: Positive Youth Response	8.12	0.94	218
.35	M50	M50: Youth's Service Involvement	7.71	1.34	219

2. Pastor and Youth Minister Survey Themes: Congregational Characteristics (Reliability: .67)

A	B	C	D	E	F *
.58	M25	M25: Climate of Warmth and Openness	6.63	1.29	222
.45	M43	M43: Freedom to Disagree	6.75	1.34	220
.40	M24	M24: Congregational Support for Youth Ministry	7.19	1.47	217
.39	M44	M44: Awareness of Mission Statement	7.25	1.97	219

3. Pastor and Youth Minister Survey Themes: Effectiveness of Congregation's Ministry to Parents and Youth (Reliability: .89)

A	B	C	D	E	F *
.72	M27	M27: Youth Evangelism	5.23	1.62	217
.72	M42	M42: Youth Ministry Effectiveness	6.08	1.29	219
.71	M31	M31: Support of Families in Conflict Situations	4.16	1.56	194
.70	M30	M30: Strengthening Parent-Youth Relationships	4.41	1.52	208

A = Dimension to Theme Correlation; B = Dimension Number; C = Dimension; D = Mean; E = Standard Deviation; F = Number of Respondents

.66	M29	M29: Equipping Parents	4.70	1.31	210
.60	M32	M32: Training Leaders	5.83	1.52	215
.58	M33	M33: Emphasizes Life as a Calling	6.67	1.23	216
.58	M28	M28: Nurturing Praying Youth	5.73	1.86	219

4. Pastor and Youth Minister Survey Themes: Leadership of the Lead Pastor (Reliability: .83)

A	B	C	D	E	F*
.79	M38	M38: Pastor Creates a Healthy Culture	7.39	1.41	123
.79	M39	M39: Mission is to Make Disciples	6.94	1.40	119
.61	M41	M41: Pastoral Support for Youth Staff	7.76	1.26	121
.45	M23	M23: Mentoring	6.26	1.34	91

5. Pastor and Youth Minister Survey Themes: Obstacles within Youth Ministry (Reliability: .72)

A	B	C	D	E	F*
.59	M26	M26: Disconnect Between Youth and Adults (Reverse-scored)	7.21	1.81	208
.52	M37	M37: Youth and Parent Disinterest (Reverse-scored)	6.39	1.78	121
.51	M36	M36: Limited Personal Support (Reverse-scored)	7.34	1.83	121

6. Pastor and Youth Minister Survey Themes: Training Youth for Ministry (Reliability: .67)

A	B	C	D	E	F*
.57	M15	M15: Life-Related Group Conversations	4.76	1.20	217
.56	M17	M17: Youth-Led Activities	4.33	1.76	214
.42	M47	M47: Equipping Peer Ministers	3.32	1.91	217
.33	M45	M45: Classes on Tradition, Morality, and Justice	4.89	1.46	218
.28	M46	M46: Frequency of Mailings	5.19	1.27	220

*A = Dimension to Theme Correlation; B = Dimension Number; C = Dimension; D = Mean; E = Standard Deviation; F = Number of Respondents

7. Pastor and Youth Minister Survey Themes: Other Items

A	B	C	D	E	F *
NA	M21	M21: Frequency of Evangelism Training	2.93	0.97	218
NA	M14	M14: Life-Related Individual Conversations	5.53	1.30	218
NA	M18	M18: Frequency of Music and Bible Study Opportunities	6.25	1.59	219
NA	M34	M34: Peer Ministry	5.80	1.51	58
NA	M35	M35: Religious Absolutism	4.66	1.58	220
NA	M22	M22: Adult Mentor Training	3.87	1.53	218
NA	M16	M16: Frequency of Service Activities	3.88	0.92	220
NA	M19	M19: Sports and Games Frequency	3.10	1.20	220
NA	M20	M20: Youth Ministry Planning Frequency	4.31	1.40	213

*A = Dimension to Theme Correlation; B = Dimension Number; C = Dimension; D = Mean; E = Standard Deviation; F = Number of Respondents

APPENDIX FIVE

how the qualitative study was conducted

Thomas H. Berkas and Hal C. Weldin

T his appendix provides a brief overview of the process that was used to gather and then analyze the data from the site visits of the twenty-one congregations that were visited as part of the Exemplary Youth Ministry study. It breaks this process down into three phases: preparations, doing the site visits, and analyzing the data. For each phase an explanation is provided of what we were seeking to do as well as how we did this portion of the study. In addition a variety of tools used in this process are included in the appendices which are located at the end of this appendix.

The qualitative site visits were designed to learn in greater depth and detail how specific congregations are doing exemplary youth ministry. They also sought to identify patterns of approaches used in these congregations.

Phase 1—Preparations for the Site Visits

What Were We Seeking to Do?

Our primary task was to use a modified grounded theory approach (Strauss & Corbin, 1990) that employed a site visit process that employed ethnographic data collection methods (Fetterman, 1989) that were designed to gather a significant amount of data in a short amount of time. This part of the site visit was focused on gathering information about what was the genius of the twenty-one exemplary congregations that were visited. A second objective was to do follow up research regarding the quantitative data gathered from each congregation.

How Did We Do This?

In this initial preparation stage of the study we scoped out what needed to be done with regards to the resources that were available to do the task. This included a series of planning meetings held by the study's research and advisory teams and in conjunction with the design work that was being done by the quantitative research team. In addition, as this research effort progressed, learning from the quantitative study was applied to the qualitative design.

A key reality of the site visit portion of this study was that it needed to be done in such a way as to maximize the resources available for the quantitative aspects of this overall research effort. This resulted in some methodology decisions that were made in response to these realities (for example, deciding to not transcribe the interviews for analysis, but instead sending along a scribe on each of the site visits who was tasked with collecting field notes in real time).

The selection of the congregations that were visited was done through an initial nomination process done by the Advisory Council's denominational representatives of sites they felt would be most beneficial for us to visit from the 131 congregations which had responded to the survey research done in the quantitative part of this study (for additional information about this see Brekke, 2005). They were specifically asked to identify those congregations within their denominations from differing geographic areas of the United States which had a clear reputation of doing excellent youth ministry.

The twenty-one that were visited (three from each of the seven denominations representing small, medium, and large congregations) were selected on the basis of seeking to ensure a geographic diversity of sites. Using color-coded post-its (for denominations and sizes) on a map of the United States, we chose congregations to visit based on a maximum distribution of locations across the country. Of the twenty-one that were selected, only one was unable to participate in this study. In this case a substitute congregation was selected by the denominational representative from those congregations from his denomination which had completed the quantitative study.

In order to be able to collect the site visit data in a short amount of time in a way that maximized the use of our Advisory Council, we decided to have the denominational representatives be the Interviewers on our site visit teams. In so doing we were able to instantly tap into their knowledge of this research effort, their denomination, and of youth ministry. We deliberately decided to have the denominational representatives lead as the interviewers after extensive conversations about the pros and cons of having people with either a great deal or very little background understanding of the sites. We decided to go with the denominational representatives in order to take advantage of their extensive understanding of youth ministry within their denominations. This also minimized challenges that outsiders would have had in understanding and interpreting the cultural and linguistic idiosyncrasies of each denomination.

To respond to the range of experience that the interviewers had in this type of a data gathering process, we created a training event that was designed to get them all up to speed on the data collection processes that we were going to use during the site visits. At the same time we identified five Scribes whose task was to accompany the interviewers on the site visits, making sure each interview was tape recorded, and typing up the field notes of close to transcript quality for each interview. Teams of two allowed us to do up to five or more interviews per site visit with the field notes available soon after the completion of the visit for use by the interviewer in the write up of their executive summary. This also allowed us to gain an additional perspective of the congregations visited as, since the scribes were all Lutherans, they were most often from a different denomination than the congregation being visited.

In preparation for the training of the site visitors we identified the key areas to cover in this session. The site visit process was initially created through a series of pilot site visits that we did of several different congregations that were not a part of this study. We used this experience to design the overall process which included the creation of the human consent forms for the Adults and Youth, a demographic survey that requested information about gender, age, ethnicity, and connections of the interviewee to the congregation and different interview guides or protocols for each of the interviews which were to be done during each site visit. This included individual interviews with the Senior Pastor and the Youth

Director(s) and focus group interviews with the Adult Volunteers, the Youth, and their Parents. This combination of interviews from different key players in each congregation's youth ministry program helped us to triangulate our findings about each congregation from a variety of perspectives.

The questions used in these interviews were developed using a standardized open-ended interview approach (Patton, 2002). The focus groups were designed using methods recommended by Krueger (1994). The interviews and focus groups were all designed to focus on what was the central objective of the site visits which was to gain a better understanding of what the above mentioned key informants from each congregation identified as the genius of their youth ministry efforts. They also sought some additional information about the interviewees' vision for the congregation as well as any areas of their congregation's youth ministry efforts that they felt still needed improvement.

In addition to the guides provided for the interviews, an additional observational protocol was given to the site visit teams that asked them to seek out and write up a variety of data not gained directly through the interviews. This included questions about the congregation itself (history, size, budget, paid staff, etc.) the setting and context of the congregation, the congregation's facilities (both overall and those for the youth), and evidence (from written reports, what's on the walls, bulletin boards, and doors, what's observed during worship, etc.) of how the congregation related to its youth. This information was added to the site visit reports by the scribe.

Training of the site visitor team was done on a Friday/Saturday session held in Minnesota in November, 2003. The first day was dedicated to discussing various aspects of the site visit process. The second day was then done on site at Lord of Life Lutheran in Maple Grove, Minn., with the various interviewers doing actual interviews of pastors, the youth director, parents and youth, with the remainder of the interviewers observing what happened while the scribes took turns gathering tape recorded and typed up interview data from the interviews. This was deliberately done using a hands-on manner with follow-up debriefing to identify and respond to variations we observed in how the interviews were conducted.

Based on what we learned from this training event, we then finalized the site visit manual, seeking to have the site visit process designed in such a manner that even as the interviewers modified the language used in the interviews they conducted, they did this with the clear understanding that what we were seeking was to identify the genius of each congregation's youth ministry effort. A manual explaining and outlining the entire site visit process (Berkas & Weldin, 2003) was then sent to each of the interviewers and scribes for them to review in preparation for their upcoming site visits.

At this point in time the seven interviewers were responsible for setting up the site visits for each of the three congregations chosen for visits from their denomination. These were scheduled and all done between January and April, 2004. The interviewers worked with the congregational contact at each site to prepare for the site visit, asking them to talk over the purpose and process of the site visit with the congregation's senior pastor, as well as schedule the various interviews and invite the participants to them. In the case of the interviews with the youth, the congregational contacts were also asked to send out the human consent forms for the youth to their parents before the site visit occurred.

Phase 2—Data Collection during the Site Visits

What Were We Seeking to Do?

The primary task of the site visits was to gather as much qualitative (interview and observation) data as possible from various of the key stakeholders of each of the twenty-one congregations that were visited. This was done in order to gain a much richer and deeper understanding of how each of these congregations was doing their youth ministry efforts.

With regards to what was to be accomplished during these site visits, there were primarily two tasks. The first was to conduct either individual or focus group interviews with various of the key players within each congregation's youth ministry efforts. This included the senior pastor(s), youth director(s), adult volunteers, youth, and parents. While the questions asked during the various interviews varied slightly, they all sought to gain an understanding of how each of these individuals and groups described the genius of their congregation's youth ministry efforts. The task of the site visit team was to capture as much of the richness of this from the various congregations that were visited as was possible during their visits. A second objective was to do some follow up research from the quantitative data gathered from each congregation.

How Did We Do This?

The twenty-one congregations were visited over a weekend, taking from one to three days per visit, dependent in part on the size of the congregation. These were all done between mid-January and mid-April 2004 using the following process:

> In preparation of the site visit – *The interviewer was tasked with making arrangements for the site visits with the three congregations of their denomination. Based on when these were scheduled, we identified one of the five scribes to*

accompany the interviewer on each of the site visits. Where background materials were available on the internet about the congregations to be visited, the site visit teams were encouraged to familiarize themselves about the congregation they were going to visit before they did the site visit.

Friday of the site visit – Travel to the congregation. Often did an initial walk around the neighborhood and the facilities upon arrival. Possibly also did one or two interviews depending on how the site visit was scheduled.

Saturday of the site visit – Generally did three different interviews, with time between the interviews spent by the interviewer and the scribe debriefing each other on what they had seen and heard, noting any additional information that needed to be noted down in the field notes as well as further insights that should be gathered during the visit.

Sunday of the site visit – Observed worship and possibly did one additional interview followed by travel home.

Within one week of the site visit – The scribe was tasked with providing typed up field notes of the various interviews to the interviewer.

Within two weeks of the site visit – The interviewer wrote up an executive summary of the site visit and then had it checked for accuracy by one or two of the key contacts at the congregation.

Within one month of the site visit – The interviewer and scribe submitted their site visit report to us.

During the individual and focus group interviews, the interviewer was responsible to conduct them using the interview guides developed for this process, adding any additional probes or follow-up questions that they felt would provide helpful additional information. They also provided a human consent form to any of the adults who were interviewed and collected from the youth or youth director the human consent form that was to be signed by both the youth and their parents before the interview began. They also had each person interviewed fill out a brief demographic survey before the interview began.

As this was happening the scribe was responsible to tape recorder the interview as well as type up field notes of what was said, with the goal being to capture as much of the key dialogue as was possible (the scribes were chosen for their ability to very rapidly key in data on laptop computers in real time during the interviews). Thus, while we did not create transcripts of each interview, the scribes did capture seven to thirteen pages of close to transcript quality field notes per interview.

Finally, after the site visit was done, the scribes cleaned up their field notes and sent them to the interviewer whose task was to write up a five- to ten-page executive summary of each site visit for each of the three congregations from their denomination that they visited. This summary was then checked by one or two key contacts from the congregation per Patton's (2002) recommendation that review of analysis be done by inquiry participants (p. 560). Once any changes had been made to each summary by the interviewer, they were then sent to the scribe who combined them with the field notes in a site visit report that was sent in to us for processing and analysis.

This site visit process resulted in interviews with Senior Pastors at all but one of the twenty-one congregations which were visited, and interviews with the youth director(s) and focus groups with the adult volunteers, youth, and parents at all of the sites. Site visit reports ranged in length from fifty to eighty pages, for a total of over 1200 pages of field notes and over 130 pages in the collection of just the site visits' executive summaries (Berkas & Weldin, 2004).

Phase 3—Analysis of the Site Visit Data

What Were We Seeking to Do?

The primary tasks here were to both better understand the individual depth and richness of the data on the genius of the youth ministry of each of the congregations visited, as well as be able to compare the various sites in order to be able to distinguish similarities and differences between them.

How Are We Doing This?

The analysis of the site visits was initially done using several different methods. Initial analysis of findings was done by the interviewer and scribe as the site visit was occurring. Optimally, this was done at the end of each of the interviews and if possible on the ride home (if the team was traveling together for at least part of this trip), with the scribe adding the reflections of the interviewer and themselves about the site visit to the field notes.

A second follow-up analysis occurred once all of the site visit interview field notes were typed up and presented to the interviewer. At this point the interviewer used this data and their own notes and reflections to write up their executive summary of the site visit. These executive summaries were then shared with one or two key contacts from the congregation visited for additional feedback. Once they had been reviewed by the key contact(s) and modified as necessary, they were integrated into the site visit report by the scribe and sent to us for analysis.

After all of the site visits had been submitted to us, we began the process of organizing this data for further analysis. This was done initially by collecting each of the executive summaries in a booklet that allowed us to be able to easily access and reference them (Berkas & Weldin, 2004). These executive summaries were then used to conduct an initial theme analysis of the data. This was initially done by several different researchers individually who then met together as a team at Luther Seminary in July 2004 to identify the major themes we found in the site visit data. These themes were then compared by Roland Martinson to data analysis that was being done of several other data streams from the quantitative side of the study. From this meta-analysis he identified the major themes of this study. These major themes were then studied in greater detail by the team of researchers who read the data specifically with the task of fleshing out each of these key themes. This information was provided to Roland Martinson and Wes Black, the lead researchers on this effort, for further analysis.

Since then Martinson and Black have done additional analysis of the data. In addition a journalist was hired to write up a story of each of the sites from each of the site visit reports. Finally, we have recently begun to do additional qualitative analysis of the site visit data using Crawdad (2005), a qualitative data analysis software program that will provide us with additional insights and perspectives on this data.

Limitations of This Study

There are several limitations of this study. The first was in the selection of the twenty-one sites that were visited. While the initial design was that these would be selected on the basis of the results from the quantitative study (the "best of the best"), this was not possible given that the timeline of the quantitative data gathering process had to be extended due to challenges faced in collecting this data. Therefore, what was done instead is that the denominational representatives from the Advisory Council were asked to identify from the list of 131 congregations which had responded to the quantitative study those sites they felt were most worthy of site visits. From this the twenty-one sites were selected using a process that ensured geographic diversity for each of the sizes and denominations. It should be remembered that due to this sampling process, care must be made in the use of the themes identified from the site visit data.

Second there were insufficient resources to do a fully grounded theory or even a case study of each of the congregations visited. For this reason, while an open-ended approach was used to identify what we described as "the genius" of each congregation's youth ministry efforts, there were only resources available to do a single, weekend long site visit of each congregation. In order to respond to this limitation, five to seven interviews from pastors, youth leaders, adult volunteers, youth, and their parents were done during each site visit to maximize the amount of information that was collected from multiple perspectives while on site. In addition, the executive summaries, which were written up by the interviewers using the extensive field notes collected during the site visit, were shared with one or two of the key contacts at each congregation visited for their feedback.

A third limitation was in the large number and varied backgrounds of the interviewers used in this study. While several had extensive experience in conducting interviews, for others this was a newer experience. This was responded to by providing both hands-on training and a manual on the process and the interview protocols to be used during the site visits. Scribes were also sent along on the site visits whose task it was to help the interviewer follow through on the site visit process as it was designed. They also collected field notes and tape recorded the interviews, ensuring that we had a significant amount of data to work from in the analysis. While some of the interviewers did not have extensive previous experience in interviewing previous to this experience, as they were all members of this study's Advisory Council, they all were very knowledgeable about this research effort, their denomination, and the field of youth ministry.

Throughout the entire site visit process, we sought to have the site visit teams focus on the youth ministry program of the congregation being visited. A lesson learned through this research process is that while in some ways within some of the congregations visited the youth ministry program can be viewed as running anything from somewhat to in a few cases very independently of the rest of the congregation, in many of the congregations the youth ministry programming was integral to the congregation itself. This meant that clearly defining the boundaries of the content to be collected and analyzed from these site visits is not possible, making the collection and analysis of this data quite complex.

A final limitation is in the analysis of the data. Given that data was collected from at least five different types of stakeholders in three different sizes of congregations from each of seven different denominations, this resulted in over one hundred interviews that were conducted and in over 1200 pages of field notes and executive summaries that were typed up. There is still much to learn from this data. For the initial analysis of the data a process that first had several individuals and then a team of data analysts look at the executive summary reports, first seeking out the major themes which arose from them and then exploring each of these themes in greater depth. These themes have been compared, modified and strengthened by work that Roland Martinson and Wes Black are doing in integrating the learning from both the quantitative and the qualitative data from this study. Finally, further analysis of the entire set of field notes using Crawdad (2005) is currently being done to help us better understand and interpret our data.

Strengths of this Study

There are also several significant strengths of this study. The use of interviewers who were well-grounded in youth ministry and in their denomination meant that they could formulate follow-up questions and probes on the fly that deepened our learning from each of the site visits. This has also meant that these members have been able to make use of initial learning from these site visits much earlier in this research process than if they had to simply wait for a different set of researchers to do the research and then write it up for their use.

The use of scribes capable of collecting a large amount of data in a short period of time means that this study was both very effective and very efficient in gathering not only stories from the various congregations but also a deeper sense of the depth of the genius of each of these congregation's youth ministry efforts. This data becomes a rich source of learning about what these different congregations look like and how they operate in real life. By working in teams of two, the teams were able to both reflect with each other on what they were learning (both during and after the visit) as well as support each other in what was an ambitious data collection design.

This study looked at three different sizes of congregations from each of seven different denominations. Because at least five different perspectives (senior pastor, youth director, adult volunteers, youth, and parents) were sought on the youth ministry efforts at each of the sites visited, this means that there is a great deal of data from multiple perspectives for each denomination as well as for each of the three size categories of congregations. This provides us with multiple triangulation opportunities in the qualitative data analysis.

Another strength of this study was that the site visit process which was used was found to be a robust design that collected in a quick and cost-effective manner a great deal of data from each of the twenty-one congregations that were visited. Sending teams of two on weekend site visits means that we spent a total of about forty days in the congregations that we visited. As we continue to learn more about the use of Crawdad (2005) as a means of quickly analyzing and reporting on this data, this is a research methodology that has potential uses in other settings that are looking for a quick method of gathering and analyzing a large amount of data.

A fifth strength of this study is the power of the stories that were collected. The ability of the stories gathered to invite the reader into the data and then reflect on and learn from it has been a very interesting aspect of this research effort. While as noted above care must be made in how this site visit data is used, there is much to be learned from immersing oneself in it.

A final strength of this qualitative study is that it was done in conjunction with a very in-depth quantitative study. This has resulted in the ability to be able to contrast, compare, and triangulate findings between the various types of data that have been gathered. The qualitative data in particular offers us the opportunity to be able to discern some of the details of the specific faces, places, and methods of youth ministry being used by some of the congregations from which the quantitative data has been gathered.

Conclusions

This study sought to maximize the use of available resources in the hands-on collection of a rich set of data from each of the congregations visited using a modified grounded theory approach. As limitations were identified, responses were sought to minimize their impact. The site visit process used proved to be quite robust in its ability to gather a great deal of data in a short amount of time. The stories gathered in this process have proven to be a very powerful aspect of this study.

References

Berkas, T. H. & Weldin, H. C. (2003). *Site visit manual for the Exemplary Youth Ministry Study.* Saint Paul: Luther Seminary.

Berkas, T. H. & Weldin, H. C. (2004). *Complete set of executive summaries from the Twenty-One EYM Site Visits.* Saint Paul: Luther Seminary.

Brekke, M. J. (2005). *The study of exemplary congregations in youth ministry: How the quantitative study was conducted.* Minneapolis: Brekke Associates, Inc.

Crawdad Technologies LLC. (2005). Retrieved June 30, 2005 from www.crawdadtech.com

Fetterman, D. M. (1989). *Ethnography: Step by step.* Applied Social Research Methods Series, 17. Thousand Oaks: Sage.

Krueger, R. A. (1994). *Focus groups: A Practical Guide for Applied Research* (2d ed.). Thousand Oaks: Sage.

Patton, M. Q. (2002). *Qualitative Research and Evaluation Methods.* 3d Edition. Thousand Oaks, CA: Sage.

Strauss, A. & Corbin, J. (1990). *Basics of Qualitative Research: Grounded Theory Procedures and Techniques.* Thousand Oaks: Sage.

APPENDIX SIX

summary of the qualitative findings

F rom the combined findings of field visits and interviews with pastors, youth ministers, volunteers and youth in twenty-one congregations with a history of establishing mature faith in youth, nine characteristics, each representing many distinct relationships and practices, emerged. These nine dimensions further align as three distinct dimensions of congregational life and ministry. In each congregation all these aspects of ministry work together to generate a "congregational youth ministry culture" that is larger more influential than its parts.

Theological and Strategic Commitments: Three of the emerging characteristics describe understandings of God's life and activity, the nature of faith and the directions of ministry that follow from these convictions:

1. Sense of the Presence and Activity of a Living God
2. Emphasis on Spiritual Growth, Discipleship and Vocation
3. Promote Outreach and Mission

Qualities of Ministry: Three of the emerging themes describe the manner and excellence with which the people and the congregation involve themselves with each other in ministry:

4. Reflect Congregational Priority and Support for Youth Ministry
5. Foster Significant Relationships and a Sense of Community
6. Develop Committed Competent Leadership

Uniquely Integrated Practices: Three of the emerging characteristics describe ministry practices and their unique and synergistic alignment in each of the congregations. Even though common youth ministry practices exist across the congregations, each congregation custom designed and integrated those practices in their context:

7. Focus on Household or Families
8. Common Effective Youth Ministry Practices
9. Custom Designed, Integrated Approaches to Youth Ministry

Theme 1. Sense of the Presence and Activity of a Living God

Worship

- *God, mystery, living active presence*
- *Connection*
- *Engagement*
- *Reverence*
- *Reception*
- *Movement*

- *Practicing, participating in God's presence*
- *Expectation*
- *Experience*
- *Music's role*

Prayer

- *Aware of and practicing God's presence*
- *Communication*
- *Working out life with God*

God's Presence in Everyday Life

- *Human capable of bearing Divine*
- *Divine – human encounter*

God's Action

- *Word – study – God speaks, "creates," acts*
- *Sacraments – God gives self and God's benefits: claims, blesses*
- *Creation capable of bearing Divine*
- *Masks of God, God comes in the hiddeness of the ordinary*
- *Call/vocation*

God Talk

- *God "subject of sentences," actor in our lives*
- *Language about God, fresh, mundane, non-religious and sacred*
- *Dietrich Bonhoeffer*

Witness

- *Speaking of living in God's presence day to day*
- *God/human relationship expressed in being and doing*

Attitudes of

- *Expectation*
- *Humility*
- *Openness*

Theme 2. Emphasis on Spiritual Growth, Discipleship and Vocation

Life of Faith

- *Ongoing God-human relationship*
- *"Faith is a busy, active thing" (Luther)*
- *"Knowledge, acceptance, action" (Luther)*

Know and Follow Jesus

- *Scripture*
- *Prayer*
- *Holy Communion*
- *Body of Christ*
- *Gospel narrative of life of Christ*
- *Life of the Early Church/Christians*

Bible Study

- *"Story of God"*
- *Living word*
- *Prayer and power of Holy Spirit*

Vocation

- *Call*
- *Identity – destiny*
- *Faith in daily life*
- *Understand*
- *Equip*
- *Exercise*

Discover and Develop Spiritual Gifts

- *Discernment*
- *Enrichment*
- *Servanthood*
- *Leadership*

Mentoring

- *Model*
- *Dialogue*
- *Guide*

Theme 3. Promote Outreach and Mission

"Tell" the God-Jesus Story

- *Speaking/telling/writing*
- *Music*
- *Media*
- *Drama / Mime*

Bear Witness – Martyria

- *Speaking of living in God's presence*
- *Relationship expressed/professed*
- *Activity observed*

Send and Go

- *"Others": open, respect. declare, dialogue*
- *"There": Join God where God is already at work.*
- *Campus, mall, work, peers, etc.*

Serve Others

- *"Neighbor": family, community, world*
- *Jesus – "least of these" – "Little Christs"*
- *God – Discern God's will*

Care About Each Other

- *Respect*
- *"Know"*
- *Respond*

Bridge Boundaries

- *Race*
- *Language*
- *Culture*
- *Class*
- *Religion/Faith*

Invite Others to the Community

- *Friends*
- *Neighborhood*

Live, Speak and Act in Faith

- *"Wherever"*
- *Authentic, wholesome and compassionate "real life"*

4. Reflect Congregational Priority and Support for Youth Ministry

Pastoral Leadership

- *Pastor(s) understand(s) youth ministry.*
- *Pastor is committed to excellence in youth ministry.*
- *Pastor supports youth ministry throughout the congregation.*
- *Pastor values, knows and understands youth.*
- *Pastor "mentors" youth ministry leadership team.*
- *Pastor articulates and models a living faith.*

Youth Accepted and Involved

- *Individuals, groups and leadership value youth.*
- *Youth are welcomed into congregational ministries.*
- *Young people's gifts are discerned and utilized in ministry.*
- *Young people are recruited for leadership.*

Congregational Budget

- *Significant percentages for youth ministry*
- *Youth are involved in establishing congregation's budget.*
- *Youth are expected to be strong stewards of their monies.*

Campus and Buildings

- *Congregation's campus and buildings serve youth well.*
- *Youth are encouraged to utilize all facilities including the sanctuary.*
- *Innovative ministries are housed.*
- *New facilities are imagined for outreach with youth.*

Youth Ministry Staff

- *Paid and volunteer leaders are supported.*
- *Paid and volunteer leaders have long tenures.*
- *Professional youth leaders are well compensated.*
- *The youth ministry leadership team is well trained.*

High Expectations and Accountability

- *Expectations are clear and rigorous.*
- *A culture of evaluation.*
- *Leadership responds quickly and effectively to challenges.*
- *Congregation is open and willing to take risks.*

Theme 5. Foster Significant Relationships and a Sense of Community

Welcome and Hospitality

- *Youth are accepted.*
- *Worship, preaching, environment reflects youth consciousness*
- *Schedules reflect young people's life rhythms.*
- *Youth given one-on-one attention.*
- *Displays of physical affection*

Authentic Adults

- *Adults are transparent and vulnerable.*
- *People model being real.*
- *Faith talk comes naturally.*
- *Highs and lows are spoken and worked.*

Congregational Community

- *When gathered the congregation enjoys each other.*
- *Conversation and ministry reflect compassion and wellness.*
- *Communication is direct, honest and affirming.*
- *Youth are integrated into relationships and ministries with all generations.*
- *Real sense of "Being the Body of Christ," "The People of God."*

Mentoring

- *Adults seek out and converse with young people about their lives.*
- *Intentional strategies of linking youth and adults put significant adult guides in young people's lives.*
- *Older youth mentor younger youth.*

Congregational Openness

- *Individuals, leadership and groups are open to new ideas.*
- *Leaders are willing to risk.*
- *Conversation is direct and transparent.*
- *Diversity is expected and valued.*
- *New people are invited and welcomed.*

Conflict Acknowledged and Resolved

- *Differences are valued and worked.*
- *Leaders model diversity and definition.*
- *Conflict is "in the open" and moved toward resolution.*

Theme 6. Develop Committed Competent Leadership

Pastoral Leadership

- *Pastor(s) knowledgeable and supportive of youth ministry and youth ministry leaders*
- *Pastor's intentional and creative longevity*
- *Pastor models servant leadership.*
- *Pastor develops and mentors youth ministry leadership.*
- *Pastor develops a congregational intergenerational leadership team.*
- *Pastor fosters a climate of open communication, affirmation and accountability.*

Youth Ministry Leadership

- *Prime youth minister (paid or volunteer) is knowledgeable and competent.*
- *Youth minister senses a primary, lifelong call to youth ministry.*
- *Youth minister's intentional and creative longevity*
- *Youth minister develops a team; team leads the youth ministry.*
- *Youth minister(s) is/are called, challenged and strongly supported spiritually, relationally, professionally and economically.*
- *Is regularly "home grown."*
- *Utilize interns*
- *High expectations, support and accountability*
- *Youth minister is open to evaluation and responsive development.*

Adult Volunteers

- *See their ministry as a "calling."*
- *Are leading on the basis of their gifts, passion and strengths.*
- *Are consistently trained and mentored.*
- *Many and diverse: "Every believer is a minister with a ministry discovered and called through prayerful discernment and discovery of gifts."*
- *Participate in casting vision, strategic planning and evaluation, invested.*
- *Are affirmed and nurtured by youth, parents and the congregation.*

Youth Lead

- *Every young person is considered a potential leader.*
- *Youth's gifts, passions and strengths are discerned and employed in youth ministry as well as throughout the congregation.*
- *Youth of varying ages are recruited for leadership and mentored as they assume greater levels of responsibility.*
- *Peer Ministry Training is Regularly Available to All Youth*

Leadership Teams

- *Prime youth ministry leaders serve on congregational leadership teams.*
- *Youth ministry is team-led.*
- *Youth ministry events, practices and programs are team-led.*
- *Team leaders are carefully selected, trained and supported.*
- *Parents are invited onto leadership teams and advisory councils.*

7. Focus on Household or Families

Nurture Mature Faith in Parents and Grandparents

- *Effective worship, preaching and teaching nurtures Christian maturity in adults in households and families.*
- *Pastor intentionally develops disciples through preaching and teaching.*
- *Strong Christian Education for parents and grandparents*
- *Congregational care tends personal hurt and pain.*

Congregation/youth ministry provide family education

- *Enriches marriages across the life cycle.*
- *Parent education prepares families for raising all ages of children and youth, particularly teenagers.*
- *Congregational care tends family hurt and pain.*
- *Divorce recovery ministries available.*
- *Single parent and blended families accepted, supported and strengthened.*

Parents Are Participants in Youth Ministry

- *Parent's advisory councils are utilized.*
- *Parent's gifts, passions and strengths are discerned and utilized in youth ministry.*
- *Parents are encouraged to support their child's participation in church and youth ministry.*
- *Youth ministry provides intergenerational, especially parent-teen events and practices.*
- *Parents are trained in mentoring.*

Families Are Partners in Ministry

- *Families are understood as "Domestic Church" or "Church in the Home."*
- *Parents, grandparents and other adults in households and families are educated and equipped to be in faith mentors to/with their children.*
- *Families are provided resources for use in caring conversation, prayer, faith talk and service.*

8. Common Effective Youth Ministry Practices

Worship

- *Sunday evening youth worship*
- *Midweek youth worship*
- *Youth-Adult worship planning and leadership team*
- *Worship retreats*
- *Shared leadership in congregational worship*
- *Coffee house and café worship*
- *Worship integrated with Bible study, retreats, adventure trips, etc.*

Prayer

- *Prayer groups*
- *Prayer bracelets*
- *Pray-a-thons*
- *Prayer partners*
- *Internet prayer "meetings"*
- *Personal and corporate prayer*
- *Prayer ministry*
- *Prayer integrated with Bible study, retreats, adventure trips, etc.*

Bible Study

- *Small group*
- *Weekday (Wednesday evening, etc.), Sunday evening, Sunday morning*
- *Retreats, adventure trips, travel trips, conferences, confirmation*
- *Focus of discipleship*
- *Youth-adult co-led*

Small Groups

- *Life conversation, Bible study, mission, and prayer "format"*
- *Adult led; youth-adult co-led*
- *Foci: study, discipleship, fellowship, healing and growth, worship, prayer, etc.*
- *Variety of places and times*

Service Projects/Mission Trips/ Immersions

- *Local, regional, national and international*
- *Peer and intergenerational*
- *Youth group, families and congregation*

- *Weekly, yearly and ministry "cycles"*
- *Youth-adult co-led*
- *Great variety of goals, strategies and activities*

Mentoring

- *Adults mentoring youth*
- *Youth mentoring youth*
- *Prayer mentors*
- *Confirmation mentors*
- *Service project mentors*
- *Leadership mentors*
- *Discipleship*

Music

- *Worship bands*
- *Outreach bands*
- *Youth choirs*
- *Musicals*
- *Ensembles*
- *Outreach singing groups*
- *Core of worship, retreats and community building*

Drama

- *Drama teams*
- *On worship leadership teams*
- *On retreat leadership teams*
- *Peer and intergenerational*

Adventure and Travel Trips

- *Backpacking*
- *Whitewater rafting*
- *Mountain and road biking*
- *Running*
- *Pilgrimages*
- *Global travel*
- *Peer and intergenerational*

Recreation

- *Sports teams*
- *Bowling nights*

- *Gyms*
- *Skate parks*
- *Exercise clubs*

Fellowship/Community Building

- *Lock-ins (often a combination of practices)*
- *Pictorial "directories"*
- *Coffee houses*
- *Seasonal parties*
- *Dances*
- *Peer ministry*
- *Retreats*
- *Travel trips*

Camps, Conferences, Congresses, and Gathering

- *Seasonal, yearly, bi-/tri-annually, and ministry cycles*
- *Utilized for youth leadership Development and training*
- *Occasions for renewal*
- *Utilize combinations of practices*

Designated Youth Spaces

- *Youth "rooms"*
- *Youth buildings*
- *Youth houses*
- *Game rooms*
- *Gyms*
- *Storefront outreach centers*
- *Youth coffee houses*
- *Youth computer rooms*
- *Individual and group music practices rooms*

Discipleship and "Discipling"

- *Focus: deeper faith formation; more disciplined life in Christ*
- *Faith formation for leadership*
- *One-on-one and small group*
- *Youth with youth; adult with adult; adult with youth*

Outreach Ministries

- *Campus missionaries at high schools*
- *Outreach to the homeless: food, clothing, shelter, companionship, worship*

- *Outreach Teams: parks, other churches, international churches, etc.*
- *Advocacy teams: focus on justice issues both local and global*

Communication

- *Newsletters*
- *Email, list serves, etc.*
- *Websites*
- *Blogging*
- *Instant messaging*
- *Letter and note writing*
- *Phoning*

9. Custom Designed, Integrated Approaches to Youth Ministry

Context and Culture Matter

- *Local, national and global youth culture studies and "utilized."*
- *Local context is "mapped" and youth ministry responds specifically.*
- *Partnerships are developed with other churches and institutions in the community.*

Common Practices Are "Custom-Designed"

- *Ministry practices are tailored to better fit the mission of the particular congregation in a specific place. The "character" of the congregation matters.*
- *Leaders committed, knowledgeable and creative enough to redo generic resources.*
- *Local "expressions" of common practices generate new practices.*
- *Creative "naming" reflects core values, youth culture and context.*

Common Practices Are Integrated

- *Congregational youth ministry leaders incorporate common practices into an intentional overall strategy of ministry that extends across the youth "life cycle."*
- *Impact of common practices enhanced through strategic repetition and relationship to other practices.*
- *Common practices are not primarily programs, but focus on building community and relationships.*

APPENDIX SEVEN

content analysis report:

pastor and youth minister

Merton Strommen

T he following is based upon an analysis of the written responses to a series of four questions given to the youth ministers and pastors of congregations involved in Exemplary Youth Ministry study. Approximately 204 respondents submitted answers to these four questions.

The purpose underlying this analysis is to discover from what they write, why their approach to youth ministry is especially effective.

The procedure I used was straight forward. First, I read the answers given to each question and recorded each response that was unique. I tried to be faithful to what each writer described by using his or her words When a comment made by a respondent duplicated a previous response I made a tally mark by that response.

When I had finished reading their responses to each of the four questions, I discovered that I had written over eighty separate entries for the first three questions and forty for the fourth question. This means there was a wide range of comments for each of the questions. I then proceeded to group their comments into clusters and in doing so, discovered that several distinct and meaningful answers emerged for each question.

Through this analysis, I discovered several things:

- *First, there is wide spread agreement with respect to what is essential for an effective youth ministry.*
- *Second, there is considerable variation, even creativity, in the activity of these exemplary congregations.*
- *Third, the elements contributing to effectiveness tend to cluster in meaningful ways.*

I view this report as important because it gives a bird's-eye view of the thinking of people who are heading up the finest youth ministries in the country. What they have said in their comments is thoughtful and insightful. A summary of what they said represents a preliminary glance at what is to come.

In the report which follows, the numbers used are nothing more than rough estimates of the importance one might give to answers of respondents. About 40% of the congregations are represented by two reports, one from the youth minister and the other from the senior pastor. The remaining congregations are described by one report. The 204 respondents are describing no more than 134 congregations.

Question 1

Your congregation has been identified as one that is doing job of nurturing youth to mature Christian faith. Why do you think your congregation's youth ministry is able to accomplish this while so many other congregations struggle at it?

Overview of the answers

- *It is the vision and strong support given by our congregation.*
- *We credit the outstanding leadership given by our youth minister.*
- *Our effectiveness is due to the dedicated participation of volunteer adults and parents.*
- *It is effective because of the strong evangelical emphasis of our program.*
- *An important consideration is the wide variety and nature of our youth programs*

A. Answer: It is the vision and strong support given by our congregation.
(A total of 134 comments contributed to this conclusion.)

86 respondents singled out their congregation's vision and commitment to a youth ministry. Their comments included the following:

- *Because there is a high values of importance put on student ministry.*
- *Youth ministry is a priority here—a consistent vision.*
- *It is a purpose-driven vision.*
- *Our congregation is very caring and supportive of youth.*
- *It is kid-friendly—its climate is one of caring and concern for youth.*
- *Congregation values youth as a vibrant part of the family of faith.*
- *Good congregational spirit and a willingness to get involved with youth.*

Twenty-seven respondents especially noted that the youth ministry is well-supported financially. One person reported that a third of its congregational budget is for youth ministry. An additional six respondents referred to the fact that their congregation provided good facilities.

Some congregations have a history of sustained support over time. A total of thirteen respondents spoke of their congregation's long tradition of quality youth ministry—a history of caring for their youth and families.

Note should also be made of the thirteen respondents who singled out the pastoral staff as being especially supportive of the youth minister (s) by being both encouraging and involved.

B. Answer: We credit the outstanding leadership given by our youth minister(s).
(Ninety comments lead to this conclusion.)

Seventy-seven respondents singled out the leadership being given by the youth minister or pastor. The comments included the following:

- *He/she is committed to establishing a close relationship with the youth.*
- *Our leader has been serving for a number of years—a long tenure.*
- *Our youth minister is experienced, well trained, and extremely competent.*
- *Our leader has established a high level of trust with both congregational adults and the youth.*
- *Key leadership works well together and involves the whole church by doing mission together, training youth and adults, and worshiping together.*

Some congregations have several youth staff members. Hence thirteen respondents simply referred to them as committed, well-trained youth leaders.

C. Answer: Our effectiveness is due to the dedicated participation of volunteer adults and parents.
(121 comments contributed to this conclusion.)

Sixty-one respondents called attention to the dedicated assistance being given by volunteer adults. Their comments included the following:

- *Their love and passionate commitment for youth.*
- *Their willingness to be trained--to attend monthly or weekly orientation sessions.*
- *Their longevity—little turnover in personnel.*

Twenty-five respondents took note of parental involvement—their commitment to the youth ministry—some of whom (years ago) were in the ministry.

Twenty-eight respondents commented on the strong emphasis in their congregation on a close relationship between youth and adults—how it is kept central in whatever is done. Theirs is a relationship based youth ministry that includes a mentoring program in which an adult mentor is linked with a young person.

Seven respondents make special mention of the close-knit families that are producing youth of a mature faith. Mention was also made of godly people in the congregation who surround the youth and provide exemplary role models.

D. Answer: It is effective because of the strong evangelical emphasis of our program.
(Sixty-eight comments encourage this conclusion.)

Sixty-eight respondents characterize their youth ministry in ways that reflect an evangelical emphasis. Typical of their comments are:

- *Our goal is that they know Christ and make Him known.*
- *We go beyond knowing the faith to living it.*
- *Out teens are enthusiastic about their Lord.*
- *We are conscious of our need for God's intervention.*
- *Our focus is on Jesus Christ and the gospel.*
- *We disciple our youth to walk with God.*
- *We feature small, weekly Bible study fellowship groups.*
- *We are equipping them for a life of faith.*
- *Ours is Bible based, Christ-centered teaching and preaching.*
- *Ours is a commitment to long term spiritual goals.*
- *We encourage spiritual renewal and commitment.*
- *We ask a high commitment of our youth.*
- *We have established a strong prayer base.*

E. Answer: Another important feature is the wide variety and nature of our youth programs.
(109 comments lead to this conclusion.)

It was impressive to read about the many different type of events and program features that characterize the youth ministries of the congregations under study. Respondents refer to these programs as making a significant impact on the spiritual development of their youth. Listed below are a few of the activities they chose to identify:

- *Peer ministry.*
- *A focus on intergenerational participation.*

- *Annual retreats and summer mission trips are big events.*
- *Many youth are involved in service projects*
- *We cooperate in our youth activities with neighboring congregations.*
- *There is freedom and trust to be creative and take risks.*
- *An early involvement of children prepares them for later participation in the youth ministry.*
- *A strong, innovative confirmation program emphasizes disciple making.*
- *Youth are involved in leadership positions and given a sense of ownership in the youth ministry.*
- *There is a strong emphasis on being a part of the church family.*
- *The religious education given in parochial school (grades 1-8) is a distinct plus.*
- *We provide a safe, loving environment where youth can explore their faith.*
- *Ours is a strong Biblical, educational program.*
- *Youth are involved in all aspects of church life—they feel a part of the congregation.*
- *Our senior youth ministry program is a weekly bible study fellowship that uses scripture to provide answers to youth's questions.*
- *Ownership of the youth ministry is given to the youth, parents, and youth workers.*

Question 2

Describe any key structural/organizational components to your youth ministry.

The answers given to this question varied considerably. Some addressed the structural or organizational aspects of their youth ministry whereas others focused more on program considerations. Here is their answer to the question:

- *Leadership is vested in a governing body that works with the Youth Minister.*
- *A team approach involving youth and adults characterizes most youth ministries.*
- *Sunday School and Confirmation are viewed as preparatory.*
- *The structure for a ministry year is supplied by the program elements.*

Given below in greater detail is an account of how these four conclusions emerged from the written accounts.

A. Answer: Leadership is vested in a governing body that works with the youth minister.

(Eighty-two comments contribute to this conclusion.)

Thirty-nine respondents identified some type of Board, Commission, Council, or Committee that has been established to provide oversight and direction. The names chosen for these elected or appointed governance groups are legion:

- *Youth Executive Board*
- *Youth Ministry Committee (or Team)*
- *Adults and Youth (Parents and Youth) Committee*
- *Youth Council*
- *Planning and Evaluation Committee*
- *Board of Faith Formation*
- *FISH Bowl Design Committee*
- *Youth Connection Ministry Team*
- *S.S. Leadership Organization*
- *Church Leadership Team*

Twenty-nine respondents identified a pastor or full time youth minister as the key link to facilitating the vision of the overseeing Board, Committee, or Council.

Eleven respondents made special reference to a mission statement that served as a focus for the youth ministry and the basis for determining purposes and process. One spoke of their ministry as not personality driven but organized so that ministry would continue even though the youth minister were gone.

Three respondents spoke appreciatively of a cooperative arrangement with other congregations in their area that has enabled them to carry out a ministry not possible if tried alone.

B. Answer: A team approach involving both youth and adults characterizes most youth ministries.

(A total of 102 comments contributed to this conclusion.)

Thirty-five respondents identified a Student Ministry Team approach as characteristic of their youth ministry. A team consists of volunteer adults who work with a number of youth in planning and carrying out one or more major youth events. They meet weekly to plan-pray-and evaluate—often prior to an evening youth event. These teams are sometimes referred to as Lead Teams.

Twenty-eight respondents referred to the key role of volunteer adults who work as part of a leadership team or as a leader of a small fellowship, cell group. For some adults theirs is primarily a ministry of prayer and giving the youth emotional support. These leaders, chosen and trained by the youth minister, often meet weekly (or monthly) for training and encouragement.

Twenty-two respondents indicated that theirs is a decentralized youth ministry where the youth meet mostly in small groups (5–8 youth and one adult leader). Their focus is on Bible study, discussion, games, and fellowship. These discipleship, cell groups (sometimes youth led) meet weekly.

Thirteen respondents referred to the important role of parents who serve on a committee or on a Ministry Lead Team or as adult leader of a small group.

Four respondents identify a Wednesday night gathering as an attractive evening for all.

C. Answer: Sunday School and Confirmation are viewed as preparatory.
(Thirty-three comments make special reference to these two historic educational activities.)

Twenty-four respondents made special reference to the contribution Sunday School makes in preparing children for later involvement in the youth ministry. Some spoke of a building block approach where there are clear objectives to be achieved for successive age groups beginning with third grade children. To illustrate, one spoke of how his congregation focuses on baptism and first communion for grades 3–6; on the catechism and Bible, grades 7–9; on faith development, grade 10. Note was made of the strong Bible teaching and discussion approach used on Sunday morning.

Nince respondents identified confirmation as an important entry point in the youth ministry. The training and preparation gained through confirmation is deemed of great importance. One congregation waits with the confirmation ceremony until the student's Junior year.

D. Answer: The structure for a ministry year is supplied by program elements.
(A total of 113 program related comments were made in answer to this second question.)

Twelve respondents identified annual retreats as an important part of their ministry. Some of these are five day camps, others are one day planning retreats that are used to kick-off the year.

Eighteen respondents referred to annual summer mission trips and service projects which have been found to energize the youth.

Nineteen respondents noted how the youth are both trained and empowered to take leadership positions as well as participate in deciding what is to be done.

Twenty respondents spoke warmly about events where youth are able to gather in safe and loving environments for a weekly fellowship experience as well as for monthly recreational events (for example, skiing, camping).

Sixteen respondents referred to how theirs is a relationship-based ministry that features adult-youth mentoring and a program of peer-ministry.

Twelve respondents singled out the weekly worship experiences and prayer times as a significant element in the life of their youth.

Ten respondents gave special attention to their youth's involvement in some form of youth music either choir, band or musical drama. One referred to the fact that ninety youth participate in a high school choir that practices two hours each week. During a student's four years in the choir this person will have participated in two annual domestic tours of two weeks each, one overseas tour of three weeks, and one two week service project. These events have proven to be a great success.

Six respondents referred to program features that provide a discipleship emphasis.

Question 3

Compared to other congregations in your area, what is distinctive about your youth ministry?

Overview of answers

- *The dedication and long-tenured service of our adult youth leaders*
- *The high priority our congregation gives youth ministry.*
- *Our strong mission-oriented purpose of seeking to change lives.*
- *The focus we give to developing youth's capabilities.*
- *It is the attractiveness of our youth ministry .*

A. Answer: The dedication and long-tenured service of our adult leaders.
(Eighty-three respondents identified this as a distinctive feature.)

Thirty-five of the respondents made specific reference to the outstanding leadership of their youth minister—"great youth leader," "dynamic person." Their comments often included a reference to long-term service: "been with us for sixteen years."

Forty-three respondents singled out the consistent, dedicated work of committed volunteer adult leaders and characterized them as persons strong in their faith and love of young people. One congregation reports having over one hundred adults involved in youth ministry.

5 respondents made special note of the 110% support they receive from the senior pastor. They characterized this person as one who has a heart devoted to young people.

B. Answer: The high priority our congregation gives youth ministry.
(Fifty comments centered on this answer.)

Twenty-eight respondents had words of praise for the way in which members of their congregation show love and concern for youth They note that a high priority is given to youth ministry. In addition, their accepting attitude has established an atmosphere which youth can sense—that church is a safe, and friendly place. Youth are made to feel a part of the congregation.

Thirteen persons singled out the financial support of the congregation ("no competition for funds" or "no need for fund-raising") plus the good facilities that have been made available for the youth. For some this includes a Youth Center or Youth House.

Seven respondents were conscious of the strong support given by the parents who are not involved in serving as volunteer leaders.

Two respondents note that their youth ministry brings unchurched families to the church.

C. Answer: Our strong mission-oriented purpose of seeking to change lives.
(120 comments centered in this answer.)

Thirty respondents especially identified the mission-oriented nature of their youth ministry. This is made evident through annual mission trips, excellent mission opportunities, and an emphasis that has made students mission minded.

Thirty-nine respondents see their ministry as purpose driven—a clear vision drives the program namely, to help youth discover a life-changing relationship with Jesus Christ. Their program emphasizes discipleship not entertainment or fun and games (ten respondents especially commented on this).

Sixteen respondents especially single out the strong focus on service. For some there are monthly service activities and for many there are annual summer projects that involve the youth for an entire week.

Thirteen respondents refer to a strong outreach emphasis. Youth invite unsaved friends to their youth meetings where there is often a spiritual challenge to commitment.

Fourteen respondents made reference to a strong prayer emphasis, their focus on scripture, and retreats and camps that encourage spiritual renewal. One referred to unique worship times expressed through art, music, prayer, or storytelling.

D. Answer: Our focus is on developing youth's capabilities.
(Sixty-seven comments emphasized this answer.)

Fifteen respondents commented on their leadership training of youth, their focus on ministry skills, and their encouragement of leadership roles. They want their youth to accept responsibility for the youth ministry and gain a sense of ownership.

Thirteen respondents especially singled out youth's involvement in worship. Some view worship as the center of all activities. Some have a youth-only worship service on Sunday morning. Others involve the youth in the all-church morning service.

Ten respondents told about the youth music, bands, and youth choirs that meet regularly for practice and presentation. For some this is a front-line ministry—a team-building activity.

Fifteen respondents speak about their small group, cell approach which focuses on the study of scripture and the discussion of youth issues. This approach also includes a contemplative approach with spiritual exercises.

Fourteen respondents made special reference to their program of adult mentoring of youth and their training of youth in peer ministry. Their emphasis is on welcoming all.

E. Answer: It is the attractiveness of our youth program.
(Sixty-two have comments regarding this answer.)

Twenty-seven respondents refer to the well-publicized, wide range of activities and learning experiences that are available at their church. They are comprehensive and youth led causing the program to gain a good reputation. A holistic approach focuses on a ministry to, with, and by all youth—not just a youth group.

Fourteen respondents frankly admit that their larger size and more kids is in itself an attraction. One congregation that draws 2500 youth from seventeen different towns knows that some travel as much as forty miles to get there.

Thirteen make reference to the strong bonds established when youth feel they are youth family and when their primary friendships center in this family. These friendships motivate them to attend meetings in order to see their friends. There is a closeness in their group and a receptiveness to newcomers.

Eight respondents see their ministry as attractive because it is well run—good organization, sustained excellence of programs, good communication, and cooperative working relationships with nearby congregations.

Question 4

Please complete this thought: The youth ministry of our congregation would die if . . .

Note: Nineteen respondents either dismissed this thought by saying it couldn't happen to their youth ministry or to say it would die only because their church dies. The remaining respondents made comments that can be summarized as follows.

Overview of responses

It would die:

- *If our congregation loses its vision and the high priority it places on a youth ministry.*
- *If the ministry's emphasis shifts away from its focus on Jesus Christ.*
- *If we lose our committed, loving, and dedicated adult leaders.*
- *If we marginalize the youth of our congregation.*
- *If we eliminate certain program features that have been singularly successful*
- *If God no longer blesses what is being done here.*

A. Response: If our congregation loses its vision and the high priority it places on a youth ministry.
(Seventy-seven comments centered on this response.)

Fifty-seven respondents gave their strongest response by indicating that death would come to the youth ministry: if their congregation stopped caring about its youth, was no longer supportive of its youth ministry, had lost its commitment to youth, and as a result had stopped investing in them. Their strong response underscores the importance which youth leaders credit to a congregation's vision for a youth ministry and the priority they give it.

Twenty respondents see a related activity as also being devastating—that of cutting funds to eliminate a salaried youth minister and thus demonstrate the lower priority they give a youth ministry. Their cutting back on budget allowances will force the youth into a fund raising mode.

B. Response: If the ministry emphasis shifts away from its focus on Jesus Christ.
(Seventy-eight comments centered on this response.)

Forty-four respondents see death if the emphasis of the youth ministry is no longer on discipling youth—in pointing youth to Jesus Christ. They believe that when Christ is no longer the center and people have stopped believing that the Christian life is the best way, death is eminent.

Thirteen respondents see that demise happening when there is no longer prayer for the youth and no longer an emphasis on the Bible and the spiritual aspect of a youth ministry such as the use of spiritual exercises and a contemplative approach.

Fourteen respondents feel that it is when the key focus of the youth ministry — namely, mission—has been lost. When mission is forgotten, caring and reaching out to others stops. When there is no longer a personal touch-the taking of time to get to know the youth. When there is no longer a desire to serve.

Seven respondents made special reference to death as the outcome when the ministry reverts to entertainment, to fun and games.

C. Response: If we lose our committed, loving and dedicated youth leaders.
(Sixty-seven comments referred to this outcome.)

Twenty-five respondents made special reference to the volunteer adult leaders. If they ceased to care about youth, lost their passion for and commitment to Christ, if they were no longer interested in serving, it would be the youth ministry's death knell. Without question these people are an important reason for the effective youth ministries of the 134 congregations in this report.

Fifteen respondents identified the loss of their youth minister and the congregation's inability to replace him or her, as the most devastating loss. To depend only on volunteer leadership without the help of a paid staff worker was seen as most problematic.

Twenty respondents made reference to a poor staff leader as being capable of killing a youth ministry. Reference was made to a youth minister who was on an ego trip, or involved in moral failure, or incompetent, or involved in turf battles, or one whose attitude was a turn–off for youth.

Seven respondents commented on the ultimate loss if parental and family support were withdrawn from the youth ministry.

D. Response: If we marginalize the youth of our congregation.
(Twenty-five comments referred to this.)

Twelve respondents saw the killing effect of an adult-driven program where youth are not involved in decision making and leadership positions. A similar effect would come if the youth ministry is not integrated into the congregation's life.

Seven respondents saw a similar effect of isolation when the youth are not involved in the congregation's worship life or given a chance to share their faith. Worship should be at the center of activities.

Six respondents made direct reference to the chilling effect of youth's loss of interest in their youth ministry. There is little adult leaders can do if the youth no longer wish to participate.

E. Response: If we eliminate certain program features that have been singularly effective.
(Nine comments were given with no more than one to each of the following topics.)

- *Loss of variety in the youth program.*
- *Eliminating the peer ministry program.*
- *Dropping the after school program.*
- *Neglecting Sunday School or midweek worship.*
- *Eliminating the chances for youth to be together to talk and listen to each other.*
- *Separating confirmation from youth ministry.*
- *Becoming event focused instead of people focused.*
- *Not having dynamic preaching.*
- *Few chances for youth to get together.*

F. Response: If God no longer blessed what is being done.
(Eight comments referred to the deadly effect if God should remove His Spirit and blessing from what is being done.)

NOTES

Chapter One

1. These characteristics of vital Christian faith were identified from two studies: *Effective Christian Education*, which assessed evidences of a committed Christian faith in youth and adults (*Effective Christian Education: A National Study of Protestant Congregations*, Peter Benson and Carolyn Eklin [Minneapolis: Search Institute, 1990]) and *Five Cries of Youth*, which described the concerns, behaviors, and beliefs of high school youth (*Five Cries of Youth*, Merton Strommen [San Francisco: Harper, 1988, 1974]). Through factor analysis of the thirty-eight-item "faith maturity" scale from the Effective Christian Education Study, the EYM team found that there were four primary, well-defined factors within the faith maturity scale, corresponding to characteristics 1, 2, 3, and 6 above. *Five Criesw of Youth* identified a similar set of factors related to the faith maturity of youth and also identified factors corresponding to characteristics 4, 5, and 7. All seven factors were considered by the study team to be necessary to fully describe youth of vital, committed Christian faith.

Chapter Two

1. Robert Lewis and Wayne Cordeiro, *Culture Shift: Transforming Your Church from the Inside Out* (San Francisco: Jossey-Bass, 2005), xxi.
2. Ibid.

3. Nancy Ammerman, "Culture and Identity in the Congregation" in *Studying Congregations: A New Handbook*, Ammerman et al., eds. (Nashville: Abingdon, 1998), 78–82.

4. Robert Michael Franklin, "The Safest Place on Earth: The Culture of Black Congregations," in *American Congregations Vol. 2: New Perspectives in the Study of Congregations*, Wind and Lewis, eds. (Chicago: University of Chicago Press, 1994), 258.

5. Ibid., 281.

Chapter Five

1. Smith, Christian with Melinda Lundquist Denton, *Soul Searching: The Religious and Spiritual Lives of Teenagers* (New York: Oxford University Press, 2005), 57.

2. Ibid., 57.

3. Ibid., 261.

4. Ibid., 267.

5. Lytch, Carol, *Choosing Church—What Makes a Difference for Teens* (Louisville: Westminster/John Knox Press, 2004), 199.

6. Benson, Peter L. and Carolyn H. Eklin, *Effective Christian Education: A Summary Report on Faith, Loyalty, and Congregational Life* (Minneapolis: Search Institute, 1990), 38.

7. Wuthnow, Robert. Growing Up Religious (Boston: Beacon, 1999), xxxi–xxxii.

8. Richards, Lawrence O., *The Bible Readers Companion* (Wheaton: Victor, 1991), 123.

Appendix Two

1. Luther Seminary. Proposal to the Lilly Endowment Inc. in support of a study of exemplary congregations in youth ministry: a proposal. 2001, St. Paul, MN.

2. Benson PL, Eklin CH. *Effective Christian education: a national study of Protestant congregations : a summary report on faith, life, loyalty, and congregational life.* Minneapolis, Minn. (122 West Franklin Ave., Minneapolis 55404): Search Institute; 1990.

3. Strommen MP, Gupta R. *Five cries of youth.* New and rev. ed. San Francisco: Harper & Row; 1988.

4. Strommen MP, Gupta R. *Five cries of youth: issues that trouble young people today.* 2nd rev. ed. San Francisco: HarperSanFrancisco; 1993.

5. Strommen MP. *Five cries of youth.* 1st ed. New York,: Harper & Row; 1974.

6. American Religion Data Archive. *Effective Christian Education: nat study of protestant congs 1991* [data file], 2002.

7. Strommen MP, Jones KE, Rahn D. *Youth ministry that transforms: a comprehensive analysis of the hopes, frustrations, and effectiveness of today's youth workers.* Grand Rapids: Youth Specialties/Zondervan; 2001.

8. Froehle BT. *New Directions in Youth Ministry: a national study of catholic youth ministry program participants.* Washington, D.C.: Center for Applied Research in the Apostolate, Georgetown University; July 1996.

9. Benson PL, Williams DL, Johnson AL. *The quicksilver years: the hopes and fears of early adolescence.* 1st ed. San Francisco: Harper & Row; 1987.

10. American Religion Data Archive. *Young Adolescents and Their Parents: a national study,* 1984 [data file], 2002.

11. The Youth Ministry and Spirituality Project. *The Youth Ministry and Spirituality Project.* San Francisco Theological Seminary [website]. Available at: www.ymsp.org.

12. Youth and Religion Project. *Youth and Religion Project.* University of Illinois-Chicago [website]. Available at: www.uic.edu/depts/soci/yrp/index1.html.

13. National Study of Youth and Religion. *National Study of Youth and Religion.* The University of North Carolina at Chapel Hill [website]. Available at: www.youth Fandreligion.org/.

14. Strommen MP. *A Study of generations: report of a two-year study of 5,000 Lutherans between the ages of 15-65, their beliefs, values, attitudes, behavior.* Minneapolis, MN: Augsburg Publishing House; 1972.

15. Schuller DS, Strommen MP, Brekke M, Association of Theological Schools in the United States and Canada., Search Institute (Minneapolis Minn.). *Ministry in America: a report and analysis, based on an in-depth survey of 47 denominations in the United States and Canada, with interpretation by 18 experts.* 1st ed. San Francisco: Harper & Row; 1980.

16. Strommen MP, Andress S. *Five shaping forces: using organizational dynamics to do more with less.* Minneapolis, Minn. (122 West Franklin, Suite 215, Minneapolis 55404-2466): Search Institute.

17. Egbert W, ed. *What Lutherans can learn about outreach.* Minneapolis, MN: Augsburg; 1987.

18. Strommen MP. *Four Imperatives: Youth and Family Ministry.* Minneapolis: Augsburg Youth and Family Institute; 1991.

19. Brekke MJ, Brekke ML. How the study was conducted. In: Strommen MP, Jones K, Rahn D, eds. *Youth Ministry that Transforms: a comprehensive analysis of the hopes, frustrations, and effectiveness of today's youth workers.* Grand Rapids: Zondervan; 2001:341-360.

20. Loevinger J. A systematic approach to the construction and evaluation of tests of ability. *Psychological Monograph.* 1947;61(4):iii-49.

21. Loevinger J. The technique of homogeneous tests compared with some aspects of scale analysis and factor analysis. Psych Bull. 1948;45:507-529.

22. DuBois P, Loevinger J, Gleser G. The construction of homogeneous keys for a biographical inventory. San Antonio: USAF Human Resources Center, Lackland Air Force Base; 1952.

23. Mosier C. Machine methods of scaling by reciprocal averages. Proceedings of the Research Forum. 1946.

WORKS CITED

Chapter Two

Ammerman, Nancy T. "Culture and Identity in the Congregation." *Studying Congregations: A New Handbook*. Edited by Nancy T. Ammerman, Jackson W. Carroll, Carl S. Dudley, and William McKinney. Nashville: Abingdon, 1998.

Franklin, Robert Michael. "The Safest Place on Earth: The Culture of Black Congregations." *American Congregations Volume 2: New Perspectives in the Study of Congregations*. Edited by James P. Wind and James W. Lewis. Chicago: University of Chicago Press, 1994.

Lewis, Robert and Wayne Cordeiro. *Culture Shift: Transforming Your Church from the Inside Out*. San Francisco: Jossey-Bass, 2005.

Chapter Five

Anderson, David. *From the Great Omission to Vibrant Faith*. Bloomington: Vibrant Faith Ministries, 2009.

Anderson, David, and Paul Hill. *Frogs Without Legs Can't Hear: Nurturing Disciples in Home and Congregation*. Minneapolis: Augsburg Fortress, 2003.

Benson, Peter L. and Carolyn H. Eklin. *Effective Christian Education: A Summary Report on Faith, Loyalty, and Congregational Life*. Minneapolis: Search Institute, 1990.

Lytch, Carol. *Choosing Church—What Makes a Difference for Teens*. Louisville: Westminster/John Knox Press, 2004.

Smith, Christian with Melinda Lundquist Denton. *Soul Searching: The Religious and Spiritual Lives of Teenagers*. New York: Oxford University Press, 2005.

Wuthnow, Robert. *Growing Up Religious*. Boston: Beacon, 1999.

Chapter Six

Jones, Jeffrey, "Leading for the Future." *Congregations*, Winter 2006 (Alban Institute).

THE AUTHORS

Roland Martinson

Roland Martinson is academic dean of Luther Seminary and has served there since 1977 as dean of students and professor of pastoral theology and ministry and pastoral care. In 2001 he was named Carrie Olson Baalson Professor of Children, Youth and Family Ministry. Rollie was the convener of the leaders of the seven denominations for the Exemplary Youth Ministry Study and the project director of this landmark study funded by the Lilly Endowment. He has been a life-long enthusiastic youth minister, as well as a trainer and supporter of youth ministers, youth ministry, and the church. He was a participant the Search Institute's original "Effectiveness of Christian Education" study.

His works include: *OMG: A Youth Ministry Handbook* (2010); *Coming of Age* (2006); *Gearing Up for Youth Ministry in the 21st Century* (1992); *Effective Youth Ministry, A Congregational Approach* (1988); *Bringing Up Your Child and Ministries with Families* (1986); and *A Joyful Call to Ministry* (1982).

Wes Black

Wesley Black is Professor of Student Ministry and Associate Dean for the Ph.D. Program in the School of Church and Family Ministries, Southwestern Baptist Theological Seminary, Fort Worth, Texas. He has served in local church and denominational youth ministry since 1967. Before coming to his present position, he was youth specialist in discipleship at the Baptist Sunday School Board (now LifeWay Christian Resources) in Nashville, Tennessee.

Wes is the author of several books on youth ministry, including two textbooks, and numerous articles in journals, periodicals, and curriculum pieces. He has been involved in the national research study of Exemplary Youth Ministry, involving seven denominations, from the beginning when it grew out of the Faith Factors study. Wes has also done extensive research in a personal project, The Faith Journey of Young Adults, exploring the factors in the problem, "Why do some teenagers drop out of church after graduation and some do not?"

He and wife Sandi, a licensed professional counselor, lead youth leadership conferences, workshops and conferences for parents of teenagers, and marriage conferences. They are both involved in their church's youth ministry through a parent ministry group that meets on Sunday nights.

John Roberto

John Roberto is president of Lifelong Faith Associates and editor of the journal Lifelong Faith. He is the project coordinator for the Faith Formation 2020 Project. John works as a consultant to churches and national organizations, teaches courses and conducts workshops in faith formation, manages the LifelongFaith.com website and has authored books and program manuals in youth ministry, family ministry, and intergenerational faith formation. He created the theory and practice of Generations of Faith—an intergenerational, lifelong approach to faith formation; and administered the five-year Lilly Endowment funded project to develop lifelong faith formation in Catholic parishes across the U.S. His latest publications include *Faith Formation 2020* (LifelongFaith Associates, 2010), *Living Well: Christian Practices for Everyday Life* (LifelongFaith Associates), and *Becoming a Church of Lifelong Learners* (Twenty-Third Publications). John was the founder and director of the Center for Ministry Development, where he worked for 28 years.